I AM FROM HAITI

I AM FROM HAITI

By *Rodrigue Mortel, M.D.*

As told to Judith T. Witmer, Ed.D.

Published by *The Mortel Family Foundation*

ISBN 0-9705364-0-2

Acknowledgements

I dedicate this book to Ceil and my children who have spent days and nights without me, but have been a constant source of love, support, and encouragement.

I am forever indebted to Dinah, my sister who dropped out of school in order for me to go on.

There are no words to convey my profound gratitude to George C. Lewis, Jr., MD who gave me a chance by accepting me in the obstetrics and gynecology residency program at the Hahnemann Medical College and Hospital, and to John L. Lewis, Jr., MD who took a gamble by offering me a fellowship position at Memorial Sloan Kettering Cancer Center. I also want to thank Leo J. Dunn, MD who guided me through major decisions in my career over the past twenty years.

The Pennsylvania State University provided the perfect environment in which I grew to be a leader and Dr. Harry Prytowsky gave me the opportunity to serve. I would not have succeeded, however, without the support of a hardworking core of faculty and residents. Their performance at the local and national level made me look good.

There would have been no book if it were not for Judith T. Witmer, EdD. For years she has been encouraging me to tell this story. She finally pressed me to organize my thoughts and brought her writing skills to bear on the production of the manuscript.

I owe a special debt of gratitude to William Cardinal Keeler, Archbishop of Baltimore, a longtime friend. He generously read the original manuscript and provided positive feedback and helpful suggestions.

I am particularly thankful to the members of the *Association des médecins haitiens à l'étranger* (AMHE). Their interest in my career and their continued encouragement mean a great deal to me.

I have been privileged over the past 28 years to work with a very loyal and dedicated staff. Their patience and ability to coordinate my ever-changing activities are indeed remarkable. May all of them find here an expression of my deep gratitude.

Mary Dewey is the administrator that I always dreamt of but never thought existed. She always brings her incredible organizational skills to bear on the outcome of every large project I embrace. I owe her a debt of gratitude.

Finally, E. Nan Edmunds of the Public Relations Department at The Milton S. Hershey Medical Center critically reviewed the manuscript and offered meaningful suggestions. To her, I am most grateful.

Rodrigue Mortel, MD

Foreword

"Father Vic, over there is where I used to study every night during my high school years here in Port-au-Prince." The "over there" was the sidewalk under the florescent lights of a local gasoline station. The speaker was Dr. Rodrigue Mortel. It was November 1997. We had just completed a six-day, fact-finding tour of the Diocese of Gonaives in preparation for Cardinal Keeler's dream, the Haitian Outreach Project that would bind that Diocese in a closer link with my own Archdiocese of Baltimore. During those six days I came to realize that I was in contact with a great soul. I learned of Dr. Rod's deep love for the Lord, for his family, and for his native land—all blended together with an infectious *joie de vivre*.

My contacts with Dr. Mortel since that delightful tour of Gonaives have only served to reinforce my initial impression of this marvelous man. Our most recent meeting took place in July 2000 as I was leading a small group from Baltimore for volunteer work in Gonaives. Dr. Rod had insisted that on the way from Port-au-Prince we stop for refreshments in his native town of St. Marc. It was there that he showed us the school that he was having built on his own property to help educate the neediest children of St. Marc. As he guided us amid the workers and construction materials, I couldn't imagine him being any happier even if he had won the biggest Big Game Lotto in history. Back in our Land Cruiser on the "washboard" road to Gonaives, I kept recalling what William James had said years before: "The greatest use of life is to spend it for something that will outlast it." These pages recount the story of one such life. Read and be inspired!

Msgr. Victor Galeone
Director, Propagation of the Faith
Archdiocese of Baltimore

Foreword

It all started on an ordinary day. I was scanning a pile of successful Haitian Physician resumes for a database. I suddenly lost perspective of time and urgency when I started reading with more attention the resume of Dr. Rodrigue Mortel. I had heard his name before, at least thirty years ago. Someone must have referred to his name as an example of a hardworking and dedicated medical resident. This time, I was in the situation to understand and appreciate the value of this man's journey. While I was reading his resume with admiration, I was impressed by both its length and its content. My mind drifted into the deep thinking of how interesting his journey must have been. Think of a life of a young physician graduated from the medical school of Haiti, making his way in the United States medical universe as an immigrant from African descent three decades ago!

Many Haitian professionals are successful, at home and abroad and in different fields and context. The explanation for their success is never the same but always implies strong determination and crucial timing. In Dr. Mortel's case, however, his resume seemed to imply that the determination and the timing were not only crucial but also exceptional. I was fascinated. His resume magnetized me because it brought together three of my strongest beliefs: my motherland, Haiti, is rich in extraordinary brains; my people are very strong and courageous and our next generation of Haitian-American is capable to do even better than we did. Because I venerate profoundly my motherland, because I strongly believe in Haitian success, because I very much want our Haitian-American children to succeed, Dr. Mortel's resume shined into my eyes in a very emotional way. I had just found my hero through a resume. Next, I had to meet a man so proud of his country that he introduces himself, "I am from Haiti."

Let's make it clear that there are many intelligent and courageous Haitians destined for extraordinary life like this one. Many more than statistics have calculated and reported. Many more than anyone on earth could think of. However, since resources for Haitians are always very scarce and opportunity for education and promotion almost always providential, too many of our men and women have lived and died with their potential undeveloped to full capacity. Too many never live long enough to even know that they have a potential. In that sense, Dr. Mortel is a survivor, a national symbol of success. A symbol of what life could have been for so many more Haitians, if . . .

When I met Dr. Mortel for the first time at *an Association des Medecins Haitiens à l'Etranger* (AMHE) convention by the beach of the Haitian *Club Med*, I shook the hand of a very unassuming man in bathing suit and barefoot, profoundly modest and down to earth. He didn't particularly enjoy my compliments and rapidly changed the subject toward his family life, giving credit to his wife and his two daughters to whom he is so grateful for accepting that his professional life interferes so much with their family life. For some reason, I didn't see any contrast between the simplicity of the man I met and his impressive resume.

I knew after that meeting that I would dedicate my book, The Bonplezi Family, to that man. His life experience has reinforced my faith in my country, in my people and in our collective experience. And I wanted him to know that. When, later on, I read more about his life, I wished that his life story be told and published in many languages for everyone in search of an inspiring story to enjoy. Any human being from anywhere on earth would find something inspirational, touching, moving, motivating or challenging in the biography of Dr. Rodrigue Mortel. He has not only realized the American dream; he has triumphed against all kind of adversity and has maximized all the opportunities that God has laid on his path. His journey is paved with challenging contrast like growing up with financial difficulties in a surrounding of high moral values, like being raised by parents with limited level of literacy but with thirst for his professional achievement. His Christian faith and self-confidence are the essence of the success of his incredible journey.

Today, Dr. Mortel speaks about his life as if the best is yet to come. I believe so, knowing how ready he is to share and to give to others as much as God has given to him.

Besides himself, Dr. Mortel is a prototype of the Haitian Dream, a role model for our youth, a patriot who is a living proof of our motherland potential and a man of great leadership capability who can inspire anyone. His journey is worthy to be celebrated and honored. His book is for people who want to look up to success as a difficult but attainable challenge. His book is for people who are walking on difficult roads but with high determination. His book is for readers in search of an exciting and uplifting experience to follow. His book is for any youth who aspire to become a winner, any youth who would follow in his footsteps, any youth who, in turn, might also say, "I, too, am from Haiti."

May his story reach your heart and comfort your soul. May his story energize you in your own journey. May his success help you foresee your own success with faith and more confidence.

Maude Heurtelou, MS
Specialist, Educational Materials Development
Vice-president, Women Writers of Haitian Descent

Table of Contents

* A New Penn State Cancer Center: My Vision
* Denise: A Study in Courage
* Penn State Cancer Center: The Reality

SPECIAL FACETS

I AM FROM HAITI

An Introduction to Haiti

Haiti—its very name suggests mystery and intrigue, tropical islands lush with vegetation, peace and happiness, islanders in the sun, fishing, boating, siestas, festivals, and a love of living.

A beautiful country, Haiti is full of contrasts, extraordinarily lovely with many pristine beaches and mountains still untouched by civilization. Until the 20th century Haiti was described as a tropical paradise with endless ranges of spectacular mountains, neatly planted trees, and rolling plains of pale green sugarcane, mangoes, bananas, and apricots. Bougainvillea and oleander grew in abundance, alongside and intertwined with many other varieties of trees and flowers. Like a rare gemstone set in precious metal, this paradise island is surrounded by a clear, blue-green sea with cooling breezes. It isn't any wonder that it became France's wealthiest colony, its fertile soil and thousands of plantations spewing forth sugar, coffee, cotton, and indigo.

Yet something happened to this once beautiful island. Something destroyed the dream. The haunting beauty became a barren wasteland and the lush greenery became unfertile, dry earth. Abundance waned, and hunger prevailed. The once happy people, self-sufficient and proud, became a nation barely able to eke out an existence from their ruined land.

1

In area, Haiti is a little more than ten thousand square miles (approximately the size of Maryland) with a population of seven million people; its capital and largest city is Port-au-Prince, with more than two million people packed into an area that is not nearly large enough to contain the ever-increasing influx from the rural areas. Eighty-five percent of the population of Haiti is rural and more than fifty percent of the economy is agricultural. With its 700 people per square mile, Haiti is the most densely populated country in the western hemisphere.

The country occupies the western third of the Caribbean island of Hispaniola, with its only land neighbor, the Dominican Republic, dominating the remaining two-thirds. The next nearest island is Cuba which lies northwest of Haiti. The climate is tropical with an average temperature of 80 degrees. Annual rainfall varies from 20 inches on the coast to 100 inches in the mountains. One would expect vegetation to be abundant; however, because of the deforestation that has taken place during the past sixty or more years, there is no vegetation. When it rains, there is nothing to retain the water and along the shoreline one notices darkness just beneath the water. This is silt, island topsoil that has been washed away into the sea.

Haiti is said to be one of the most extraordinary nations in the Western Hemisphere with its open-air markets and unique cultural tradition developed by a proud nation of liberated slaves. Its people are artistically creative and one could easily be convinced that the art is a reflection of their joy, but because of immense poverty, there is not much in Haitian life about which to be joyous. Haiti has the lowest per-capita income in the Western Hemisphere and is heavily dependent on foreign aid.

Historians generally agree that the original inhabitants of Haiti were four tribes of Indians. No complete historical record of Haiti exists, and, through the years, many of the country's artifacts were sold to foreign museums. During various political uprisings much of what was written was destroyed by fire. Intentionally or unintentionally, private libraries and government buildings were often the target of political attacks. One of the most disastrous losses to the history of Haiti was the burning of the finest library in the country, which included many rare books, especially a life's work, nearly completed, *The History of Haiti.*

Most of the population are of African descent, except for small minorities of Europeans and the resulting mulattos. The official languages are French, taught in the schools and spoken in government offices and business organizations, and Creole, spoken by all and much more widely used than French. One of the most striking characteristics of Haiti is its division into two distinct social classes. The class lines are so very rigid that many say the only way to describe the separation of the élite and the masses is by using the word "caste." For the peasant caste, life is spent in following the traditional ways of the village. What matters is food, family and friends. There is virtually no hope to get ahead, no future to work toward. There is only today.

The literacy rate in Haiti is among the lowest in the Western Hemisphere. Eighty-five percent of Haitians are totally illiterate and only 20 to 30 percent in rural areas complete their primary education. Only five percent of the youth attend high school and the number who attend university is infinitesimal—lower than that of any other country in the civilized world: **two-tenths of one percent**.

Those who can afford to send their children to the available private and parochial schools do so, as many privately-operated schools provide a better education than the public schools. Parents who can afford it send their sons away from the villages to board with relatives in the larger towns and cities so that they can attend better schools. Even with the number of private schools, however, there are not enough schools to accommodate large numbers of students, and many children will never have the opportunity to complete their basic education and, thus, have almost no hope of ever attending the public university.

The predominant and official religion of Haiti is Catholicism, the religion of the original European settlers. However, the practice of voodoo, a blend of West African beliefs infused with Catholicism, still continues. As in all religions, voodoo helps its believers deal with the passages through life, such as birth, death, and all hurdles in between. The major feasts of the Christian year are closely synchronized with special dates and ceremonies of voodoo. The attitude toward voodoo is mixed. Many abhor it, yet few can ignore it. There is a saying in Haiti that ninety percent of the population is Catholic but everyone believes in voodoo.

Sickness and disease run rampant in Haiti and for four of every five Haitians, mere survival is a full-time pursuit. Because of often non-existent sanitation and hygiene in addition to malnutrition, diseases such as malaria, typhoid, tuberculosis, and a wide range of skin diseases continually decimate the population, greatly impacting life expectancy which is quite low, age 47 for women and age 45 for men.[1] With a severe shortage of medical care, the infant mortality rate is more than ten percent with 110 deaths per thousand births (compared to 13 deaths per thousand births in the United States). The rate of doctors to patients is one to approximately 10,000 persons.

Potable drinking water is at a premium even in urban areas where only 46 percent of the population has access to drinkable water. In rural areas only three percent have safe water. The majority of water is gathered at a central area along the road to which the villagers gather to fill their vessels. Even this water source, however, cannot be counted upon to be available every day, nor is it always potable. Many of the villagers use the drainage ditches which are seen alongside every road as a source of bathing, washing clothes, and, in some cases, drinking water.

The infrastructure of Haiti is deplorable. The government controls but does not maintain any of the systems which are needed to assure the smooth operation of a country. All government appointments are political, with managers and directors being placed into positions for which they have no training or experience. There are only a little more that 1,100 miles of paved or improved streets and roads, and 1,300 unpaved miles for more than 10,000 vehicles in the country. There are two major ports and one major airfield.

Electricity at a very basic level is available in the towns and cities, although it was not until the 1950s that electricity was available to cities such as St. Marc. Electrical service is, however, subject to rationing and regulation. Telephones are not common to any but the wealthy. For example, until 1991 in the city of St. Marc, with a population of approximately 50,000, there was only one telephone to serve the entire town.

The capital city of Port-au-Prince is what most people think of when they hear the word Haiti. Crowded, colorful, dusty, hot, exciting, depressing, frightening, intriguing, and screaming with traffic - all are terms which describe this center of Haitian life and politics. As in most modern cities, in Port-au-Prince there are too many people and too few services, as the population of the city has exploded. The cathedral is the tallest and largest building in the city. Behind this "pastel, two-towered tropical fantasy with stained-glass windows and plastic flower garlands"[2] is found the old slum, inappropriately named Bel-Air, where migrants to the capital first gather.

The worst part of the city is its slums and, during the rainy season, a river of mud and sewage runs through the nearby marketplace. The living quarters are shacks, reminiscent of the slave quarters on the worst southern plantations in the United States during the 19th century. Children are everywhere, hopelessly milling about, with little to occupy their time. On the flats, opposite the large slum of La Saline, is Fort Dimanche, the prison from which it is said no one has ever returned.

In Pétionville, high above the city, only the less expensive homes of this upper-class neighborhood can be seen, as the houses of the wealthy are hidden behind high cement security walls. Villas, high in the mountains, provide a comfortable lifestyle for the small percentage of the population who can afford luxurious living. The air is cool, there are shade trees, a nearby public park, and walls high enough for protection. Pétionville once offered some of Haiti's liveliest hotels, a casino, a nine-hole golf course, tennis courts, boutiques and art galleries, and some of the capital's best restaurants. The well-known Barbancourt Rum distillery is nearby.

Most Haitian cities are located on the coast of the country; these cities all have surrounding villages for which the city is the economic center. For example, Saint Marc, a coastal town north-northwest of Port-au-Prince, serves as the hub for seven villages. It

was in one of these villages, set in a rural lush area known as the
Artibonite Valley, that Lamercie Antoine, my mother, was born near
the beginning of the 20th century.

Notes

1. 1993 figures from *The Grolier Multimedia Encyclopedia.*

2. Amy Wilentz, *The Rainy Season: Haiti Since Duvalier* (NY:
Simon and Schuster, 1989), 83.

Chapter 1: Village Life

In the countryside, life was simple, routine, and busy. Deep in the Artibonite Valley of central Haiti, in the village of Savary, for generations my mother's family had farmed and taught their children the skills they would need to survive. Lamercie Antoine, the only daughter of the family, and later to be my mother, was expected to do her share of the family work as soon as she could walk. A willing child, she readily took her place beside her own mother. The peasant hut in which she lived with her parents and four brothers was crowded, but to my mother ("Cicie," as her family called her) this was home, a place filled with family that included a wide range of relatives, direct and auxiliary, on the sides of both parents. Cicie was surrounded by the safety of family, knowing little of the world beyond her own village.

The division of labor in Haitian families is pre-determined, with the men tilling the fields and the women taking care of the gardens and handling the household tasks, so there was no doubt as to Cicie's role in the family, both as a child and in her presumed future. The women took care of the family garden, retaining a portion of it for the needs of the household and selling the surplus at the local market, using the money to buy clothing and other necessaries for the family.

7

"It takes a village to raise a child" is more than just rhetoric in Haitian culture. All elders are responsible for and hold rights over those who are junior. This oversight is especially true in the rearing of children. Any adult in the village has the duty to correct or reprimand any child. Punishment for departing from the code of behavior is both prompt and painful, beating with sticks being the most common physical punishment. One of the most disparaging insults one can make is to tell someone he or she is "without manners." Showing respect for elders and complying with their will are the best ways a Haitian child can remain in good standing within the family.[1] If by mischance a young person is not as attentive as an elder expects, the elder might make a pronouncement such as, "Watch out for your own old age! You mistreated me in my old age, and you will suffer in yours."[2]

Expansive hospitality is also characteristic of Haitians. Guests are honored and the hosts will go to any extreme within their means to feed and entertain them. Haitian peasants are incredibly generous, sharing whatever they have, always offering the most comfortable bed and/or the best bedroom to their guests. The homes are usually very crowded, but, without fail, families demonstrate that there is always room for another, be it one more guest to spend the night or one more relative to stay "until things get better."

One of the strongest driving forces in Haitian culture is the desire to own property. Families are very reluctant to sell their land even when it no longer is productive and the money offered for it might buy the seller a chance for a better life. When a person is asked why he or she will not sell the land, the usual response is, "I have children. I cannot sell." There is an inherent desire in all families to retain the land as a legacy to one's children, adhering to the hope that some day the land will again provide.

Money is important for the prestige that wealth reflects and not for the display of possessions it might permit. Villagers do not use banks and those who have money will keep it at home, very often hidden from all other members of the household. It is often difficult to identify a person of wealth, for he, more likely than not, will be plainly, if not poorly, dressed. He usually will not put a lot of money into improving his house. He may upgrade from a thatched roof to tin, but will not add indoor plumbing if he lives in a village or town where his neighbors do not have this luxury. Rather, he will buy land, pay for elaborate ceremonies and rituals held for family ancestors and family gods, and educate his children so that they may eventually move to Port-au-Prince and there attain social and political positions of importance.

Frequently the houses in the villages were built in clusters so that all family members could live in close proximity. Most of the houses were, and remain, similar in style and appearance. The Antoine home was no exception and was indistinguishable from every other house in the village. The tiny pastel houses, constructed of mud and wattle, often appear to lean against one another as if for support. The *ti-kay* (little house) of Lamercie Antoine's family, like most of these houses, was meager, consisting of one small room whose walls had been built from bits of wood, banana leaves, cardboard, and corrugated tin. Occasionally one of the houses in the cluster would boast a new door which stood out amid the dilapidated appearance of the surrounding houses. As a rule, however, everyone in the village was poor, and no one saw much difference in the way anyone else lived.[3]

In front of each small hut was a broad thatched roof (*tonnèl*) larger than the house itself, open to the air, and supported at four corners and the center by irregular poles of stripped sapling. Family members spent time here when they were not working in the fields or off to the market. To the rear of the house, and sometimes behind a cactus fence, was the cooking area marked by a triangle of three stones upon which to place the cooking pot fueled by burning sticks of wood. Although not common in most villages, some yards also boasted a brick oven in which bread would be baked. All yard area was shared by everyone.

The furnishings in the Antoine hut were as simple as the construction of the outside. Inside was a double bed, a table, a stool, two or three patched chairs, an iron pot or two, and calabash bowls. Cicie and her brothers, as was common for all children, slept on mats on the floor. Clothes for the family were stored under the bed mattress and Cicie had her own special corner of the mattress under which she stored a few private treasures. Other family possessions were kept in the rafters above the bed in boxes or makeshift containers.

Much like the houses in which they lived, the lives of the villagers were simple and self-contained. From the time she was old enough to be of help, Cicie rose at dawn with her mother as she prepared the morning coffee. With only this beverage for breakfast, her father and brothers headed to the family field where they worked most days until sundown. During the hottest part of the day there was a break from the fieldwork when Cicie and her mother would take a humble meal to the workers. Boiled plantain and sweet potato, occasionally supplemented by smoked herring, were the common foods for this meal, taken any time between ten and noon.[4] Time was judged only by the sun, as clocks and calendars were neither available nor needed.

Cultivating the field and harvesting were the men's major occupations. Farming practices were, and continue to be, very primitive as there is no farming equipment. The concept of crop rotation is not understood and a farmer continues to plant the same crop in the same field until the harvest yield is quite evidently producing very little; only then does he change to another type of crop or allow the land to lie fallow.

When a large field was to be cultivated, a cooperative work system called *combite* was used, although this commune system was far more prevalent during the time of harvest than at the time of planting. Combite made it possible to have more labor available at one time in one field with the men all working together, starting at one end of the field and moving across the field in a column. This communal activity accomplished together what one man alone, or only with his immediate family, could not. Each family, in turn, would help another family who needed additional manpower. Men who did not have large fields to be cultivated or harvested joined the combite for a small wage or for part of the crop they had helped cultivate or harvest.

Life in the villages was repetitious, year in and year out, the only variation being the dry season (December to February) when the work of field cultivation and harvest was replaced by tasks such as repairs to the hut or hand implements. Meanwhile, the women occupied themselves with household tasks, pounding grain or working in a small garden near the house. The rule of life in the villages was and still is unremitting labor for the female from the time of childhood. She cooks and makes clothes, labors in the fields after the men have cleared them, does the family washing in the nearest stream, and carries water for drinking and cooking.

Nearly every Haitian peasant woman also has the experience of going to market to sell the vegetables, trinkets, or other wares her family may produce, and to buy necessities. Cicie and her mother often joined these women in their continuous procession, coming down from the hills, swinging majestically along, with a great load on their heads, or riding on the haunches of a tiny donkey loaded with bulging panniers. At market, the women frequently would sit all day in the broiling sun before returning home for the night and perhaps preparing for the next day's market in yet another neighboring village. The only exception to this almost daily routine would occur when the women went to market in Port-au-Prince; there, those who came from the villages sometimes slept nearby for the night, in order to complete their purchases and sales and to enjoy talking to friends. Even those with small children took them along to market. Such was the early life of Lamercie Antoine and all other village girls and women in the early part of the twentieth century.

During this time it became more and more difficult for the women to get their goods to market. When it rained the streets were quagmires, as even at best the roads were in very poor condition, making it difficult to move goods and services. Wooden carts, not in the best condition to begin with, were quickly damaged if anyone were foolhardy enough to try to take them on the broken roads. Many of the bridges were unsafe, although the travelers continued to use them. There were no alternative routes except through the fields and woods and rivers. Such a journey could be both arduous and unsafe. Finally in 1911 the government ordered the repair of streets and roads, the replacement of telegraph wire, and the construction of new telegraph lines. These improvements, which continued for only one year, nevertheless greatly improved some of the traveling conditions.

It has at all times been an on-going struggle for most Haitians just to find enough food to feed a family. Foraging for daily sustenance thus occupied much of Cicie's day, and most people ate whatever they could find, until their hunger was appeased, with no regard for the nutritional value in the food. This lack of proper nourishment directly affected the health of the people, yet there was no health system to care for those who were ill. From the time of the country's formation until around 1915, there had been a total of barely twenty physicians in all of Haiti who were properly trained. Dr. Robert P. Parsons describes Haiti in 1915 as "an unspeakable hotbed of diseases, ranking second to none in the world. . . . the mass of three million people, sick, suffering beyond all power of words to describe, crippled, and weakened from the ravages of a host of diseases, pitifully helpless and hopelessly resigned to their lot."[5]

Growing up, Cicie never saw a doctor and she learned very early that disease was regarded as mystical. The villagers believed that if God (the Christian God) had sent the illness, it should be borne, for God's will was unchangeable. If, on the other hand, the illness were the result of magic worked by an enemy of the family, the identity of that enemy and the magical means used must be ferreted out so that countermagic could be employed. Thus, the importance of the voodoo practitioners was acknowledged and their advice heeded. In a blend of religious rites and homely practices of folk medicine, combined with the belief brought by the patient to the cure, the voodoo priest held control.

Childbirth did not vary much from the practice found in most primitive countries. Following childbirth, women remained in the house for many days and sometimes as long as a month. The room in which they stayed was kept in darkness and the new mothers discouraged from leaving bed. The newborns were swaddled and were as confined as their mothers. On the other hand, for some new mothers, pressure to return to the fields or the marketplace led them to stop nursing their infants too soon, instead substituting fruits and solids which the infants' digestive tracts could not handle. Occasionally, babies whose mothers were without homes were born by the roadside, on the way to market, or even in the marketplace. Most of these babies did not survive.

Cicie spent every day of her early childhood learning and working alongside her own mother. She hoed and weeded, carried and fetched, always under the hot tropical sun. While she was laboring daily in the country, little girls in the aristocracy of the nearest city were starting school. Cicie knew about schools, but as there was no school in her village, gaining a formal education was out of the question. Thus, instead of sitting in a classroom, Cicie began a life of labor with little thought or hope for any other life. She imitated the life she saw, learning Creole from her mother and the other village women, unburdened by the need for rules of grammar and the correction to "proper syntax" of the French language being studied by her city counterpart.

Regardless of her routine, Cicie yearned for something unnamed, a chance for something else. Because she had seen nothing of the world beyond the village, she did not think in terms of "better," yet she longed for what would be termed improvement. She knew that some children were sent to live with relatives in towns or cities where they attended school in exchange for helping with the work in the home where they were guests. She watched as her younger brother left the village to live for a time in St. Marc with a relative of her family. She quietly observed that when her brother returned to the village, there was an air of anticipation and excitement; attention was paid to him and what he had learned. He could read! From his schooling, he told his sister stories of Haiti, of life beyond the village in which they lived.

Cicie longed to follow the path of her brother, but being the only daughter of the family she may have been concerned her mother would never be able to manage the household and field chores without her help. When her brother was home, she would ask him questions, questions she was unsure how even to frame. One thing, however, became an obsession. She desperately wanted to read and to learn more about the things her brother told her. Apprehensive without being able to define that feeling, when she was eight years old she gathered the courage to ask her mother. "Man-man," she most likely began, "lekòl. . . ," and her voice no doubt would have broken as she formed the word for "school." Her mother, with tears in her eyes, would have replied, "Ssshhhh. Wi, ane pwochen." Next year! A glorious promise which would have sustained her through the daily routine of the following months. I can only imagine how her little cache of hidden treasures secured under the corner of the mattress began to increase in eager anticipation of starting a new life and going to school!

Arrangements were made for Cicie to move to St. Marc with a family known to the Antoines. This widespread form of placing children, which continues even today, usually involves children who are called *restavek* (children who stay at someone else's house.) Restavek are the children, often of peasants, "given" to friends who live in a town or city. To give a child in this manner is in most areas of Haiti viewed as a token of friendship, and it is expected that the children will be regarded by the host family as their own. Sons are sent to families willing to take them. Daughters, on the other hand, would be sent to live only with a family whose principles and values were well known to the sending family. Preferably, daughters were sent to households with daughters near their own age. Thus, this restavek arrangement appeared to be just the solution for Cicie's desire for an education.

St. Marc

Saint Marc, my mother's destination, is best viewed from a fort located in Port Guêpes which provides a superlative vista of the city, and from which one can see the entire bay between "La Table au Diable" and Cap St. Marc.[6] St. Marc is one of seven cities (not including Port-au-Prince) in Haiti upon which surrounding villages are dependent. It, like its six sister cities, is a port with all the commerce therein entailed. Primitive even today by western standards, it has not changed much from the 1930s. The church is still central to the life of the people just as the market life is central to its economy.

The year following her mother's promise to her, Cicie gathered up her small parcel of belongings. and her uncle took her to the receiving family in St. Marc. Wide-eyed with excitement, she would have been silenced by the size of the city. Had the Antoine family had money, her room and board would have been fully paid and she would have helped a little around the house of her hosts and concentrated intensely on her schooling. However, because her family had no money and could send only rice to the host family, the first year she spent with that family she was told she would be expected to work and not go to school. Disappointed, she nonetheless worked hard, hoping for her chance to go to school the following year. She listened intently when the children of the household talked to one another about school. She could not understand much of what they said for they spoke among themselves about what they were learning and sometimes, as if in spite, spoke in French, the language used in the schools. However, she admired their uniforms when she laundered them and she respectfully tended to the books the children would bring home. Several times she was sent to "L'École" to deliver forgotten books or notebooks. Lingering in the doorway, she tried to imagine herself there in the classroom, as her mother had promised, "next year."

That promised next year for school never came for Cicie. The family she worked for told her they needed her at home. No further explanation was given. She had no one to speak on her behalf and the living arrangement simply continued as it began. She worked for her keep and that was that. As time passed, there was no more talk of school.

Without benefit of an education or any means of information as to what was happening in Haiti either politically or militarily, Cicie's life was unaffected by the turmoil caused by most political events in her country, including what was referred to as the American Occupation. Nonetheless, the impact of that occupation would reverberate throughout, and very likely beyond, the century in which she lived.

In 1915 when a report came out of Haiti that the country was out of control, President Woodrow Wilson of the United States felt it necessary to enact his new policy of human rights in the Caribbean, and on 28 July, following numerous cablegrams, radiograms, and telegrams between Port-au-Prince and Washington, the United States Marines landed in Haiti. Accounts differ as to what occurred in the early days of the American Occupation. Contemporary reports of that time do not paint a very pleasant scene, recounting constant upheaval, with street robberies, assaults, general disorder, and gunfire. Later writers recount that with the occupation calm and tranquillity were restored to the country and especially to the capital of Port-au-Prince. While the overall impact of the American Occupation turned out to be negligible, what the Occupation left in its wake was the perception in the mind of every Haitian that Americans were biased against Haiti.

Marriage and Family

Unaffected by the turmoil caused in her country by the American Occupation, Cicie Antoine continued living with her host family in St. Marc for many years. Occasionally she would return to Savary to visit with her family, but never again to make her permanent home with them. As a young woman in the first quarter of the 20th century she had only two options for her life: one was to start her own family and the other was to make her home with someone else's family. There was no such thing as "being on one's own." Her only preparation for adulthood was for marriage and the work of the household, and the only expectation was to take a suitable and proper place in society by establishing her own family and carrying on the tradition of her people. The only questions on her mind were "how" and "with whom." She wondered if she would find a suitable partner with whom to share her life and start a family, and she wondered if she would ever marry in the Church.

There are two ways in which a new Haitian family is formed, the first through a marriage sanctioned by the Church, in token of which a ring is thereafter worn by the wife, and the second by the means of the institution known as *plaçage*, wherein a man and a woman who desire to live together simply establish a new household. In the villages *plaçages* are far more common than marriages solemnized in the Church. Regardless of its beginnings, however, the Haitian union between a man and a woman is viewed as permanent. Nonetheless, it should be noted that the prestige of a Church union is of enough significance that it motivates later weddings at which the children and sometimes grandchildren of the couple act as attendants.

Sometime during the late 1920s Lamercie found herself being courted by Demarant Mortel, a self-employed tailor. Even though she was 24 years old at the time and late by Haitian standards to find a husband, once Demarant's marriage proposal was acceptable to her, customary procedure dictated that she send him to her parents. Had this been a typical family arranging a church marriage, a *lettre de demande* would have been delivered from the man's parents to the parents of the woman. This letter would have been written on flowered paper with a lacy border and wrapped in a green silk handkerchief, "for hope." In keeping with the Haitian practice of hospitality, refreshments would have been provided. A visit would then be returned by the prospective bride's family who would carry a response to the young man's family by means of a red silk handkerchief, "for victory." A wedding would follow the formalized acceptance, after the man had accumulated the requisite necessities to establish a household. A *plaçage* union, however, did not observe these customs, and no formal wedding took place for Lamercie and Demarant.

Demarant, originally from a village north of St. Marc, had been born to Mortumise Mortel in 1899. Because his parents were not married at the time of his birth, Demarant took the surname of his mother's family. As Demarant's father later married someone other than his mother, he retained the name of Mortel. Later, his mother also married, but this man did not adopt Demarant, choosing only to recognize the children he and Demarant's mother later had together. Therefore, Demarant Mortel could hold no expectations of receiving inheritance from either his natural father or his mother's husband. Further, he was denied the extended formal schooling provided to his half-siblings and he himself reached only the equivalent of a fourth grade education after which he appren-

ticed himself to a tailor. There he learned the trade that would provide him with the equivalent of $30 per year, barely enough upon
which to begin a family.

At the ages of 24 and 31, respectively, Lamercie Antoine and
Demarant Mortel set up house together. Theirs was a monogamous
union, cemented by mutual affection and interest in the future of the
children they expected to have. Within a year, their own family was
established with the birth of a daughter, Dinah. Lamercie was
pleased and proud, vowing that this child would fulfill the unreal-
ized dream she herself had carried for almost twenty years. This
child would go to school.

Baby Rodrigue

Four years later I arrived, born in the one-room house (whose dimensions were no more than 12 feet square) my parents rented for $1.50
per month, which was 60 percent of my father's approximate
income. This house still stands in St. Marc, changed only in color
from what it was more than sixty years ago—now painted pink with
green shutters. My exact date of birth can't be confirmed, as birth
dates were not recorded by peasants who neither read nor kept a calendar. What is known is my date of baptism in early January 1934;
because a child is baptized a month or so following birth, it is presumed I was born in December of 1933. The third of December was
selected as my official date of birth which is the date recorded by the
government official who arbitrarily assigned a date based on the general recollection of my parents to the official's question, "How many
days ago was the child born?" To record my birth cost my family two
gourdes (40¢). This payment assured me a birth certificate, a requirement for later entering public school.

The Mortel family was complete with both a daughter and a
son. My parents, I was later told, were delighted, as Haitian fathers
are said to prefer their daughters, and mothers their sons.[7] Although
my parents regarded us children as a blessing, they held no greater
expectations for us than an education, marriage or gainful employment for Dinah, and perhaps a career for me. Little could anyone

have known that I, then only a new baby, christened Rodrigue Mortel, was destined for far greater things than my mother could imagine, achievements beyond her comprehension, and honors of which she had never heard.

As in most Catholic countries, Haitian godparents are carefully selected and play an important role in the life of their godchild. To this day I hold great affection and respect for my godparents: Mme. Eliante Romeus, who was my aunt, my father's half-sister, and Dr. Clement Lanier, who became a prominent principal of the high school when he retired from the practice of medicine. Warm affection is nearly always reciprocated by the godparents, and a child will likely take problems to godparents for advice before or instead of discussing them with parents.

I recall being a happy child, surrounded as are all Haitians, by family. There were many children to play with and, from the very beginning, I knew how precious I was to my mother and my sister Dinah, four years my senior and just enough older to find me an intriguing plaything. As was the custom, I was taught to sit up near the end of my third or fourth month, and by the time I was six or seven months old I am told I could sit up quite well; when I was ten months old, Dinah took me by the hand, teaching me to walk and later allowing me to hold one end of a stick for support. Like all children in Haiti, I was never left alone. Instruction in expected behavior began in the fourth or fifth month, with words such as "Sit up, little lazy one," and later, in being taught to walk, with "Come, lazy one! Come on!" As a rule, children do not receive physical punishment until they are somewhat older; for example, once a child can crawl, he is cautioned to not cross the threshold, but if he does, he is reprimanded only verbally. If, however, after several scoldings, the unwanted behavior continues, the child is smacked with a hand to his backside. Later, words alone are usually enough to serve as a reprimand. To this day I remember the neighbor who corrected my table manners.

My early years were free from care, and, other than living in poverty and having no toys, we children in the neighborhood were content. We played simple games such as hide-and-go-seek or soldier, using sticks for horses and arranging ourselves into a military unit with the older children barking orders for the younger ones to follow. Because a real ball was a luxury unheard of among the villagers, when we children were big enough to play any game with a ball, we used an orange. No money was available for anything except essentials; consequently, gifts of any value were neither expected nor provided. I vividly recall the only Christmas gift I ever received as a child: a bright red, penny balloon.

When Dinah and I were ages seven and three, the family moved to a three-room house because we needed to provide a home for several cousins who had moved to St. Marc from the country. These cousins were sent as restavek, just as our mother had once been sent to live with friends of her parents. This meant there were now nine people living together in three rooms without running water or electricity, which at that time did not exist in St. Marc. The children all slept on mats on a dirt floor, and often had little clothing. We had school uniforms and "church clothes," and for play wore whatever was no longer serviceable for school or church. While we had shoes we wore to church and school, we were not permitted to wear them for play. As a result, there were many injuries to toes.

Soon Dinah went to live with our Aunt Eliante, my godmother and the half-sister of our father. Because my father's business as a tailor was not profitable, it fell to my mother, whom we called "Manman," to provide for the remaining eight members of the extended family for which she was now responsible. I helped with the chores which included walking some distance to get water and carrying the container home balanced on my head. The bond between my mother and me grew; I felt extremely close to her and she was the center of my world. Perhaps I should explain this closeness to my mother, as I was not what people think of as a "mama's boy." In Haiti, home for a child has traditionally been the abode of his mother—a fact reinforced by the law's insistence upon legal relationship of maternity rather than paternity. The mother-child relationship among Haitians has always been close and, in many cases, stronger than the marital relationship between husband and wife.[8] So by both law and tradition, as well as by love, we were and continued to remain very close.

Life in the Country

Manman strongly believed in family ties and determined that her family would not lose touch with their larger circle of relatives. Each summer she took Dinah and me to visit aunts, uncles, and cousins in her home village deep in the Artibonite Valley. These relatives, like all peasants, lived in small communities of fewer than one hundred persons. Sometimes the villages consisted of only four or five houses. Very isolated, their only contact with the outside world was through trips to the nearest market towns, at most populated by only a thousand persons. Bound to the soil, plagued by poor health, mentally unstimulated, and ruled by a government whose very existence would be threatened by improving the lot of the peasants, these primitive people remained unprogressive, struggling through a daily existence with little thought for their future.

Manman's place of birth and the dwellings in which her family lived would be described by most western cultures as hovels. The houses, unchanged for generations, are set back off the main road, built directly upon an earthen foundation, with stick framing (wattle) upon which a mixture of mud and/or a native sort of plaster or ashes (daub) is applied. This stick framing is not the "two by fours" to which Americans are accustomed; in Haiti, stick framing means *stick*. Perhaps "small stripped branches" might be a truer description of the building material with which the houses are framed. Approximately one to two inches in diameter (however, not consistently this size), these sticks or branches are rarely straight. In fact, foreign visitors who see these bundles might ask what the "bunch of branches" are used for. Ranging in length from four to six feet, again with no consistency of length within a bundle, the sticks are purchased along the roadside and carted to the place where a house is to be built.

Families build their houses close together, either in rows or in clusters. It is tradition that a son and his wife build a house on the same plot of land as the house of his parents. There is no definite design plan or any intent to align any of the dwellings in rows or in any order, and the only upgrading of a dwelling consisted of improving dirt floors to concrete; changing thatched roofs to metal; replacing doors; or adding a tiny addition on an already existing structure.

Within the compound of these cluster dwellings can often be found the family tomb, also brightly colored. A villager often took more pride in building a family tomb than in improving his house, for a tomb demonstrated reverence for one's ancestors and marked a man as a good son. In many instances, the tombs rivaled the houses in the amount of square footage. In the words of novelist Graham Greene, "In the small yards the family tombs looked more solid than the family huts. The dead were allotted mansions of a better class than the living—houses of two storeys with window-embrasures where food and lights could be placed on the night of All Souls."[9] In the tombs can be found numerous chambers for multiple family members and over a period of time, as a tomb became filled, space was made for the newly deceased by moving the bones of the earlier ancestors and piling them in a corner. While family tombs still exist and are tended to by the family, today the dead are interred in cemeteries.

Drainage ditches, dug parallel to the road when it was initially built, form a natural barrier between the area of the houses and the road. The villagers (or perhaps road crews) placed or built walkways of concrete or mortar across the drainage ditches so that persons can cross from the road to the houses. Those who built houses after the mortar walkways were installed have had to devise their own bridge construction of wooden slabs or woven, sturdy branches.

Life in the country in the 1930s and 1940s was just as harsh as life in the city of St. Marc. The Artibonite Valley, however, was richer than most areas because it is irrigated and many visitors to the country are surprised to see the lush green rice paddies, the livelihood of many of the peasants. My mother herself owned a small parcel of land on which she grew rice, traveling by mule, horse, or truck from St. Marc to tend to her crop. After harvesting the grain, my mother and the other rice growers would dry it in the sun, raking it painstakingly until it was ready for the mill.

Regardless of the primitive conditions, we looked forward to vacations and treasured those days spent with aunts, uncles, and cousins. These visits often extended over several weeks so that the children could form a bond and the adults could catch up on all the happenings both in the village and in the city of St. Marc. Along with my cousins and sister, I was taught to greet every person with equal respect, a lesson that has remained with me throughout my life.

Among the villagers I was treated with special regard because I lived in the city. After I started school, I occasionally wrote letters for my country relatives who could neither read nor write. During one summer Dinah and I tried to teach our cousins what we had learned in school. This was, of course, not very successful as we had been taught in French, a language neither used nor understood by the unschooled peasant children. At the time I did not realize the full extent of the privilege of an education; it was only much later that I learned Dinah and I were among a very small percentage of Haitian children who attended school on a regular basis.

Even more important to families than schooling was religious education. As such, a very important day for Haitian families is First Communion. Families will scrimp and save in order to celebrate the First Communion of a child. The day is filled with feasting and the singing of hymns, with the host families opening their homes to friends and relatives. Another favorite Holy Day is the Feast of Corpus Christi when people in the villages walk to the nearest town or city to celebrate the first Thursday in June. A colorful parade of children, who earlier in the year had made their First Communion, march through the streets, strewing *flamboyant*, red blossoms from the flowering trees by the same name. This is a beautiful and happy sight with the special meal following the Communion Mass remembered as one of the best: pumpkin soup made from a thick pumpkin base with chunks of spicy marinated beef and pieces of carrot, potato, and cabbage. Later, in days of hunger, I longed for this flavorful meal.

I remember how fascinated I was with all the things I experienced, and the stories, customs, and traditions taught me by my cousins. I still laugh every time I think of the *amitié*, a stringy, vine-like vegetation that grows everywhere in the country. The story goes that if a boy or young man states the name of a girl he likes as he strings this vine along a hedgerow, he will later know if the girl likes him by whether or not the amitié sticks to the shrubbery. I also enjoyed the rain because I was allowed to stay outside during a rainstorm in the country, taking advantage of the fresh, cool rain water. We would run and play, using the falling rain as a natural shower.

We were devout Catholics and I served as an altar boy for a period of four years, attending at the daily 5:30 a.m. Mass and for special events such as weddings and funerals. For my services I was rewarded 60¢ per month, part of which was withheld to help defray the cost of my school books. Like many altar boys, I was intrigued with the Church and set my sights upon becoming a priest. This possibility of entering the priesthood, coupled with my own impending First Communion and my mother's desire for me to be a socially acceptable student at the parochial school operated by the Christian Brothers, led to the Church marriage of my mother and father on 26 August 1944. I was almost eleven years old at the time, and Dinah and I were part of the wedding party. This was a joyous time, sanctifying the marriage and legitimizing the children in the eyes of the Church and society.

Such joy, however, was short-lived, for in October of the same year, an event occurred which served as the turning point of my life. October 9, 1944 is a date I will never forget, for it marks the day of humiliation, anger, and, ultimately, very strong determination. On this warm autumn afternoon our family was evicted from the home we had been renting for $4 per month. I watched my mother cry in hopelessness and despair because she could not pay the rent.

Here we were—eight of us, living in the streets of St. Marc. Not only had we no place to live; worse, there was no money to feed the eight people for whom my parents were responsible. I stared straight into the face of mortification and despair—humiliated in front of family and neighbors, frustrated that my father could not provide for his family and that I was not old enough to help my mother. At that moment I was overcome with the frightening perception that what I was watching was the stark reality of being a poor Haitian.

While my mother did not blame anyone for this misfortune, I silently vowed that I would do whatever it would take to prevent my mother from ever losing her home again. I was only eleven, but I never, ever again wanted to see my mother in such despair. Her own words of disappointment and bitterness at our plight became the motivating force that set the course for the rest of my life: *If I had had an education, this would not have happened.*

Education, drive, ambition—in concert with a strong religious faith—became the guideline for my life's plan. While I had not yet verbalized or defined these four elements and was not always aware that they were directly guiding me, they were the commanding principles that determined my every decision. These ideals led me, as an adult, to discover and realize that God had given me a great gift: intellectual ability, spirituality, and vision. It was, however, education which allowed me to utilize this gift.

I resolved to study hard at school and to help my mother at home as much as I could. Following the eviction, our family found temporary refuge with friends until my mother became a market woman. She bought unfinished rice from the villages and rented space in St. Marc to dry the rice. My job was to rake the rice twice a day, carefully turning it over so that it would dry evenly. Once the rice was prepared, sorted, and milled, my mother re-sold it, along with tomatoes and other vegetables, at the various markets in the surrounding villages. The nearest market was a distance of approximately five miles and the farthest close to eight miles. She often walked; other times she rode a donkey or traveled by public transportation in the back of a truck. Later, she traveled by train every other week to Port-au-Prince, a distance of fifty miles that took eight hours. I still remember the pangs of separation at her leaving, and I missed her terribly. I loved the summers when she would take me with her.

In addition to the pain of separation, I felt the physical pang of hunger, which was even more acute than the ache in my heart. There was very little or nothing for breakfast and sometimes not much for the noon meal, even though it was the main meal of the day. I learned to save a part of that sparse noon offering for the evening meal, as chances were I would have nothing more to eat that day. I remember that my mother made gruel from the left-over flour of the corn meal, adding water and a bit of sugar from cane. This was the main daily sustenance for the family. The only other food that was available was the chaff or powder left from the rice my mother sold at market. There was never enough for me to feel completely satisfied against rumblings of my stomach.

My mother kept a hectic pace, traveling from market to market, selling, buying, and then re-selling, bargaining to make the best profit she could. Everyone in the household helped in the preparation of the goods for market, and everyone sacrificed, saving for the future, adding coin by coin in order to have a house of our own. Finally, by 1947, nearly three years after being evicted, the family had earned and saved money enough to purchase a tiny house for $175.

Notes

1. Karen McCarthy Brown, *Mama Lola (A Voodoo Priestess in Brooklyn)* (Berkeley, CA: University of California Press, 1991).

2. Melville J. Herskovits, *Life in a Haitian Village* (Garden City, NJ: Anchor, Doubleday, 1971), 28.

3. Jean-Bertrand Aristide, *Jean-Bertrand Aristide: An Autobiography* (Maryknoll, NY: Orbis Books, 1993), 15.

4. Robert D. and Nancy G. Heinl, with revisions and expansion by Michael Heinl, *Written in Blood (The Story of the Haitian People)* (Lanham, MD: University Press of America, 1996), 315.

5. Ibid., 272.

6. Ian Thompson, *Bonjour Blanc: A Journey Through Haiti* (London: Hutchinson, 1992), 257.

7. Leyburn, James G. *The Haitian People.* New Haven: Yale University Press, 1966, p. 119.

8. Brown, 244.

9. Graham Greene, *The Comedians* (NY: Viking Press, 1966), 277.

Chapter 2: Education

Public education in Haiti is unsatisfactory at best, with an 85 percent illiteracy rate, the highest in the western hemisphere. Rural schools, in particular, have been extremely poor in quality and can be counted on for neither a good education nor continuity of operation. With almost every new political or military uprising throughout the five-hundred-year history of Haiti (and its century-and-a-half history of public education), the schools have closed for periods of time, ranging from a few weeks to a few months. Throughout history some rulers held public education in high regard, yet others maintained a pervasive fear of an educated peasantry. The conflicting forces of those who saw universal education as a benefit and those who saw it as a threat was a constant hindrance to any continuity of the educational system. Thus, there was an continuous see-sawing of support for public education. Rulers such as Lysius Salomon, who improved the three Lycées, the law school, and the medical school, and also reopened numerous rural schools,[1] were followed by such shameful actions as that of Pierre Nord Alexis, who set fire to the finest library in the country and, in the process, destroyed the first history of Haiti, nearly completed after twenty years' labor by its author. This act was deplored by even the staunchest foe of the author who wrote, "To blot out the works of the spirit is to proclaim the sovereignty of ignorance."[2] Yet despite their rhetoric, few Haitian political leaders ever held to their promise of an improved educational system.

Preparatory School

Amidst this unsettled public educational system, I began my formal education in L'École Frère Herve, the school provided by the Order of Christian Brothers and known by the parishioners as simply "The Brothers." Like most children, I went to the school where I was sent, without any thought about why I was there. It was only when I became a university student that I recognized how pivotal this decision, made by my mother, would be in the life I was to know. Years later I understood how privileged I had been to have received an education at all.

From the start I was a very good student. I liked school and, while the lessons came easily to me, I did not realize until the end of first grade (Level 7 in the French system used by both parochial and public schools) to what extent I excelled in my studies. I recall that on the last day of my first year of school I was given a report card to take home to my parents. This report included my grade level assignment for the following year. While my mother could not read, my father did recognize numbers and saw immediately that while all the students in Class 7 had been assigned for the next year to Class 6, I was scheduled for Class 5. Angered at what they thought was a demotion to a lower grade level, my parents proceeded to whip me. Even I didn't know that to be assigned to Class 5 meant I had performed so well academically that I was being "skipped" a grade. This was my first practical lesson in the value of knowing how to read.

I continued to do well at the Christian Brothers and, after passing the national examination from grammar school, I began level six at Lycée Sténio Vincent in St. Marc. My mother somehow knew that if I ever hoped to be admitted to the university, I would have to attend the Brothers' (Secondary) Preparatory School in Port-au-Prince. There was one drawback, however: the problem of money for tuition.

I went to Port-au-Prince for an interview, well mindful that the

Brothers' schools were selective, particularly at the secondary level. Because I had no political connections, I was refused admittance without being given a reason for the refusal. While greatly disappointed, I was told I could apply again the following year; at that time I did not realize that the refusal of admittance was also a tactic to discourage me from ever attending the school. I returned to St. Marc and the following year again went to Port-au-Prince for an interview at the Brothers' Preparatory School. This time I was told the administration did not think I could pay the tuition, but the real reason is that I was from St. Marc, and not a resident of Port-au-Prince, whose citizens received preferential treatment.

Angered by being denied admittance to the Brothers' secondary school, I became an indifferent student and stopped studying. This was a great disappointment to my mother, but the appeal of good friends and good times temporarily overrode any motivation I had. I convinced myself that I would do just fine once I put my mind to studying, but in the meantime, I began to cut classes and hang out with the wrong crowd. As with many students who fall into a pattern of indifference, the consequence of my inattention to studies did not became a reality to me until I was assigned to *repeat* level four. This time there had been no misreading of the grade assignment. This time I really had failed to pass.

With this "wake-up" call, I knew I would not be given another chance to redeem myself. I dared not fail a second time or I would have to leave the school. I resumed my studies with great intensity, and the following year was one of four new students admitted to Lycée Toussaint Louverture in Port-au-Prince to take the places of students who had failed and would not be returning. As the other students in the level three class had started their secondary schooling (level six) at the Lycée, we four late entries knew we would have to scramble to catch up with our classmates. With hope and promise, I packed my few belongings, much as my mother had done thirty-five years earlier when she had left the safety of her family and traveled to St. Marc, her young heart filled with the hope of attending school. Boarding the train for Port-au-Prince, I said to myself, "Manman, I'm going to school for both of us."

Port au Prince

Port-au-Prince is regarded as the mecca of Haiti, and it is the desire of every Haitian family to have one of its members living in Port-au-Prince, both for the advantages to the individual and for the potential assistance that person can give to other members of the family in the future. Rural families make every effort to send their most promising offspring to Port-au-Prince to begin a "migration network." Manman had sent Dinah to the capital city two years earlier to learn a trade; had she remained and had I not gone to Port-au-Prince, Dinah would have been our family link for possibly all of us moving to the city. While Dinah did well in her training, she was fully aware that if her younger brother would be accepted into a school she would be expected to come home, as there was not enough money for both of us to board away from St. Marc. Dinah never resented being called home, as it was a fact of life among the poor that the male would take precedence in attending school. My sister later told me she knew I had the potential of making a better life for all of us; in addition, she has always expressed her love for me and would have made any sacrifice to advance my future.

Manman worked harder and longer at her market trade, believing that I must succeed no matter the sacrifice required of her. One can only imagine what went through her mind when at age seventeen, I left home for Port-au-Prince. She had heard from her friends that sons in their youth could find themselves in trouble in the capital city. Thus, she prayed daily for my safety, trusting that her early guidance would steer me in the right direction.

Unmindful of the political turmoil in Port-au-Prince, I was full of excitement at being on my own for the first time, even though I was hampered by poverty. Through friends of the family, I found a place to room and board with a middle class family at $20 per month. This amount was more than my mother could readily afford, and I knew I would have no extra money. I began to understand the family sacrifices that allowed me to pursue my education. More importantly, I was fully aware that I could not disappoint my mother, as every day was a struggle for her. As a paying guest of the family with whom I boarded, I was given only a small cot in a hallway as my sleeping area, but even this was more than I had had back home.

Despite my good manners, my peasant background was a very clear factor in the family's not completely accepting me into their household. At first I was puzzled by the coolness shown me by my hosts; I thought that I must have offended them. I didn't know how to approach them, for I had no experience in such matters and it surely would have been thought rude to address the situation openly. I did my best to be pleasant, not to be any extra trouble to anyone, and not to call attention to myself. This was not difficult to do, for my studies kept me quite occupied. One day, I realized the reason for the concern of my host family. What I had first thought was sisterly teasing with the daughter of the family turned out to be a strong attraction she had for me. Her family was not pleased at this. While the words were never spoken, I could clearly sense the parents' discomfort. This feeling became more evident near the end of my first school year when they told me to find another place to live.

Stinging from the snub, I began to understand prejudice for the first time; however, this prejudice was not one of color, but of class. It was obvious that this family held no expectation that I would ever become successful. Their attitude was a hard lesson for me to face and it was difficult seeing that other people did not have confidence in my ability. However, I learned from this experience. Rather than continuing to be embarrassed, I became even more steadfast in my determination to "be somebody." What that would be, I wasn't yet sure. Like many young boys, I was (and still am) fascinated with the idea and excitement of flying. I had envisioned myself in uniform, either dipping a wing in salute over my schools in St. Marc and Port-au-Prince, or flying my mother to any place in the world she would like to go. That, I thought, would be the ultimate adventure. Never minding that I had not been nearer to airplanes than seeing them fly overhead, I viewed the airplane as a symbol of freedom and power. I imagined that my friends and family would be proud of me.

Pride, I had discovered from the incident of being rebuffed in the home of my host family, was a very strong motivator. I took that lesson to heart and developed for myself my own definition of pride. For me, pride would not be arrogance, but rather tangible achievements. I was determined to seek pride of *accomplishment* and not pride of birth. I further decided at this early age that I would avoid the kind of pride which placed others in an inferior position, as I had been made to feel in the household where I had been rejected.

It was at this point that I began to formulate what course my life must take. The idea to enter medical school became more definite with my study of biology and my fascination with the harmony by which the various body systems operate. I thought about what it would be like to be involved in restoring the body functions if one or more systems were to break down. I then vowed I would study and do whatever it took to be accepted at the Medical School of Port-au-Prince. I told no one of this target, but it became the driving motivation during the next several years of my life. I developed my goal into three objectives: (1) to attain the status of a medical doctor, the highest prestige I could bring to myself and to my family and the highest stature in the eyes of my country; (2) to prove to the family where I had boarded the first year that I was a worthy individual, not to be lightly dismissed; and (3) to personally test myself and my abilities.

It was also at this time that I began to sense that I had the ability to focus on a goal and then develop all the steps it would take to achieve that goal. This skill of being able to envision enabled me to project an outcome and to perceive what was required each step of the way to ensure success of that goal. Earlier in my life I had not understood this talent, thinking everyone had the same kind of power to envision. However, as I matured I realized that among my acquaintances there were no others who shared this gift. Initially I used this talent only in my studies; later, it helped me to plan my career. As I would come to learn, the real importance of this envisioning became central to the humanitarian projects to which I would eventually devote my life.

Once I acknowledged my goal of medicine, I quickly found a place to board with another family. This time my cousin (also a student) and I were able to rent an entire room, with each paying $20 per month. This was relative luxury compared to my previous cot in the hall, but I was soon to discover that a small room in a crowded tropical city teeming with people could become very, very hot and quite airless. Both my cousin and I found the conditions very difficult, as our room was dark and scarcely large enough for two. Having no other choices given our impoverished condition, however, I began to go to the public parks and study under street lights.

The street light under which I spent most of my student life stood near the National Palace. This lamppost still stands and I have never forgotten "my" light with its striped pole of red and blue on silver metal. Here on "my" concrete park bench it was quieter than in the crowded, hot, noisy house where it was impossible to study. Hungry, poor and alone, I studied, my stomach often empty, my eyes straining to read under the dim light. While I longed for the shade of a tree and the closeness of family in St. Marc, there was no thought ever given to going home, just as there was no choice of rooming in a more suitable lodging.

At Lycée Toussaint Louverture in Port-au-Prince, I was a much different student than I had been in St. Marc. This time I was determined to succeed. By my second year I was the one the teachers sent to the blackboard when the government school inspector made an official visit to the classroom. This singling out by the teachers and its resulting praise from the government inspector built my self-confidence and made me even more resolved to concentrate on my studies. Now it was not just a matter of completing my secondary school education, but of excelling as well. I was resolute in my determination to be first in my university classes. I realized this would be quite a feat for one who had taken his early education in public and parochial schools, and I knew that the competition I would face from those who had received their education from private schools would be formidable. Nonetheless, decisive and finally confident in my own abilities, I not only passed the first Baccalauréate Examination, but I placed *first* in the entire nation in mathematics for the B section.

Because there was neither time nor money for pleasure, "enjoying the experience of college" was never a consideration for me and most of my friends. Certainly, I liked the company of my fellow students, but there was very little leisure or funds for socializing. The only diversion the young people had was the camaraderie of one another. We enjoyed each other and shared what few resources we had among us. One of our favorite pastimes was the infrequent, but welcomed interruption of our outdoor study sessions. I still laugh when I think about how we fellows would "take a breather" by watching and talking to the girls as they passed by on their way to school, to a study session, or just out for a stroll. Sometimes these "chance encounters" would lead to conversation or to walking with the girls to a quieter spot where we could be alone and put studies aside for a brief time.

Occasionally on a Friday or Saturday night, the university students would get together for a street party outside someone's house or we would find the money to attend one of the several public dance halls which were open just for dancing on Friday and Saturday nights. In these dance halls there would be a band playing a mix of Latin American and Caribbean music; at smaller private parties, the young adults danced to records or to whatever music was playing on the radio. The source of the music did not matter; it was the socializing that was important.

"Pocket money" was scarce because I had no steady source of income and had never even heard of an "allowance." For the most part, I was dependent for spending money on what my mother could provide on the days she came to the market in Port-au-Prince. Occasionally, other family members would be visiting the capital for business purposes and would hand me loose change or even a dollar—whatever they could spare. I especially looked forward to the occasional business trips one of my uncles made to Port-au-Prince; he and I would travel around the city and, before leaving for home, my uncle would give me a dollar or so. Without this support, limited though it was, I would have been in dire financial straits.

I tried only one venture in earning extra money, one which held some promise and, while not exactly within the boundaries of legitimate business, was a typical practice in Haiti and many other countries with high tariffs on luxury items. I began buying cigarettes from a man who bought them in bulk from crew members on American cruise ships docked in the harbor. Because the ships were considered a "free port," the original handler could buy cigarettes at a low price and sell them privately to a "middle man," thus avoiding the Haitian import tax. I, in turn, would sell these cigarettes to my fellow students and then purchase more with my small margin of profit. When after three months my business reached the grand operating sum of nearly $100, I confidently gave the money to my contact at our usual meeting place, a system which by then had become routine. This time, however, my contact did not return. I saw neither the man nor my money again.

Following the embarrassment of losing time and money in this unsuccessful business venture, I quickly restricted my adventures to attending classes. During my final year of classical studies in philosophy there was barely time to sleep. Along with my good friend Ulrick and several other students, I concentrated on studying not only for the second Baccalauréate examination but also for the Medical School entrance exam, as we did not have the time or money to spend on an extra year's study preparation. Because of this strict study plan, we two friends easily passed the Baccalauréate exam, earning bachelor's degrees. Rather than celebrate, however, we immediately focused on our next task, devoting our time cramming for the Medical School entrance exam scheduled for three months later. Our study schedule became more intense as we structured a routine to which we religiously adhered. Every other night we studied through the night, sleeping only alternate nights, once in each 48-hour period. This pattern continued for three solid months.

Nearly 500 students, from all over Haiti, took the Medical School entrance exam in 1954, most for the first time, some for a second time, a few for a third. Of that number, only 40 were accepted for admission to Medical School.[3] Between Ulrick and me, both of whom had spent almost every waking minute of the past three months together studying, only one of us earned a coveted slot among the chosen few. Ulrick went to study medicine in France and I took a place among the 40 new medical students, members of the Medical School Class of 1960. To make the victory even sweeter, the family who several years before had asked me to leave their home, now heartily embraced me.

Medical School

In October 1954 just as Hurricane Hazel made her debut on the island of Haiti, I began my six-year journey of studies at the Medical School of Port-au-Prince. I had not been in class for more than two days when the hurricane hit, the worst natural disaster to ever visit Port-au-Prince. No one in living memory had seen so much water on land nor had anyone ever seen a hurricane strike with such force. Port-au-Prince is usually well protected by the mountains to the north and east and by the island of La Gonâve to the northwest, so hurricanes rarely make it over the mountains to reach the capital city. There was complete confidence that this hurricane would do no more than bring rain, just like most all other hurricanes had; hence, the damage of Hurricane Hazel was compounded by its surprise. No one expected the intense rage of Hazel, and the people of Haiti were ill-prepared to deal with the catastrophe. Beginning on 11 October, Hurricane Hazel first struck at the southwest corner of Haiti near Port-à-Piment, tore through Cayes, and nearly destroyed Jérémie to the north of Port-à-Piment, leveling everything in its path and claiming at least a thousand victims. Cutting a swath east through the Canal du Sud, it headed due east, bombarding the capital city with a ferocity hitherto unseen in Haiti.

The medical students watched the devastation from the top floor of the Medical School as the turbulent water surged by, carrying with it broken furniture, parts of houses, indistinguishable debris, and many human victims, all swirling in one massive river. Roofs were ripped from buildings, roads crumbled, and bridges collapsed. It was impossible to tell where the bay began, as water swirled and churned in and from all directions. We medical students could do nothing but watch in fascination and horror. Our morbid humor could do little to cover our terror as we cracked poor jokes about being the first medical class to be obliterated even before the initial set of examinations had been taken. Hurricane Hazel and the devastation she brought remains one of the most vivid remembrances shared by those of us who were fellow students during this horrific catastrophe.

In mid-May of 1955, scarcely a half year after the devastation of Hazel, we again watched from the windows of the Medical School, this time focusing on the undergraduate students from the lycées as they rushed through the streets of Port-au-Prince in a student revolt. The hospitals began to fill with injured students and police, and all the young medical students, including me, were pressed into service. We recognized some of the younger lycée students, friends of ours, among those we were helping to treat. It was difficult treating young men not unlike ourselves, and I remember thinking how little separated them from us. "It could just as easily have been any one of us," I thought, and I reconfirmed in my own mind the senselessness of such street uprisings. Even though siege and countersiege had been my experience as a Haitian, I knew that such a way of life for a nation made no sense. Medicine, I believed, should be for healing people suffering from disease, not battle wounds.

The following year was better for the medical students as we began to gain confidence in our roles. The class none of us have ever forgotten was gross anatomy; the group of whom I was part was assigned the only female cadaver. Because of the nearly intolerable odor of formaldehyde and my intense fear of dead bodies, I spent a gloomy two weeks trying to become accustomed to the unwelcome task of dissection. To everyone's surprise, our group became skilled in anatomy and very familiar with our cadaver, whom we named Martha. By All Souls Day we had her standing, guiding the body in a dance with a male cadaver. This second year of medical school also marked the time when most of us wanted everyone to know that we were "medical students," wearing our short white coats, and draping our stethoscopes around our necks in full view of any passer-by.

It was during this time that I began to doubt the quality of the Port-au-Prince Hospital when the President of Haiti decided to travel to the United States for a medical check-up in a Philadelphia hospital. I found myself wondering (but not daring to ask, for to utter such words could place me in jeopardy), "Why would President Magloire not schedule his routine check-up in the Port-au-Prince Hospital? Did he believe the facility was sub-standard? Did he not have faith in the quality of care he would receive there? Did he not trust the medical staff? Why would Magloire not use the medical system for which he held responsibility?"

Despite this unease, by the end of the first trimester of my first year in medical school I stood second in my class. Throughout my entire six years I never ranked below number five. The top five medical students remained consistent throughout our years together, interchanging positions, none of us ever wavering from the top five rankings. Remembering my earlier pledge as a public school student that I would do just as well, if not better, than my peers who had been schooled with much higher expectations in the parochial secondary educational system, I still smile to recall that of these five outstanding scholars, three of us had attended lycée while two were products of the Brothers' School in Port-au-Prince. With each successive year of superior class rankings, my confidence in myself and my abilities increased as did my drive to reach my full potential, unaware of the long and arduous pathway I faced in the near future.

As exciting as it was to be in medical school, the political rumblings in Haiti were unsettling and became even more so during my second year, even though I was not directly affected by politics. A rising political figure, François Duvalier, Haiti's soon-to-be "president-for-life," had gone into hiding from 1954–1956.[4] Duvalier, a quiet country doctor, born amid middle class genteel poverty, the son of a justice of the peace, would never have been thought to be destined for either greatness or infamy. A classic example of the rhetorical question, "Does history make the man or does the man make history," he was a man who found himself in the right place at the right time.

In the early 1950s Duvalier had been known by most Haitians as the doctor who had eradicated yaws. He gained this reputation not because he personally had led a drive against the disease but because he had worked with the American public health missions in its war on the disease through the use of penicillin. Based solely on his ability to speak passable English, he had been made director of the Rural Clinic of Gressier where he had tried hard to make people think he was a great country doctor. Duvalier had served as Under Secretary for Labor and, later, Public Health and Labor Minister in an earlier government. Following the election of Magloire, however, he voluntarily returned to his medical mission. There he began to prepare in earnest for the time he would become the leader of Haiti, transforming himself from a country doctor to a politician. He honed the qualities which would later serve his purpose: (1) total lack of personal loyalty to anyone, even those who helped him; (2) universal mistrust of individuals, yet demanding trust from everyone associated with him; (3) skill to lie and break promises without any hint of facial expression; and (4) ability to identify the weaknesses of others.[5]

In September of 1956, while Duvalier was quietly but carefully planning his political moves, President Magloire returned from his medical check-up in Philadelphia (with a side vacation trip to Niagara Falls). Two months later, Haiti witnessed its first terrorist bombing against Magloire's government. This assault was both unexpected and frightening, even for a country whose history is rife with violence.

Shortly after the bombings, a series of events led to Magloire's resignation. Despite his back-door attempts to remain in office by declaring himself in charge of the army by virtue of his former military rank, Magloire's plans were thwarted by a three-day general strike which paralyzed the country. He was forced into exile, complete with a military escort to a waiting DC-3 which took him and his family to Kingston, Jamaica. Immediately following Magloire's departure, the capital shut down and, on 12 December 1956, the Supreme Court Chief Justice of Haiti became Provisional President, to preside in that high office for only fifty-five days. For the next nine months numerous governments rose and fell—five within only six months. Throughout January 1957 the government was at a standstill.

During the time of suspended government services, classes at the Medical School were not held with any regularity. The interruption of classes was further compounded by the poor quality of some of the instruction being delivered by newly repatriated Haitian physicians who found positions in the Medical School. These repatriates taught in the old French/Haitian way—by rote memorization requiring the medical students to learn everything word for word. Without textbooks or laboratory classes, we had to write down every word spoken by the medical lecturers, as we had no other means by which to obtain information. In turn, all this written data had to be memorized. There was very little understanding of what was being taught and copied into notebooks. Those of us who asked for further explanation on the lectures were rebuffed by the professors. As students, we had little recourse but to share our anger among ourselves; there was no student advocacy committee or board of appeals to which to turn.

One professor in particular stands out in the collective memory of my medical class. During every class Dr. D___ stood in front of us, opened a medical textbook, and proceeded to read to us. The routine never varied. He just read aloud, class after class. We were worried as to how we would study for an examination. My friend Charles Benoit and I reclaimed the light pole under which I had studied as undergraduate. There, every night we would doggedly read, study, and try to synthesize the information from our notes. On the night before the exam, we took our places on "my" bench and began a final read-through of the thick notebook filled with notes we painstakingly had taken in cramped handwriting. Trying to review the entire book was a difficult task, but we approached our work with diligence and hope.

About ten o'clock we were hungry and decided to take a quick break for a milkshake. I ordered a small one and Charles opted for a large. We then scurried back to our studies, knowing there was no time to lose. Around midnight Charles became ill, complaining of a stomach ache. I, feeling just fine, laughed at my friend, cajoling him to get on with the studying. "Come on," I said. "This is no time for malingering. Just put your stomach out of your mind and get back to work." Charles protested that he just didn't feel right, and I continued to push him to study. Finally in exasperation Charles spouted a proverb at that time unknown to me, but one which after this incident I never forgot: "At the turkeys' funeral the chickens don't laugh." Around three in the morning, I realized the "chickens" had come home to roost in my own stomach and it was Charles' turn to laugh. However, there was no time for recriminations. Trying to complete our studying in time for the exam only hours away took every iota of will power. It was at that point we two ailing friends resolved that, once an opportunity arose, we would take some kind of action against the poor teaching we had had to endure.

Our chance came after Magloire lost power. Frustrated with the expectation that we were to recite information without any understanding of it, we students took matters into our own hands, seeking action we believed appropriate. Our class wrote a letter to Dr. D___ and other classes wrote to professors who also taught solely by rote. These letters, left on top of the professors' desks, asked for their resignations. Our entire class watched as Dr. D___ read what we had written to him and our eyes remained upon him as he openly wept and left the classroom.

As exciting as it was to be in medical school, by my third year the governmental rumblings in Haiti were especially unsettling. After much political turmoil and bloodshed, a presidential election was held. As usual, cheating at the polls was rampant. Because of the high rate of illiteracy among the population, ballots in Haiti are distributed by the candidates in advance of voting and the voters carry their ballots to the polling place. If the election official is not pleased with any ballot, he can remove it or simply reject the offending vote-caster. Using these tactics, as well as other methods of intimidation, François Duvalier won the presidency in a landslide. His rule began on 22 October 1957, on the eve of year four of my medical school education.

Shortly after taking office, Duvalier's presidency was threatened by a failed coup against him. Sensing possible danger, he devised better training methods for his army which for the most part had sat on their hands during the attempted coup. Duvalier invited the U. S. Marines to Port-au-Prince to train his regular military army at U. S. expense and he also began to put into place a quasi-military organization answerable only to him. This private police force had as its base the political leaders who already held strong-holds of power, long-established and accepted in Haiti as a part of the political system. This loyalist police force became known as the *tonton macoutes*, a name taken from fairy tales in which the *tonton macoute* was a bogeyman, a scarecrow with human flesh who wore denim overalls and carried a cutlass and a knapsack made of straw. In his knapsack, this character always had scraps of naughty chil-dren whom he had dismembered to eat as snacks. Unlike the fairy tale creatures, however, Duvalier's *macoutes* roamed the streets in broad daylight, parading their Uzi machine guns rather than straw knapsacks. The *macoutes* owed allegiance personally and exclu-sively to Duvalier and not to their country. The *macoutes* were given license to extend their base of power to any part of Haiti and soon, *macoutes* were everywhere—in the army, in civil service, on the docks, supplementing the regular police, in the banks and post offices, and even in the schools. They carried out much of the "dirty work" for Duvalier, and, because of his protection, they became the most powerful and most loathed of Duvalier's numerous forces. In time, they came to be feared as much as Hitler's secret police, the *Waffen SS*, had been two decades earlier in Germany.

Most of the newspapers and radio stations were already con-trolled by the government when Duvalier ordered the confiscation of all radio transmitters in the hands of private citizens, and he shut down radio stations and newspapers that did not take the party line—his political party. Thus any information, unless approved by Duvalier, was not easily available, even by those who had the money to buy a newspaper or own a radio. By holding both the pen and the sword, Duvalier retained total control over his countrymen.

Political disorder continued, and the medical students had to wait for teachers to be appointed to replace those who had fled Haiti in fear for their lives. With the overall unsettled political climate, most of us kept a low profile, trying to avoid direct involvement with the ever-shifting politics. Our position as medical students was so fragile we could not risk calling any attention to ourselves or we could have been arrested on the spot. We were quite aware that there were political spies in our midst and we guarded against uttering anything that might be called anti-government. No comments, no casual remarks, no making jokes—nothing even suggesting politics was mentioned in our conversations. We learned that the less attention we called to ourselves, the safer we would be.

Duvalier's macoutes, with their dark eyeglasses, denim clothing, and red kerchiefs, continued to wield power over the people. Before long, they infiltrated even the medical school, taking places that would have gone to students who had earned their admission through the entrance examination. These macoute medical students were the only Haitian citizens permitted to carry guns, even bearing arms while attending their medical school classes. They also had scheduled daily target practice and military exercises. They did not have to worry about maneuvers taking time from their studies, as it was understood that no macoute would receive a poor grade in academic studies.

Because a curfew was in effect in Port-au-Prince, the medical students who were not able to vacate the building by dusk were confined overnight. The curfew made daily living difficult, particularly as we had so little free time and not much opportunity to leave the school even for meals and studying. Fortunately there were reading lamps in the hospital, as the students no longer could use favorite studying spots under the street lamps in the park near the National Palace. One evening several of us found ourselves unexpectedly spending the night in the hospital. We had planned to leave the building in the late afternoon for a bite to eat, fully anticipating to return in time to abide by the curfew. Unfortunately, classes ran late that day and we did not have a chance to go outside before curfew. Knowing we risked arrest if we went out, we decided instead to try to find something in the hospital for our supper.

Not having eaten since early morning when I had had only a light breakfast, I was quite hungry. My dilemma was compounded by the fact that by the time the curfew would be lifted the following morning, it would be time for the first morning class. There was no dining room or cafeteria in the hospital, and no hospital kitchen was available. I tried to find a resident from whom I could borrow some food. Not finding anyone, I finally looked in the refrigerator located in the residents' kitchen. I found a bottle of milk, presumably for the child of one of the surgical residents living there and, in desperation, I drank it. This action has bothered me to this day, but I was just too hungry to resist.

Duvalier's proposed military state did not bode well for anyone, and Haitian intellectuals and professionals began to flee Haiti as soon as they could to escape the uncertain political situation. The killings in the streets, the guns in the hospital, even alleged killing in the hospital by the macoutes—all were disconcerting to the physicians, professors, and medical students. This mass exodus was especially heavy during my last two years of medical school, and its resultant "brain drain" decimated Haiti, leaving many gaps in all professional fields, including the medical school, impacting on the quality and quantity of the education for the students. Students did their best in the face of this reduced staff, but such a situation was quite unsettling.

Still, most of the students persevered under poor educational conditions, for we had no other choice. At best, the textbooks were ponderous with their formal French and there were never enough books for everyone. The equipment was sparse and sub-standard. Because there were no laboratory facilities, we never experienced how to do basic research. There were a few old microscopes, but nothing near to what was needed for authentic laboratory work, let alone research. We had to learn physiology, biochemistry, and pathology by reading and memorizing what we could. There was no opportunity to run even basic experiments, and nothing ever could be studied in three dimensions. There was also a shortage of supplies and no one could count on anything being replenished on a regular schedule—if at all. Resourceful as only the young can be, many of us learned to improvise where we could.

In the midst of all of this tumult was the return to Haiti of a group of physicians who had been trained in the United States. They were prepared to be loyal to Duvalier and were richly rewarded for that allegiance. This was good for the students in that the physicians brought with them textbooks written in English. These books provided us with information about modern techniques being used in the western world; in addition, these new professors helped their classes learn to read English in case we ever had an opportunity to apply for a residency or study in English-speaking countries.

I knew I wanted to apply for a residency in Canada or the United States because of the reputation of the teaching hospitals. My long-range goal was to enter the United States, but the only way that would be possible would be to pass the ECFMG (English competency and medical examination). This was extremely difficult to do while remaining in Haiti because of the language barrier. I, therefore, wanted to apply to hospitals in Quebec, a Canadian province bilingual in French and English. I believed I could gain admittance to a hospital in Montreal where my French would allow me to work while I studied English.

I began my master plan, first weighing all the options and their possible consequences. I chose a summer internship rotation in the sanatorium in Port-au-Prince where room and board would be provided. In that way I could save money to pay my rent during the last year of medical school. The sanatorium offered practical experience in the medical and surgical treatment of tuberculosis. The residents and attending physicians were excellent surgeons and, through observing their techniques, I developed a great interest in the possibility of pursuing a surgical specialty. Assisting in surgery, I sensed I had dexterity as well as good hand and eye coordination. My confidence increased when one of the attending physicians told me that I should consider embracing surgery as a specialty. One day when I was having lunch with a group of attending physicians, I noticed that the chief resident, a surgeon, was watching me cut the food on my plate. He commented, "I don't mean to be staring, but I couldn't help noticing that you do not switch your knife from one hand to the other when you are cutting your food. Have you ever thought of becoming a surgeon?" Rather taken aback, I asked him to elaborate. The surgeon responded that those with an inclination to be ambidextrous often make the best surgeons, as surgical skill requires dexterity of both hands. He encouraged me to consider this specialty, saying, "You must go into surgery. You would make an excellent surgeon." This casual conversation was the beginning of a focused career goal, a plan to become a surgeon.

In the midst of the political uprisings and protests during the fall of 1959, I finally moved to more suitable quarters in a pension. Here I was later joined by my cousin Roger who seven years earlier had completed his studies in the area of ethnology and soon after had left for Paris on a scholarship. While there, Roger had been offered what promised to be an administrative position in the Bureau of External Affairs in Port-au-Prince. Pleased to be invited "home" to take a government position, he returned with high expectations. Much to his disappointment, however, the position was not what he had expected and he found that his considerable skill and talent were being underutilized. Most of his time was spent writing letters for others.

Soon tiring of this clerical position, Roger wanted to return to France. An emigration, however, might be regarded as suspect, so he and I needed to find a legitimate excuse for his return to Paris. The only plan we could think of was based on Roger's bleeding ulcer. The problem was how to convince the authorities that Roger must have treatment from a specialist in Paris. Together we crafted a plot. Hosting a small dinner party, among the guests we invited was a macoute doctor who had studied in America. The menu had been carefully arranged to trigger the bleeding of Roger's ulcer. During the meal, it became readily apparent to the macoute guest that Roger had a medical problem, and he supported my suggestion that Roger required specialized treatment. The next step was to contact a physician in Paris who agreed to accept Roger on a consultative basis. That was all we needed, and Roger was on his way to Paris, this time permanently. I recall this incident with great delight as it was a bright spot in an otherwise dreary and fruitless effort by young professionals to outsmart the macoutes. While I missed my cousin's company, I was glad for the time to concentrate on a successful final year of medical school.

The spring of 1960, what should have been a joyous time of celebration and graduation, was marked by continued political unrest. The Medical School Class of 1960 was not permitted to hold a graduation ceremony, marking this class as the only one ever to be graduated without a formal observance. The medical students, now officially M.D.s, were unceremoniously handed their diplomas in an office. There were no families, no caps and gowns, no pomp, no pageantry, no special recognition to the honors graduates, and no valedictory address. The long-standing tradition of a Commencement service held at the French Institute with the President of Haiti presiding was ignored when Duvalier canceled all events for everything even suggesting a celebration.

The ill-starred Class of 1960 also holds the unfortunate distinction of being the first class assigned to compulsory medical service in the rural areas of Haiti. There were to be no exceptions, not even to accept appointments for further study in a specialty, particularly if it meant leaving the country. This ban was effected despite the desperate need in Haiti for those trained and skilled in a medical specialty. There was only one remote hope, one possibility to reduce the rural service assignment from two years to one. A few residencies in Port-au-Prince would be opened the second year of the two-year compulsory medical service and those in service to rural areas could apply for them. Everyone suspected that those few appointments would most likely be given to the doctors loyal to the regime, but in reality class rank determined who would be first offered any of the available appointments.

As 1960 came to a close, the Duvalier regime denied all exit visas, an ominous omen and a constant worry to those who had hoped for a future which would include foreign study for a medical specialty. This ruling added pressure on those who someday might want to apply to study outside the country. All of us were helpless, as we feared making any misstep or taking any action, no matter how innocent, might be construed as anti-government.

This was the kind of future I faced even with graduating *magna cum laude*. Such restrictive measures tended to stifle any kind of initiative or plans for advanced study. Graham Greene, in the oft-quoted opening of his classic novel *The Comedians*, aptly described this Haiti of the 1960s: "Impossible to deepen that dark night."[6]

Notes

1. Robert D. and Nancy G. Heinl, with revisions and expansion by Michael Heinl, *Written in Blood* (The Story of the Haitian People) (Lanham, MD: University Press of America, 1996), 258.

2. Ibid., 308.

3. Selden Rodman, *Haiti: The Black Republic* (NY: Devin-Adair, 1954, 1984)

4. Heinl, p. 542.

5. Elizabeth Abbott, *The Duvaliers and Their Legacy* (NY: McGraw Hill, 1988), p. 61.

6. Graham Greene, *The Comedians* (NY: Viking Press, 1966), p.1.

Chapter 3: A Village Physician

Rodrigue Mortel, M.D. At last I had achieved what Manman herself had always wanted and could not have for herself: an education and status. She was as proud as if she herself had earned the medical degree. She rightly viewed it as a joint effort of her own hard labor and her son's diligence. Of course, I too was pleased to have reached this goal, well understanding that, given the statistical odds, completing Medical School was a major accomplishment, if not a near impossibility for someone with my very poor background. It is difficult for anyone who has not lived in poverty to imagine the near-impossible challenge I had faced: penniless and hungry most of the time; without family, and with only a bed in a hot, crowded room to even temporarily call my own; and no one upon whom to lean, no support system except for fellow students, most of whom were as poor as I. Even very early in my career, I realized that to have come from such poverty, with no political influence, no class status, and no one to serve as my mentor and guide, and to have completed medical school was a compelling lesson in overcoming adversity.

Humbled by my good fortune, I well knew where the real guidance and support had come from. I fully believe that even with my mother's labor and persistence and my own intelligence, initiative, and self-confidence, I still could not have come this far without the help of God. From the time I had begun to take my studies seriously in my last years at the lycée, I knew that any success I would have could be attributed to my faith. The more I achieved, the more I pledged that my life would be spent in giving back. God provided so much in giving me an education and I will return that gift to others through my work and with His direction.

Into the Remotest Villages

While not agreeing with the pronouncement that my graduating class be assigned to serve two years in rural areas as government physicians, I was not unhappy with my choice of assignment. Having grown up in St. Marc, a small city, I was grateful I would be practicing medicine in a small town rather than in one of the mountainous regions of the country. Though convinced that I would not remain a general practitioner, I looked upon these two years as an opportunity to practice general medicine while helping my countrymen. There was little chance that I would remain in Haiti, even if I were to be offered a residency in a specialty at the University Hospital. My mind was set to leave the country, for I knew my destiny lay elsewhere.

Having graduated second in my class, I was given second choice of all rural assignments. I chose the town of St. Michel de l'Attalaye, which I expected to be my home base for the next two years, on the recommendation of a distant cousin (anyone even remotely connected to the family was known as a "cousin") who had established a medical practice in St. Marc, but regularly traveled to St. Michel to see patients who requested his private services. The townspeople were not particularly satisfied with the services of the only other doctor in town and many preferred to be attended by my cousin who hoped he could interest me in joining his practice. Prior to graduation, I had traveled with my cousin to St. Michel where I could see for myself that I would be able to establish a good private practice in addition to the required clinical service for the state. Further, St. Michel was an appealing assignment because the area was relatively prosperous, thanks to the family of Louis Dejoie who had established a thriving business in the town, producing an ingredient for the manufacture of perfume. The employment rate was high, and St. Michel was said to be a prime location for a good, young physician.

These public clinics were supported by the government in order to provide medical care for Haitian citizens, both in the town and in the villages surrounding it. Even today, the clinics are all easily recognizable by their white color, trimmed in green and with a green stripe painted horizontally around the center of the structure. While St. Michel's clinic was housed in its own building, not every clinic in Haiti is self-contained; some consist only of a rented room or two. Most of the larger clinics at that time were open every day and housed two full-time nurses who could provide basic medical care on the days the doctors were seeing patients in the surrounding villages.

In addition to the public clinic hours between nine and one, I held office hours for a private practice before nine or after one o'clock in a room in the house I was renting as my residence. My government salary for clinical service was $120 per month to provide care for any of the 10,000 rural Haitians who might visit the clinics for which I was responsible. Three days a week I traveled on horseback to the outlying rural areas, accompanied by a male nurse I had hired. Upon our arrival the nurse and I always found the villagers waiting for us, lined up in front of tiny pastel houses that leaned against one another at the edge of the road. Most of the houses had hand-painted picture-signs advertising goods and services for sale: bread, beer, tailoring, hair pressing, and an occasional pharmacy. The clinic itself was usually located in the *bouk* (town center) or wherever the market was located, sometimes at the end of the town. Regardless of the place, the people were always there, patiently waiting outside the clinic or rented room (which served as a clinic) in the open market area.

I attempted to treat every ailment known to the region, and learned more about my people and their needs. There was not a wide variety of medication available, so I gave my patients medications from the small supply I had on hand, or I prescribed the medications that the villagers could obtain from the local pharmacy. The pharmacy was a business anyone could operate without being a licensed or trained pharmacist; therefore, the medications were such that they did not require the skill of a trained pharmacist, but rather were similar to basic over-the-counter drugs. If medicines were not available locally, a family member would travel to the nearest city to obtain them. Difficult cases, not treatable by the local physician, were sent to Gonaïves, the nearest city.

The following chronic conditions would usually bring patients to the clinic: malaria, infectious diseases, hypertension, serious eye trouble, chronic skin trouble, nervousness, allergies, and arthritis. Haitians, by culture, are not likely to visit a doctor unless they are suffering pain; therefore, many diseases were not diagnosed in time for successful treatment. In the rural areas I served, some of the patients preferred to rely on folk and herbal medicines and they would seek the doctor's help only for broken bones or conditions that did not improve with home remedies or did not get better after being treated by the voodoo priest.

My acknowledgment of the inherent beliefs of the rural Haitians in the power of voodoo, combined with my growing awareness of the unavailability of supplies and medication, led to my fuller understanding of the severe limitations of the general practitioner, especially in Haiti. Substandard medical knowledge, incomplete training, lack of effective medication, poorly equipped hospitals— all led to frustration. The lack of good medical information and practice increased my thirst for knowledge and determination to seek that knowledge in order to some day correct those needs.

In the Haitian villages, the doctor could not, of course, treat every patient successfully under such primitive conditions; thus, the mortality rate was high. The deceased were usually attended by persons hired by the family. When a patient died, the burial had to occur within a day as there were no morgues except in the larger cities. When a death occurred, it was announced by a *rèl*, which is a piercing cry or wail emitted by a family member to signify great loss and anguish. The news of a death was passed from house to house, and within a short time the entire surrounding area had been notified that someone had died.

As there were few morticians, preservation of the body was not common. If there would be a need to preserve the body of the deceased awaiting the return of a spouse or child, then the body would be packed in ice. For longer periods of waiting time the physician would pour formaldehyde down the throat of the deceased and then inject the solution into the veins.

Family and friends would gather at the home of the deceased for the wake which today is held on the evening prior to the funeral. Many believe that this gathering helps the deceased pass a happy last night on earth. In some villages, both mourners and visitors play the games the deceased most enjoyed in his or her lifetime. Food is not usually served, although beverages are always available; tea, coffee, and alcohol are offered, as are the favorite foods of the departed. The wake continues through the night, not ending until five or six in the morning. It is at this time that the body is prepared and dressed. Once the body is readied for viewing and subsequent burial, visitations begin and continue until the time of the funeral. This visitation or vigil is expected to be enjoyed by all the mourners, and is a mark of respect to the deceased as well as the bereaved family which takes pride in the number of people who come to share in the mourning.

Both in the past and even today, following the vigil, all mourners accompany the body to the church for the funeral service. For those who can afford it, an orchestra is hired to lead the procession to the church, and then to the cemetery, all the while playing classical music. The mourners then return to the family house of the deceased at which time a reception is held. The day after the funeral, the first day of the Novena, all family members visit the tomb to recite the rosary. In some villages, every evening for nine days, in the family home, prayers are said for the departed. On the ninth day, "the last day of prayer," the prayer is of longer duration, followed by the serving of food and beverages.

A death, while very sad for the family members, is still fairly routine to physicians who daily deal with life and death. Few, though, will ever be prepared for the experience I faced in my first year of practice, an incident that haunts me to this day.

It was a Sunday, early afternoon around one o'clock, when they came for me. I was told that the patient was a twenty-two-year-old man with a high fever, and could I come immediately. I picked up my bag, saddled my horse, and followed the two men who had been sent for me. Upon entering the house, I saw a young man outstretched on the bed. I began to examine him, and very quickly I suspected malaria because of the symptoms he presented. I couldn't be sure without a blood test, but there was no laboratory within a reasonable distance which could run the appropriate testing. I had no other choice but to simply administer the proper medication for malaria to lower his temperature. Knowing that was all I could do, I returned home and began to prepare for the next day's clinic. About 4:00 p.m., I heard a knock on the door. There stood members of the family of the patient I had just left. "Please come back with us," they requested. "Our brother has died."

I went back to their house prepared to confirm the death. I carefully examined the body, checking all vital signs. There was no heart beat and no other signs of life. Sad to say, the young man had indeed died. I felt remorse at the loss of this life, a man not much younger than I. I regretted that I had not been able to confirm the malaria I had suspected and, of course, asked myself was there anything else I could have done to save his life.

I began to express my sympathy at the death of a member of this family, especially one in the prime of young manhood. I said, "I regret that he has died." Before I could offer further condolences, a family member said, "But he is not dead." Feeling a bit awkward at this point, I nevertheless had to insist that, "Yes, he has died. I am sorry at your grief, but there are no signs of life in your son and brother."

I was not prepared for their next words. "We know who did this," they said. I asked them what they meant. The victim's brother continued, "He is still alive. If we bury him like this, he will be taken out of his tomb and made into a zombie, forced to a life-in-death of hard work on a farm. We want you to make sure he cannot awaken when they come to the grave for him." I was told, "You must kill him." Not believing what I was hearing, I hesitated for a moment before responding to this unexpected request. "I cannot kill him," I replied. "You must understand; the young man is dead." I then left the house, again offering condolences.

Six hours later I returned to attend the vigil. I was surprised to find all of the family there just as they had been when I had left earlier. "Please touch him," I was asked. This I did, only to discover to my great astonishment that the body's skin was extremely hot, much like the high fever I had found the first time I had examined him. With that touch I felt my own skin turn cold. I didn't know what to say. It was impossible for a cadaver to be warm six hours after death. Again, the family insisted that he was not dead. And again they began to implore me to end his life as one of the *living dead*.

"Whatever do you mean?" I asked, already knowing the answer.

"Please, please, you must prevent what will happen to him. Don't you understand? He has had a voodoo curse placed upon him which has left him in this trance."

Yes, I did understand. While I had had no experience with this, I had heard that such things happen. I was aware of the belief that there is a process by which a voodoo priest/doctor can produce poison that places the body in a state of suspended animation. In such cases, the body is presumed dead and is buried. Later, the voodoo priest resurrects the body which resumes its vital signs; however, because there has not been any circulation of blood to the brain during this suspended life status, the person remains in a zombie-like state. Believers of voodoo say that the voodoo priest then holds control over the person. It is further believed that these persons become the "walking dead" and whoever controls them has total power over them, forcing them to work as slaves. There is almost no hope that normal life can be resumed, although there are a few unsubstantiated claimants who profess to having been zombies who later have been "awakened."

"See, you must help us," they insisted. "He will never be our son and brother as we knew him. He faces a life that is worse than death."

I will never, ever forget their pleading voices and anguished faces.

I never did forget them and the scene still haunts me. Actually, I never forgot any of the villagers. Their lives are etched forever in my consciousness and even today I can tell you the family names of my patients, the market day of each village, and the names of the streets; I can still recall in detail every turn in the road and every horse trail, as I used both horses and an automobile in St. Michel.

I owned an old jeep that I had purchased from my distant cousin, the doctor from St. Michel. Once a month I used it to make a trip to Port-au-Prince to obtain medical supplies for the dispensary. The jeep was used only for these trips, as there were no roads from St. Michel to the outlying villages; all traveling to see patients in the government clinics was done by horseback.

Even though St. Marc is located only 30–35 miles from St. Michel, travel was so difficult that the trip (by vehicle) took four hours during the dry season and up to eight hours in the rainy season. There are seven or eight riverbeds (but no bridges) between St. Michel and Gonaïves, the nearest city, and during the rainy season they are impassable. I remember clearly my first trip from St. Michel to Port-au-Prince in August during the rainy season. I still recall how I dreaded to make this journey of 12–15 miles across rough terrain between St. Michel and Gonaïves and on roads in poor condition between Gonaïves and the capital city.

Sometimes on the return trip from Port-au-Prince, I had to stay overnight in Gonaïves because of rain or darkness. Even in rural Haiti, it was not safe to travel at night, especially outside the village areas. For that reason, I will not soon forget the time I spent the night in my jeep at the edge of one of the rivers, hoping by morning that the water would have receded enough to allow my vehicle to cross and that the rain would prevent anyone from noticing my jeep and robbing me during the night.

I enjoyed the company of numerous villagers—particularly the Baptist parishioners, and I soon became a central figure in the social events promoted by two women active in the Baptist church, both of whom took a personal interest in "this new, young village doctor" and displayed a friendly rivalry as to who could win my affections. When I was not attending events with the Baptist group, my nurse and I attended social functions in nearby villages. We both had a very good time, as he was as outgoing as I. In particular we enjoyed going to the *bal champetre* (social gathering with dancing), held under a *tonnèl*, where we danced all night. As the most respected member of the community, I, *le docteur*, had my choice of dancing partners; as the villagers told me, "the town doctor can dance with anyone he wants."

On a more practical note, I used most of my income for two major items: (1) support for my parents and sister, and (2) savings for travel to Canada for a hoped-for residency following my two years in government service. Because of the limited supply of physicians, the Haitian government encouraged those physicians serving their required time in the clinics to also establish a private practice as a way to serve more people; therefore, by working six days a week in the clinic and long hours in private practice, I was able to bring my total monthly income to between $300 and $400.

While I was establishing my practice and building confidence in the villagers, François Duvalier was losing what little confidence the Catholic Church had tried to maintain in his government. Exasperated by his refusal to stop the reign of terror for which he was becoming notorious, the Vatican excommunicated Duvalier in November of 1960. This excommunication was accompanied by a denunciation from many quarters, including the United States and the Dominican Republic. Yet Duvalier still managed to evade a coup or even exile because his own power base was strong enough to convince most of the people in his own country that he and Haiti were right and every other country was the enemy of Haiti.

It must also be remembered that educated persons in Haiti were vastly in the minority, and a large percentage of professionals had either left the country or had become part of the Duvalier regime. A citizen had only three choices: support Duvalier, keep silent, or leave the country. The uneducated had no way of knowing any information other than what they heard from the pulpit; from the government-controlled radio (and few persons had access to radios); or from the village leaders, who themselves were forced to support Duvalier, as well as the macoutes, or lose their local leadership position. Therefore, the general public heard only one side— the voice of Duvalier. There was no tolerance at all for any disagreement with the Duvalier government.

An Opportunity in Town

Near the end of my first year of service, I received word that the most desirable government clinic position was going to be open because the doctor who held this assignment had accepted a surgical residency in Port-au-Prince. My request to move to the open position was granted and I moved to Arcahaie, closer to Port-au-Prince where I could more easily arrange to apply for a study visa. I was concerned, however, that my chances for a visa would be lessened when the United States' involvement in the Cuban "Bay of Pigs" incident added to the adversarial relationship with Haiti, already strained. This event, while not directly affecting my life in Arcahaie, nevertheless would shape the political future of Haiti and further add to Duvalier's resolve to not allow Haitian professionals visas to the United States.

In the meantime I established residency in Arcahaie, pleased because of the advantages this post had over St. Michel and also because it brought me one year closer to my long-range goal of a residency in North America. Archahaie was a small town rather than a village, north of Port-au-Prince, between the capital city and St. Marc. Accessible by a paved road, the clinic brought with it an opportunity for a better house and a real automobile. I sold my jeep and purchased a 1952 Chevrolet. No longer would I always have to ride a horse to the surrounding clinics I served; this new assignment covered more towns than villages and included areas which were easily accessible by automobile.

I treasured that car and took as good care of it as possible, considering there were few service stations available. There is not much demand for maintenance of vehicles in Haiti, as it is typical for those who have automobiles to not concern themselves with upkeep but simply to operate the vehicles until they no longer run. There are inspection regulations, but they are either ignored or a person pays for the licensing without having the car serviced. There are no traffic regulations, only a general consensus that cars usually keep to the right on a two-way road or street, unless it suits the driver to do otherwise. On the wide boulevards, a car passes on *either* the right or left of the car it is passing, and at a crossroads or corner, the car that can make the turn the fastest is the car with the right of way. Defensive driving is essential for those who value their lives and their automobiles.

All along the roadways throughout the country are abandoned vehicles, ranging from small cars to busses. No one seems to have the responsibility for the removal of these disabled vehicles. After a short period of abandonment, of course, any usable parts are stripped by whoever gets there first. The shell of the car remains as just another reminder of the lack of government responsibility in enforcing regulations.

There seems to be no concern for repairs of any sort; in fact, I often tell my friends that in Haiti there is no such word as "maintenance." Roads are built, then not maintained; they just wear away. Many houses also are in disrepair and various degrees of dilapidation. Throughout the country can be found many partially constructed homes. Families build these to a minimum level of livability and then move in, even though the structures are barely habitable. Only floors, ceilings, and four walls are in place, but with no evidence of intent to install windows and doors. The builders always say they plan to finish the work some day. Rarely, however, are the houses ever completed.

Disregard for completion and maintenance extends to the pub-

lic utilities as well. The government owns all utilities and has undis-
puted authority to determine the charge to the users. The government can set any fee at all, without the oversight of a regulatory
agency. Because of this monopoly, the government also chooses if
and when repairs are made or replacement parts installed. There is
no maintenance plan and no thought given to the fact of attrition and
depreciation. Some customers wait years to have the electrical service completed from the street wires into their homes, and even in
major cities one can see frayed electrical wires strung across the
main streets. It is pointless to ask about the potential hazard of this
old wiring, as one's inquiries are met with a shrug of the shoulders.
In addition, there are few repairmen with any training, experience,
or background in the operation of any of the utilities. Likewise,
those who choose to have a telephone installed are placed on a waiting list and may wait for years to have the service connected. It is
conceivable that in one's lifetime a person could watch the wires be
strung in front of his home and never live to see the service connected to his house.

When a water main breaks, it may or may not be repaired or
replaced. If it is easier to divert the flow of water, then that is the
action taken. There is also no schedule for the collection of trash, and
garbage collects in the middle of the street. Sometimes the trash
accumulates to the point that it blocks the entrance to a street. When
that happens, people just find another way in, either by entering the
street from the other end, or by creating a new pathway wherever
there is space to get around the buildings.

This disregard for the necessity of repairs and replacement has
been common throughout Haiti's history, and the Haitian citizens
have become accustomed to this way of life. Most have had to be
personally resourceful and to make their own repairs to the extent
that is possible. The particular lack of maintenance of the electrical
system, however, would play a part in a future misfortune which fell
upon me.

During my second year as a clinical physician, I continued to
draw my government salary of $120 per month, supplementing
those earnings by establishing a new private practice in the area I

was now serving. To further add to my income, I raised chickens and sold the eggs as I made my rounds throughout the region.

Finding a house where I could keep my chickens was not difficult, as poultry requires little care. I quickly rented a house, a place with an interesting history. The house had earlier been Duvalier's own residence when he had once had a medical practice in Arcahaie. I was amused at this political irony. In addition, my next-door neighbor was President Duvalier's Minister of the Interior. One of the duties the minister held was oversight of the public utilities. He, therefore, was popular among the citizens, for he was credited as being the person responsible for bringing electricity to the town. As Minister of the Interior, this neighbor was also responsible for maintenance of the equipment for the utilities, particularly the electrical service. Safeguarding the service, of course, was non-existent, but no one in town had the courage to question the minister, lest the one asking the question lose his own electrical service. Thus, the system of non-service was perpetuated and the Minister's laxity would later have serious consequences for me.

As had been the routine in St. Michel, the clinic in Arcahaie was also open six days a week, from 9:00 a.m. to 1:00 p.m. so that I could maintain my private practice. Private patients were not seen in the clinic; rather, they came to my house for care or they arranged for me to visit family members too ill to make the trip to the doctor's office. As is typical in Haiti, patients were charged according to what they could pay or whatever goods they could use as payment to the doctor, including chickens, goats, or simply rice. This system of barter made it difficult to establish a fee schedule. A new physician could not always determine who should be able to pay, as some patients who were relatively wealthy continued to live in their village huts giving the appearance of not being any better off than their neighbors.

These villagers with the financial means occasionally made small decorative improvements to their houses, but they did not improve their overall standard of living. For some, being secretive about their wealth was a sign of humility; for others, keeping their money to themselves was intended to keep family members from requesting loans. The hiding places for money were not revealed; however, some of those who hoarded their money buried it in the ground. Even today, there are stories of men who buried their money without telling anyone, and the secret of the hiding places went with them to their graves.

During my year of service in Arcahaie, I devoted myself to two tasks: (1) caring for my patients and (2) finding a medical residency out of the country. The first task was relatively easy, as my medical skill, training, and a year's experience had given me confidence in my abilities. I faithfully made rounds to the clinics, attending to any of the 10,000 peasants in my charge. In visits to the outlying rural areas, often I was joined by a priest who heard confessions in one side of the clinic room while, on the other side of the room, I attended to patients. The two of us, one dispensing aid to the body and the other ministering to the spirit, enjoyed each other's company as we made our rounds on horseback into the mountain villages inaccessible by vehicle. I remember very clearly the nights we slept outside, under the stars, with only the sky as a cover.

My second task, seeking a residency, was more complicated because of the political conditions in Haiti. While my choice was to enter a residency in the United States whose hospitals recruited foreign medical graduates, the successful passing of a medical knowledge exam and an English language test was necessary to be offered a position. I, therefore, sought an appointment in Quebec, Canada, because of my fluency in French. I had learned from friends and the visiting professors that Montreal was a good choice for Haitian residents, not only because of the medical facilities, but also because in Montreal there was a small Haitian community of physicians. I wrote to a number of hospitals there requesting a surgical position, but received a reply from only one.

Even more attractive was the opportunity in Canada to improve my proficiency in English. While I could read the language as a result of studying American medical books, my English speaking and writing skills were not strong enough for me to apply directly to hospitals in the United States. Another consideration, as always, was money: (1) The cost of traveling to Canada was not prohibitive (while traveling to Europe was out of my reach); (2) the earning potential for a specialist was better in the United States than it was in other countries, and the best way to get to the U.S. was by way of Canada; (3) it would be easier to arrange to support my family in Haiti from the United States or Canada than from Europe; and (4) I would be closer to Haiti from the United States, in the event of any emergency. Even so, the prospect of leaving my family in Haiti and traveling to a country and culture totally unfamiliar was somewhat frightening, even though I knew the choice was right and that God was leading me.

I also knew it was absolutely essential to make connections to people close to Duvalier, people with some power or influence who could speak on my behalf. I laid a carefully wrought plan. While applying for an exit visa, I continued to keep a low profile, periodically making the trip to Port-au-Prince to present my petition for a student visa. I also held in my hand an invitation from the Hôpital de la Misericorde in Montreal to enter the fall (1962) class in obstetrics and gynecology. One of the factors in my favor was that my family would remain in Haiti. The government held slightly more assurance in those students who left parents behind, considering that the odds of their returning were higher than if the family applied to accompany the student.

Duvalier, however, remained adamant in his demand of loyalty to his regime and looked unfavorably upon any young doctors who chose to leave Haiti. Shortly after the special election to assure his presidency, the "Dessalinian doctrine of necessary involvement" was created as a cardinal principle of Duvalier policy. "Who is not on my side is against me and who is on my side must get involved" was a basic tenet of Duvalierism, and, as such, excluded any kind of neutrality on the part of intellectuals and professionals.[1] This attitude of control was leveled against all strata of the educated classes. Duvalier continued to expel priests and to order the hounding, imprisoning, and killing of teachers and their students.

When the university students went on strike, Duvalier declared martial law and jailed the parents of the students. He then restructured the university, placing it totally under state control. Among his attempts to control the intellectuals and professionals was his periodic and arbitrary closing of the universities, very often with the help of those students who supported his policies. The government eliminated faculty autonomy and placed the students under close scrutiny. In addition, Duvalier dismissed both technicians and professionals from the upper echelons of the university.

Not satisfied with firing only educators, Duvalier also went after those in high ranking positions in banking, the army, and public service. These pogroms resulted in the widespread exodus of technicians and professionals to the United States, Canada, Latin America, Europe, North Africa, and black Africa. The estimate that 70 percent of the physicians who graduated between 1953 and 1963 emigrated from Haiti reflects the seriousness of the crisis facing the country. This diaspora exacted a high toll on all Haitian professions and particularly on those individual members who for any reason wished to leave.

It was possible to buy an exit permit on the black market, but I had neither the money nor was I willing to risk everything on the chance this illegal but widespread practice would be discovered and in some way jeopardize my opportunity to leave Haiti. I probably need not have worried, as buying an exit permit was common enough for Graham Greene to note, "In the last ten years three-quarters of the doctors who graduated here preferred to go elsewhere as soon as they could buy an exit-permit. Here (Haiti) one buys an exit-permit and not a medical practice."[2]

I patiently continued to wait for a favorable reply from the National Palace. After months of hearing nothing, I began to fear the worst. Finally, after many fruitless personal interviews and reviews of my papers by government officials, I sought out a medical student I knew and asked him to speak on my behalf. Roger Lafontant, later to gain repute as a Duvalier henchman, was in the class two years behind me and was finishing his last year of medical school. I knew that Lafontant was a macoute; however, I did not know the extent to which he had betrayed his own classmates, reporting to the Duvalier forces their every word spoken and action taken against the government.

Lafontant agreed to support my petition and to request from the Palace permission for me to be granted my visa. Lafontant's intercession and support was the boost I needed. I was granted the visa and at last I could accept the offer from Misericorde Hospital. This appointment would seal my future as a specialist in "ob/gyn;" more importantly, it confirmed my conviction that I could do more for my country by being out of Haiti rather than by remaining in it.

By the spring of 1962, I began to dream of Canada and what awaited me there. While continuing service to my patients, I kept my ever-increasing elation to myself. I continued my daily routine of work, spending my nights reading about Canada and studying everything I could find in the area of obstetrics and gynecology to add to my knowledge base and to be prepared for the residency that now awaited me.

On 14 May, however, near tragedy occurred four days before the national celebration of Flag Day, a day when Duvalier was expected to visit Arcahaie, the "birthplace of the flag." A fire broke out in my house. At the time, I was in the front section of the building, which contained a waiting room and an examination room used for attending my patients. Smelling smoke, I rushed into the kitchen area where the staircase to the second floor was located. Without stopping to think of the possible consequences, I raced up the steps, hoping to retrieve my belongings. As I reached the top of the stairs, I found everything black with smoke. Knowing my efforts would be fruitless and suddenly realizing that the house was about to go up in flames, I ran down to the first floor and out the side door. I jumped into my car to move it away from the fire, not even thinking about the results if the flames should reach the vehicle. Suddenly everything was engulfed in the roaring fire that had been fueled by the gasoline stored in the house, in an area directly under the stairs. (With few gas stations, storing one's own supply of gasoline was standard practice for the automobile owners in the towns.) The fire totally destroyed my house and all of my belongings—medical equipment, supplies, clothing, books, and all personal effects. It was only later that I realized how close I had come to perishing in the fire.

It was determined that the cause of the fire was faulty wiring—

wiring that had never been maintained by the utility company, owned by my next door neighbor, the same Minister of the Interior who had been instrumental in bringing the electric utility to Arcahaie. The Minister offered a small sum of money to compensate me for my loss, but the amount was so trifling that I would not dignify the offer by accepting it. A token payment could not begin to make up for my loss.

I immediately moved to Port-au-Prince, commuting to Arcahaie for the final few months of the government service I was obliged to complete. I did, however, make it a point to be very much in evidence on Flag Day, as I was apprehensive that some persons might think I had set fire to my own house, burning it to the ground as a political statement in protest of Duvalier's visit. I felt I needed to visibly show my support to the Duvalier government, especially since I had had words with the Minister of the Interior over the faulty wiring. I was well aware that any one who had a real or imagined grudge against me (or even someone who wanted to show great loyalty to the Minister) could have made comments that might be misconstrued regarding the burning of my house.

I did not rent another house, but moved to Port-au-Prince, making the daily drive to see private patients in their own homes and others in the clinic. One Sunday, a few weeks after my house had burned, several young men came to the capital city to find me. They asked me to come to Arcahaie to attend to a patient whose husband had been fatally shot during a wedding reception held at the home of the Minister of the Interior, next door to my burned-out house. The shooting had been an accident, occurring when the men began firing their guns, a typical ceremonial gesture practiced in celebration of the marriage. One of the bullets, carelessly fired, had ricocheted, killing its victim almost instantly. I, of course, returned with the men to assist my patient and to help in any other way I could. I also offered my services to my former neighbor, the Minister, who was lamenting the tragedy that had happened under his own roof. As I wanted no misstep of mine to spoil my chances to leave Haiti, I spent the remainder of the day comforting and attending to all who needed my assistance.

Three months later, on 12 August, 1962, I stood in the airport, empty-handed except for one small suitcase, and with money enough only for a flight to Montreal. The political tension in the city was palpable because of the pending anniversary celebration of the *Cérémonie Bois Cayman*, an event which was to mark the beginning of the two bloodiest years in Haitian history. I held my breath for fear the airport would be closed, and all visas revoked. I had said my farewells to my family, barely able to contain my tears as I kissed my mother, father, and sister good-bye. It pained me greatly to leave my family and my homeland, and, although I could not utter the words (even to myself), in the quiet recesses of my heart I feared that there was a strong possibility I might never see either my family or my country again. I knew my only hope to obtain the training I needed to was to leave, but in the leaving, I risked losing everything to the very fate from which I was escaping.

Notes

1. Leslie F. Manigat, *Haiti of the Sixties: Object of International Concern* (Washington, DC: Washington Center of Policy Research, 1964), 56–57.

2. Graham Greene, *The Comedians* (NY: Viking Press, 1966), 247.

Chapter 4: Internship and Residency

Out of Haiti

When I finally arrived at the Hôpital de la Misericorde in Montreal, Canada, on 10 August 1962, carrying the suitcase containing all my worldly possessions, I was in awe of the city, so unlike Port-au-Prince, the only other big city I had ever seen. Only a few hours travel separate Canada and Haiti, yet the two countries were disconnected by a century of progress. Canada's modernization and increase in population had led to a demand for additional physicians, more than the medical schools of either Canada or the United States could meet. This shortage of doctors led both countries to advertise for physicians from all over the world. Québec was especially appealing to Haitian physicians as it had opened its arms—and its hospital training—to them. As most Québécois were fluent in both French and English, Haitians eagerly applied to Québec hospitals, secure in their own French and relatively confident in their ability to learn English.

This bilingual attraction, however, presented two unexpected dilemmas to those who sought residencies. Like many other Haitian physicians, I had counted on learning to *speak* English as well as I read and comprehended it. Through studying American medical texts, I had acquired a solid reading knowledge of English and expected to perfect my spoken skills by doing my internship in Montreal. Further, I anticipated English to be widely used in the Canadian province and I had no idea that most Montrelians would insist on speaking French.

Even in the midst of my dismay, however, I could find humor in the situation. I had just left a country whose educated classes prided themselves in speaking only French, even to the point of refusing to speak Haitian Creole. Now I found myself in a country whose language was French, in which I was fluent, but I was expecting to learn English. I asked myself and others facing the same dilemma, "How can we learn to speak English if the Québécois Canadians *won't speak English?*"

I was equally perplexed by the second dilemma I faced. While I had no difficulty at all with reading anything written in French, I found conversation to be another matter. Much to my chagrin I discovered I could not readily comprehend the conversational French of the Québécois! I had wrongly assumed that my fluency in French would be an asset to me in conversations and in learning to transition from French to English. What I had not known was that just as there are dialects throughout and within a country, so is there a great difference between the French spoken in Haiti and the French used in Québec.

Difficulty in using the French Canadian vernacular only added to the loneliness I was trying very hard not to acknowledge. Homesickness was far more difficult than the language adjustment, the change of climate, and the difference in food. I missed my family, especially my mother. A personal letter was not an option because my mother could not read, and telephoning home was out of the question as there was no telephone service through which to reach her. I feared her anxiety even if I had been able to connect with the one public telephone in St. Marc. All of the neighbors would be alarmed at the sight of a telephone messenger coming to the door of our home, as no one in the neighborhood had ever used a telephone.

I had no choice but to contain my sadness and embrace the farewell words my mother had spoken to me when I first talked about going to Canada, "You must go, my son. As heavy as my heart is, you have too much talent not to use it in the best way possible. You must leave; you are the hope of your own future and of ours." It is probably fortunate that at the time I had no idea that it would be nine years before my return to Haiti.

This wrenching parting from my family remains with me to this day and I will never forget the overwhelming loneliness I felt, especially when I think of the same sorrow I saw reflected in my mother's eyes as she struggled to contain her tears at my leaving. However, I had work to do in Montreal. My mission was to study, pass the ECFMG examination, and gain a residency in an American hospital.

I was pleased that the obstetrical part of the medical program was well-developed in the Hôpital de la Misericorde; on the other hand, the gynecology section was extremely weak and provided inadequate opportunity for a good training in the specialty. However, I realized that I had accepted the offer of an ob/gyn residency in the Hôpital de la Misericorde not because of any burning desire for that area of medicine but because it was the only position available to me. I also understood that my internship would not be recognized as anything more than additional training, and that I would, no doubt, have to begin again as an intern in another program later, this time in the United States.

I knew I did not want to be just another doctor, or even just another specialist. I was determined to make a difference, to make a significant contribution to medicine. I knew that I had the intellectual resources, as well as the motivation, to achieve. Further, I was convinced that God had plans for me to devote my life to the betterment of mankind, whether it be through practicing medicine, research, or some other avenue. Where, when, or how was not clear, but I knew Canada would mark the beginning of my journey.

When I first arrived in Québec it was the end of summer and the air was cool. Winter came early that year and in September there was snow, a new phenomenon for someone who had lived in a country whose average daily temperature is 82 degrees. I didn't own a coat; the one jacket I once had was among the possessions lost in the fire in Arcahaie. At first, I tried not to go outside when it was cold, but this decision was impractical. One day a friend suggested I visit the flea market where I bought a second-hand lightweight coat for ten dollars, all I could afford. Even though the coat did not provide much warmth, it was an improvement over no coat at all. Now I would not have to remain indoors, although I never really got used to the climate in Canada and to this day I shiver when I think of that first year in Montreal.

Fortunately, room and board were provided in the hospital complex for the medical students and interns. Hospitals such as Misericorde welcomed foreign interns because that practice allowed them to receive services from medical doctors at a very small cost of $200 per month. These hospitals attracted young medical school graduates who wanted to immigrate to and receive training in North American hospitals. Further, these Canadian hospitals were able to pay very low wages because most of the foreign medical doctors needed a "first placement" where they could learn about western medical procedures and hone their medical and language skills.

Young doctors, myself among them, had to make adjustments in every part of their lives, from the language to the traffic regulations and the mores of a new culture. One of the changes easily learned was the monetary system. To my dismay, I discovered that Montreal was an expensive city but I quickly learned to budget Canadian dollars, as I needed to send most of my small income to my family. Learning the social customs required more determination; fortunately, good manners are so much a part of Haitian culture that we quickly adapt to new surroundings.

Not so easily learned was tolerance for the meals that were not at all like those to which we were accustomed. Another intern (who soon became my best friend) and I found the hospital food very distasteful. Out of necessity, we fashioned a cooking pan from a large empty can and used that on a hot plate, preparing meals as closely as we could to what was customary fare in Haiti. In time, we were able to purchase a frying pan; this greatly improved the food preparation. No longer would we have to suffer through the meat loaf, potatoes, and gravy in the hospital cafeteria. On rare occasions, we would treat ourselves to a Chinese restaurant, whose menu was as close to Haitian food as we would find.

Neither of us could afford to purchase books and we did all of our studying in the library, much as we had studied under the streetlights in Port-au-Prince when we had been medical students. The library became our refuge and was a much more practical study site than the street in the harsh, cold winters of Canada. We spent every available minute pouring over medical books and practicing our English competency skills, determined to pass the ECFMG examination. Often we were joined by several other friends, all with the goal of securing a position in a hospital "somewhere in America."

All of us were eager for information about any aspect of life in the United States, and Haitians who had spent time in the American hospitals were very willing to share what they had learned, to both warn and encourage us. One former intern in particular tried to frighten us with stories of life in the United States, particularly in hospitals. This tale-carrier, whom everyone called "Briere," took great delight in telling stories of long hours residents spent on duty in American hospitals. He would elaborate on these stories, enjoying the reaction he got from his listeners. Emphasizing the long work hours, he filled in with stories of residents, interns, and medical students who occasionally fell into a sound sleep while on call or of those who would slip into empty hospital rooms and sleep on the hospital beds, relying on a friendly nurse to awaken them when it was time for rounds. Briere also did his best to alarm us with his reports of young doctors being dismissed for various minor infractions. Most of all, he enjoyed telling how difficult the work was in the American hospitals and how lucky we were to be in Canada rather than the United States. Briere enjoyed telling of Haitian friends who returned to Canada because they could not pass the ECFMG exam. The interns in Montreal who listened to Briere's stories had no reason not to believe him, and we listened carefully to every piece of information and every bit of advice we could get. All data, correct and otherwise, would add to my growing knowledge base of what I could expect to find in the United States.

Other than listening to the adventures of those who had gone before us, we did not have much social life. Very few of us had money, so our opportunities to socialize were limited to what we could devise cost-free. Those who had their sights set on entering the United States did not have the time to spend in amusement or idle relaxation; we were busy improving our English language and medical skills.

In the 1960s there was not a large Haitian community in the city of Montreal. Rather, there was a cluster of interns, physicians, and other professionals—all diaspora who shared a common bond and who longed for home. We enjoyed the comradeship of friends in exile and occasionally would gather at a Haitian nightclub where we could make a beer last an entire evening while debating Haiti's future as well as our own. Such companionship gave us a chance to get away from our English language studies and to converse in French or Creole.

Haitians were aware of the bias most Québécois held. This partiality was not based on color, creed, nationality, or religion, but rather on the strong dislike the citizens held against *all* outsiders. And *anyone* not from Québec was considered an outsider. There was a definite sense of "Canada for Canadians," or, rather, "Québec for Québécois." Haitian physicians who remained in Montreal to continue their training told me they found strong racial prejudice when they attempted to purchase a home; some residential areas were not open to them.

In 1962 when I began training, the Hôpital de la Misericorde was devoted completely to caring for unwed mothers. In this strongly Catholic country, unmarried pregnant girls (and women) were sent by their families to the care of the Church. Two homes in the city were well-established institutions for unwed mothers, one for girls under the age of eighteen and the other for women over the age of eighteen. Upon being admitted to the homes under a cloak of secrecy, these mothers-to-be were assigned an assumed name which they kept throughout their stay, a period ranging from a few weeks to several months. Both basic schooling for those not yet high school graduates and specialized training for those wishing to learn a trade were offered to prepare the women to take their place in the working world, without their illegitimate babies.

The assumption that unwed mothers would not keep their babies drove all procedures of the Hôpital de la Misericorde. The adoption rate was 95 percent—all babies being adopted by approved Catholic couples. The hospital was viewed as a service institution, exclusively serving their clientele while keeping a low public profile. The message of shame was evident in all regulations. Everything was insular. No visitors were allowed in the hospital and there was no family support for the delivering mother. The nurses, the Sisters of Mercy, went quietly about their duties, almost silent. The air of sin was noticeable. Few girls or women ever wanted to return for the birth of a second child, although there were some who returned more often, assured of excellent care for themselves and a good, Catholic home for their babies.

Conditions in Haiti continued to deteriorate and by spring 1963 the political situation was such that I knew I could never return to Haiti as long as the country was ruled by François Duvalier. "Everyone," Graham Greene was to write, "is some sort of prisoner in Port-au-Prince."[1] The wretched situation in Haiti also increased my resolve to help my country; nonetheless, I was realistic enough to know that I would be far better able to assist both family and country by continuing my education and preparing myself for the challenges which lay ahead.

Once I passed the required test, I researched American hospitals to find an accredited internship. Soon after, I accepted an offer from Mercy-Douglass Hospital in Philadelphia. I had no friends, no relatives anywhere in the United States; the choice of Philadelphia was purely arbitrary based only on my admiration for the Philadelphia Orchestra and Eugene Ormandy. The Mercy-Douglass offer of a rotating internship included a salary of $375 per month with room and board.

Full of excitement, I went to the American Consulate to apply for a visa to the United States. I held the contract from Mercy-Douglass in my hand, knowing that to obtain a visa I needed proof of employment. The Immigration clerk suggested that I apply for a permanent visa because Haiti was a non-quota country. However, the permanent visa application required proof of a bank account with a minimum balance of $1,000. I returned to my friends, not knowing what to do. To my great relief I was told that the small Haitian community in Montreal had an established fund which could be used for such purposes. A small donation would allow me to use this account for the $1,000 collateral needed for the visa.

Of course, I had no idea where Philadelphia was located except from what I could observe on a map. I also could not afford the $200 air fare. In fact, I could not even pay the full fare to travel by bus, so I booked a seat on a night bus that offered reduced rates. In Plattsburg, New York when the driver made a rest and meal stop, I hesitated to leave the bus and enter the restaurant. However, my hunger and the little courage I could muster overrode the warning voice of Briere who had advised me not to talk to any white people. Cautiously I walked to the serving counter where a woman greeted me warmly and offered to take my order. I will never forget how kind and friendly she was to me, a stranger in a very strange land. Feeling more confident and now questioning Briere's stories about how all white Americans would treat me, I ate my meal and then returned to the bus where I fell asleep smiling.

Getting to America

When I awoke, I was in Philadelphia, full of hope and trust at being in the United States. I hailed a taxicab as I had no idea how to get to Mercy-Douglass. I gave the driver the name of the hospital and when he asked, "Where is that?" I showed him the address I had on the envelope of a letter: "Mercy-Douglass Hospital, Fiftieth and Woodland." The cab driver shrugged, said, "Oh, Southwest" and took a long look at me as I climbed into the back seat. I checked my French-English pocket dictionary and asked as clearly as I could, "Do you know where that is?" The driver assured me he did, and sped away. There were many questions I wanted to ask, such as was I really in Philadelphia, but by the time I found the translation, my mind was racing with even more questions.

Peering out through the cab windows, what I saw was not what I had expected. Filth and garbage were everywhere. I said to myself, "This cannot be the United States. There is so much rubbish in the streets. Everything is so dirty." I knew the stories I had heard of streets paved with gold were greatly exaggerated, but I could not believe that in this land of plenty there would be so much litter. I had become accustomed to the cleanliness of Montreal and expected that America would be immaculate. Without realizing I was now speaking aloud, I repeated, "This cannot be the United States." The driver responded with, "This your first time here, buddy?"

The closer the cab got to Mercy-Douglass Hospital in southwest Philadelphia, the dirtier the city looked. I was overwhelmed at the squalor I observed through the smudged windows of the cab and I couldn't believe this was a part of America. On this early Sunday morning beer cans littered the sidewalks, and people were sitting or leaning against buildings, sleeping. Newspapers were stacked at street corners; others were unbundled, their pages separating and blowing through the streets. Refuse filled the area, with no evidence of any attempt to keep the streets and sidewalks clean. What struck me even more was how ill-dressed and careless in grooming the people were. I had seen poverty, but what I was seeing in Philadelphia was a lack of pride. I couldn't help thinking that Haitians, for all their poverty, always kept themselves clean and would be embarrassed to be so sloppy as those I was viewing. This was not the America I had expected.

The ride was long as I furiously searched my pocket dictionary, attempting to ask the driver, "Are we still in Philadelphia?" The cabby laughed, understanding the inflection more than the actual words, and said, "Never been in a city this big?" Later I realized how obvious it must have been that I was a newcomer and that the driver had taken advantage of me, taking a long, roundabout route to the hospital. After being dropped off in front of the hospital and with considerably less than the $50 I had when I left Montreal, I vowed that never again would I be "taken for a ride."

My view of the United States now tarnished, I felt increasing dismay. What had I done? With an ever-tightening knot in the pit of my stomach, I stood outside Mercy-Douglass Hospital in the grey of early morning, looking at this sordid scene, a single suitcase in hand. I lifted my eyes to gaze upon the front doors of the hospital. Mustering courage, I trudged up the stairs, head held high, doing my best to hide my disappointment. Looking back, I should have known that I could not stay at this place. Entering the old, decaying hospital with what I hoped would look like confidence, I found myself in an empty lobby, shabby and unwelcoming.

I quickly realized I need not have concerned myself with the impression I was making. As it was Sunday, no one was on desk duty. Surveying the area, I saw not a soul. I turned right, down the first hall. It was very quiet. I then continued a few yards when I heard a sound. Around the next turn I found a man mopping floors. I approached him, hoping to gain some information. I then noticed that this man was drunk and reeked of alcohol. Nonetheless, he was the only person I had seen in the hospital, so I spoke to him and told him who I was. The man, mumbling, kept patting his stomach, saying, "I'm stuffed." I heard the words the man spoke, but my French-English dictionary was not much help in translating "I'm stuffed." I kept listening to the man, turning to the dictionary, speaking to him a second time, re-focusing on the dictionary, listening yet again, and once more returning to the book which could not provide the translation.

It was a busy week for me, getting settled in my room, learning the routine of the hospital, meeting the staff, and generally trying to become accustomed to a new culture. Naturally sociable, I quickly made friends and within a few days began to feel somewhat more comfortable in my immediate surroundings. It would take much more time to become familiar with the city.

There were many surprises awaiting me, including the Selective Service System. Following instructions I had been given at the border crossing, I reported to the Selective Service Department of the Immigration and Naturalization Office where I was classified 5-A, a classification that seemed reasonable at the time. The clerk told me there was nothing to be concerned about, that all males above the age of 18 who were citizens or who held permanent visas had to be registered for possible military service. The clerk further assured me, "The only way you would be expected to serve in the military would be if the United States went to war and we would run out of volunteers and younger men." I also was told that to take my Pennsylvania medical license test I had to sign a statement of intent to be naturalized within five years. This was somewhat disturbing because, while I knew I could not return to Haiti because of Duvalier, I still did not want to turn my back on my Haitian nationality and citizenship. I asked about the possibility of "dual citizenship," but was told that was not an option. Only one thing was clear: I would not be able to be licensed to practice medicine unless I signed the papers of my intent to be naturalized.

As the newest resident at Mercy-Douglass, I was assigned emergency room duty for the Fourth of July weekend. It took no time at all to realize the weekend would not be easy. Conversation was difficult because no one on duty that three-day extended weekend knew French, and I could not interpret their "Philadelphia English." The duty nurse was in no mood to be helpful, and trying to understand the medical terminology, different in English than it had been in French, was almost impossible. I was impatient with myself and even though I had my dictionary, I could not translate fast enough to prescribe the correct medications. There I was, faced with the wide variety of cases found in the inner city. It was a terrible weekend with knifings, heart attacks, street fights, and everything from drunkenness to gun shot wounds. With very little sleep compounded by frustration and discouragement, I was trying to minister to patients with all kinds of symptoms, speaking in languages I did not understand. I had been led to believe that the assisting nurse—or someone in attendance—would be French-speaking, but such was not the case on this Fourth of July holiday.

I lost four patients that week-end. I was responsible for the deaths of four people. It was dreadful. Three of the patients died from heart attacks just because I could not translate fast enough and the names of the medications were not the same as they were in Canada and were not at all familiar to me. I was convinced that these deaths were due to my medical incompetence and lack of knowledge of the English language. It was the lowest point of my life. All I wanted to do was return to Montreal to a clean hospital, safe streets, and caring friends.

Following the holiday week-end duty, I did not want to go back to my rotation in the pediatric ward at Mercy-Douglass and asked for a day off to think things through. I took a bus to visit other sections of the city and to enter other hospitals that were much cleaner. That night I attended an open-air concert and the next day went back to the ward. To test my decision to remain in Philadelphia, I returned to Montreal the following week, visited friends, reevaluated the situation, and came back to Mercy-Douglass, convinced that I should stay in the United States where the opportunities remained unlimited.

After my experience with taxis and the long travel time by bus, I decided to buy a car. I mentioned these thoughts to one of the nurses who suggested I go to Sunny Stein Chevrolet. "Sunny will give you a good deal," she guaranteed. Trusting my new friend's advice, I headed to the sign with the bright yellow, shining sun that proclaimed: Sunny Stein Chevrolet! Best Prices in Town! I purchased a new 1963 Impala, and several days later the nurse who had recommended Sunny Stein thanked me for buying my car at Sunny's as she had earned a $400 finder's fee from the sale. The purchase of the car, I discovered, was not the "deal" I had been promised; in fact, I later found out that I had paid at least $500 more than book price. This was the second and last time I was taken advantage of in Philadelphia.

Having my own car, overpriced though it was, gave me freedom to explore areas in and around Philadelphia. Much to my relief, and eventual delight, I found the City of Brotherly Love offered much more than only a sub-standard hospital in southwest Philadelphia. I discovered Fairmont Park, the Philadelphia Museum of Art, the Philadelphia Orchestra, and many other cultural attractions. I quickly made new friends who provided companionship in which to enjoy my limited time for relaxation. I dated several young women and became part of a group of young adults with similar interests who traveled together, enjoying many of the cultural events in the city.

For very practical reasons I decided to finish my internship at Mercy-Douglass. First, I believed in honoring my commitment; second, I would lose time if I left Mercy-Douglass and had to begin somewhere else; and third, I felt the hospital had been sympathetic to my dilemma. I saw the hospital for what it was, yet I stayed to honor my contract in the first year and then remained a second year for a far more personal and important reason.

The typical track for interns is to work on a different service every two to three months. However, because I was skilled in obstetrics and gynecology, having served one year in the hospital in Montreal and as a general practitioner in Haiti for two years, I was soon placed in a supervisory position. This hand of fate sealed my future in obstetrics and gynecology.

Halfway through my first year I was becoming comfortable with the hospital routine, my supervisory duties, and American English. There were still some confusing moments, but these situations were readily resolved. One typical incident had no severe consequences, but was a reminder that a physician must always check any symptom that is not clearly understood. One night when I was on call, the nurse on duty reported that one of my patients on the floor was complaining of "headache." Hearing the word on the phone, I was not clear as to what the nurse was saying. She repeated "Hed. Ake." Still, my mind was not translating this pronunciation into the French "Hed. Auck." I looked outside where a raging winter storm was in full force. Quickly dressing and bundling up against the snow, I crossed the parking lot from the living quarters to the hospital. Making my way to the third floor ward, I met the nurse who had placed the call. She showed me on her notepad the word she had been telling me over the phone. Indeed, it was "headache," only a simple, mild pain in the head. I prescribed an aspirin and made my way back across the parking lot, none the worse for the wear, but a bit annoyed at myself for not understanding the message.

By the spring of 1964 and at the end of my first year at Mercy

Douglass, I was told that the hospital valued my work. The Director of the Department of Obstetrics and Gynecology believed I could have a very bright future in that field; however, the program at Mercy-Douglass was not an accredited one and the Director thought I would better benefit from one that was. Consequently she contacted directors of ob/gyn programs in the Philadelphia area, recommending that they consider making an offer to me. As a result of her recruitment and through her strong recommendation, I was offered a position at Hahnemann Medical College and Hospital as an ob/gyn resident. Given the reputation of Hahnemann Medical College and Hospital, the offer of a position was an attractive opportunity. I accepted the contract offer and was looking forward to moving to Hahnemann, even though the salary was only $150 per month, less than half of what I was then earning at Mercy-Douglass. However, this move from Mercy-Douglass was not to be. At least not yet.

My mother had suffered a stroke and, as it was out of the question for me to return to Haiti, I had to find a way for her to come to Philadelphia. I knew that the care available in the United States was her only hope for rehabilitation, as already the time that had passed since the stroke would prevent a full recovery. I also knew I could not afford to bring both my mother and sister to the United States and to provide care for them at the salary offered by Hahnemann. Mercy-Douglass offered me $600 per month (plus room and board) to remain there as a house physician plus all the extra duty I could handle at $25 per night and $75 per weekend. In addition, I was offered the use of an apartment for my mother and sister. Even though I longed to begin a residency in a program such as the one offered by Hahnemann, I sacrificed this opportunity.

With Mercy-Douglass as my only choice, I met with Dr. George Lewis at Hahnemann and explained that I had to turn down his offer because I faced an emergency family obligation. Dr. Lewis was understanding and completely supportive of this decision, and complimented me on my honesty with him. He indicated that they would open a position at any time I would be able to accept it. With that assurance, I could turn my attention to my family and return to work at Mercy-Douglass as house physician in the ob/gyn department.

My mother and Dinah arrived in the United States during the summer, two months after my mother had been first felled by her stroke. I made arrangements for daily physical therapy for her as an out-patient at Mercy-Douglass. Dinah accompanied her to these sessions so that she could help her continue the prescribed exercises and procedures at home. Most of the instructions could be demonstrated without language, so it was necessary for me to join them only when detailed verbal instructions needed to be given and understood, as neither Dinah nor my mother understood English. During the time of their stay, however, both picked up a smattering of conversational terms, such as "Good morning," "Hello," "Goodbye," "Thank you," and "Excuse me." I would tease my mother long after her convalescence when she continued to use "Good morning." I would say to her, "You sound just like an American!"

I enjoyed my family for the six months they were here, and spent weekends showing them around the city. I took particular care in searching for places that might remind them of the Haitian countryside and in tracking down public concerts they might enjoy. I was pleased at how well I was becoming acclimated to life in Philadelphia. On one of the Sunday excursions, we were happily speeding along the New Jersey Turnpike when I looked into the rear view mirror and noticed that I was being flagged down by a uniformed officer in a police car. Somewhat confused, I continued driving. The police car followed for a distance at which time I pulled off the road and stopped the car. When the officer asked to see my driver's license, I apologized to him in French and produced my Canadian license which was also in French. Taking a chance that the officer could not speak French or understand that the license had expired, I began a long explanation, pretending I did not understand English. Finally in exasperation, the officer waved me off with only a warning.

Because of working full-time, I contacted several other Haitians on the hospital staff to arrange for Dinah and my mother to have visits with people familiar with their homeland and their language. However, as the weather in Pennsylvania turned colder, they began to long for Haiti. They also missed other family members and were not comfortable living in Philadelphia, so both returned to Haiti where Dinah helped with our mother's continued therapy at home. By 1965 I had saved enough money to keep the promise I had made twenty-four years earlier. In the spring of that year, I built a house for my mother.

It was not easy making building plans long distance, but I knew what I wanted. Dinah made all the arrangements and supervised the construction. This house, made of concrete block, is very comfortable with a living room, small dining area, and a kitchen on the first floor. There is running water and electricity, and, except for the fact that there is no need for a heating system, the house looks much like small homes found most anywhere in the United States. It is two-storied, with three bedrooms and a bathroom upstairs. It boasts a small porch and a second floor balcony from which the town square can be seen. My mother was understandably excited and overjoyed, telling all who would listen to her story. "My son built it for me," she would say, beaming with pride. "He is a doctor in America."

I was becoming attuned to the brisk pace of city living and the pleasure of having a car to take me wherever I wanted to go. Confident that my Canadian license would continue to excuse me from the nuisance of going through the process of applying for a Pennsylvania license, I thought no more of the incident of the previous fall. I continued to drive, secure that my French would serve as a convenient excuse, should I ever be stopped again. The next time an officer pulled me over, I was on my way to Coatesville, a small town west of Philadelphia. I probably was traveling too fast on Route 30, a congested highway which originally had served as the main artery from Harrisburg to Philadelphia. The speeding, combined with the color of my skin, made me an easy target for traffic violations. When the officer asked me to produce my license, I handed him the Canadian one, expecting the same response the previous officer had given. This officer, however, was not about to listen to any arguments in French. Noting that the expiration date on the license was long past due, the officer directed my attention to that fact. When I continued to speak French, I was taken to the nearest justice of the peace who seized the outdated license and issued a fine of $75. The next day I reported to the Department of Motor Vehicles and completed an application for a Pennsylvania driver's license.

The following week, new license tucked in my wallet, I picked up a girl I was dating and pulled on to the Ben Franklin Parkway. Glancing in the rearview mirror, I saw blinking lights and could not believe that once again I was being tailed by a police car. Secure in the knowledge that I was not speeding and that I held a valid Pennsylvania license, I obligingly pulled over to the side of the road. As the officer approached, I asked him why I had been stopped. The policeman demanded to see my license as well as additional proof of identification before telling me I had been stopped because I was driving too *slowly*. My mouth dropped in disbelief and I asked the officer how that could be, that I was driving at a "normal" speed, well within the posted speed limit and in keeping with the pace of the other drivers. The officer said, "Are you trying to give me a hard time, boy?" I knew then to keep any comments to myself. The officer continued with a barrage of abusive comments, stopping short of striking me. This marks one of the few times I saw, regardless of my stature and position, how vulnerable I really was.

I remained at Mercy-Douglass through 1965 at which time I reapplied to Hahnemann Hospital and was immediately accepted, one of three ob/gyn residents admitted for that year. In July 1965 I began a three-year residency program in obstetrics and gynecology, the first black, and one of the few persons not born an American, ever to be placed at Hahnemann. My classmates were both Americans by birth; one was a graduate of Hahnemann Medical School and the other from the University of Chicago Medical School. Again, because of my years of service in the Haitian villages, extra year of training in Montreal, and two years at Mercy-Douglass, I was far more experienced than either of my resident cohorts. This was both an advantage and a disadvantage. On the one hand, the previous experience certainly helped me in understanding medical techniques and in diagnoses; on the other hand, some of the other residents (particularly those who were second or third year) resented my very presence. Until my arrival, Hahnemann's residents had been divided by ethnicity or religion between Italian-Catholics and those of Jewish heritage. With a third factor now of skin color in this mix, I often found myself in the middle of this Italian-Jewish rivalry. Each side would tell me that the other had been making comments about "blacks." I purposely made no response, doing my best to get along with everyone and to discount most of what was being said. In fact, I became very good friends with one of the Jewish residents as we shared a love for classical music as well as other interests. We remained friends until his death separated us in 1994.

There was a camaraderie among the residents and an easy fondness between the residents and the nurses, and I made friends easily. It was customary for those who had days off in common to spend some of their leisure time together, going to the movies or dances or just keeping company in the apartment of anyone who had enough space and an understanding roommate. Occasionally, couples formed from these wider groups of young people, and there were even a few marriages resulting.

However, I was not in any hurry to become involved in a serious relationship. I enjoyed dating and formed several close friendships but was not ready to return the apparent affection of one young woman in particular. G__ and I were not seriously involved even though we had been dating on a fairly regular basis. She, unfortunately, read much more into our friendship than I ever intended. She began a "campaign" to encourage me to marry her. She did not believe me when I told her I did not return her feelings and she refused to accept my rejection of her. She began to wait for me outside my apartment building, creating a scene with her crying. She even told her family in Haiti that I had compromised her, even though we rarely spent time alone. Not having experience in such matters, I did my best to ignore her and hoped that my up-coming three-month rotation at Chester Hospital would cool her ardor.

I was able to separate this personal dilemma from my professional life, although at the hospital I found another kind of quandary in that my experience in obstetrics and gynecology was resented by some of my colleagues. One instance concerned the attending physician at a difficult obstetrical problem to which I was called. This physician had given an order that I believed was contraindicated. Because it was clear to me that the unborn baby lay transversely across the pelvis with its back presenting into the birth canal, I disagreed with the physician's order to stimulate labor. Calling the attending, I reported on his examination, stating, "It is in the best interest of both the mother and the baby to have a Caesarian section." His response was unexpected: "You are only a first year resident; start the medication as ordered." I politely refused and was immediately reported to the Chairman of the Department. I explained my reasons to the Chairman and proposed that an independent obstetrician examine the patient. The attending refused the request, stormed into the labor room, and began a pitocin drip himself. In addition, the attending made his feelings known, "Dr. Mortel, you are not to be involved in the care of any of my patients, now and in the future. Is that clear?" I nodded. Following four hours of good contractions but no progress, the patient was given a pelvimetry. This procedure confirmed my findings that a Caesarian was necessary, and the C-section was then performed. Even though I had been right, the attending physician never again spoke to me.

It was no secret that because of my race some private patients refused my performing a pelvic examination on them. I always respected their wishes, as I had decided when I first arrived in Canada that I would not be bothered by such situations. I understood their prejudice and refused to feel insulted. The reaction of the attending physicians was mixed. Some asked me not to attend their cases and others insisted that, because of my skill, I be involved in their patients' care. This ability not to take incidents personally is a lesson I learned early; it has served me well.

My clinical experiences were further expanded through treating indigent patients at Chester Hospital (southwest of Philadelphia). All residents affiliated with Hahnemann Hospital spent three months of their first year residency in the ob/gyn service at Chester Hospital. Most of the time the residents were in charge of patient care only because serving the poor was not a priority for many of the attending physicians who often made themselves scarce. This provided the residents with decision-making opportunities we might not otherwise have had.

I found myself wishing this rotation could solve the problem I was having with G__. She was still persistent in her pursuit, and continued to wait for me at my Germantown apartment where I had moved at the outset of the rotation at Chester Hospital. Day after day she waited, camped out at my doorstep, shouting and crying for all in the apartment complex to hear and see. This complicated my life since I had become interested in the head floor nurse on the medical/surgical ward. We dated regularly during the three months I was at Chester Hospital, and the friendship with her helped distract me from the "G__ problem." When my rotation at Chester was finished, I kept the Germantown apartment despite G__'s demonstrations. Even though I had given her no encouragement and had never been seriously interested in her, she definitely had her sights set on me.

By the time of my second year of residency in 1966, Chester Hospital had merged with Crozer Hospital, and the Chester Hospital building closed. The residents from Hahnemann continued to travel to Crozer-Chester Hospital as part of their rotation. This year is memorable to me for two reasons—one by accident, the other by design. In the first situation, I had an automobile accident when my car hit a patch of ice. On impact of hitting the vehicle in front of me, I hit my head against the windshield of my car and broke the glass. I continued to drive the damaged car to the hospital because I didn't know what else to do. The second event was my marriage to the head nurse from the medical/surgical ward.

It was during this marriage that I began to understand the phrase "culture shock." Our entire marital relationship was marked by a clash of Haitian and African-American cultures. Most people assume that Haitians and African-Americans are alike, while in fact they share almost no similarities. Actually, I found more likenesses between Haitians and my Jewish and Italian friends. I tried very hard to assimilate into my wife's family and culture, but I was rebuffed at every turn, their prejudices evident in both words and actions. There were many incidents in which my intended courtesies were mistaken for what they called "showing off." I was consistently mocked for such common good manners as opening the door or pulling out a chair for my wife and the other women. The ethnic dissimilarities were far greater than our religious backgrounds. She was Protestant and I am Catholic. We were able to work out the religious differences, but, unfortunately, not the cultural ones.

During my second year as a resident at Hahnemann, I decided to pursue a specific branch of the obstetrics/gynecology specialty. Dr. George Lewis pointed out that gynecologic oncology was untried territory, a very promising area of sub-specialization, but that there was no one at Hahnemann who had formal training in surgical oncology. Dr. Lewis, himself a nationally-known oncologist, specialized in radiotherapy and indicated that if I were to choose surgical oncology, the two of us would make a good team at Hahnemann to cover all aspects of gynecologic oncology. Six months later, Dr. Lewis organized a three-day national gynecologic oncology symposium where I met several prominent surgical oncologists. Speaking with these surgeons solidified my choice to enter academic medicine not as a general obstetrician/ gynecologist and not strictly a surgeon, but as a gynecologic oncologist who would be not only a clinician but also a teacher and a researcher.

Dr. Lewis took an interest in me and offered to help me find a way to receive surgical training not available at Hahnemann (which was heavily weighed towards radiation treatment). Dr. Lewis suggested I apply for a National Cancer Institute scholarship, in particular a U.S. Public Health Service Award to Study Gynecologic Oncology. Further, he was so impressed with my performance that in 1967, my third year as a resident, I was named administrative chief resident at Hahnemann, a much sought-after position which I held until I completed my graduate training.

I tried not to become involved in politics during this time, but the Vietnam Conflict was nearly my undoing. Much to everyone's surprise, Selective Service numbers took on an importance unprecedented in American history, and no young American male escaped the consequences. Selective Service numbers meant that in 1967 at age 35, father of one child and another on the way, I found myself reclassified as 1-A and a prime candidate for the draft pool. Nothing in my experience had prepared me for enduring the medical examination all potential draftees faced. It was dreadful and humiliating and the most dehumanizing situation I have ever been in. This experience marked the second time I considered returning to Montreal, only this time the return would have been permanent. Fortunately, my service to Hahnemann Hospital was reviewed and designated as "essential;" thus, I was reclassified and spared being drafted.

Near the end of my third year residency, I received most welcomed and awaited-for news: the announcement of a $16,000 grant award to pay for my first fellowship year. In June 1968 I began my post-residency training with Dr. Lewis in radiation treatment and surgery. During that year I spent most of my time in the department of radiation therapy with Dr. Luther Brady, learning about radiation techniques, radiobiology, radiation physics, and treatment planning. In addition, I assisted Dr. Lewis with his clinical research in endometrial cancer and partnered with Dr. Ismail Kazem on experimental studies of the lymphatic system.

Dr. Kazem and I became good friends during the time of my residency. Then, near the end of my last year of training at Hahnemann, Dr. Kazem was selected to chair the Department of Radiology at the Catholic Hospital in The Netherlands. Because he would be leaving the United States, he gave me his Volkswagen to use while he was out of the country.

Also in 1967, a son, whom we named Ronald, was born to my wife and me shortly after we had bought a house in Mt. Airy. It was at this time that Dinah returned to the United States as a permanent resident. Much as I delighted in having Dinah with me, her presence only accentuated how different I was from my wife's family. Despite this difference, the following year we welcomed a daughter whom we named Michele, and our young family struggled in yet another effort to establish a home which could incorporate both Haitian and African-American cultures. Unfortunately, these efforts were not successful and the marriage continued to disintegrate.

An Invitation to Memorial Sloan-Kettering

Near the end of my first year of post-residency training at Hahnemann Hospital, I interviewed with Dr. John L. Lewis, Chief of the
Gynecologic Service of New York City's Memorial Hospital for
Cancer and Allied Diseases, today known as Memorial Sloan-
Kettering Cancer Center. During the interview process, Dr. Lewis
asked me why I was interested in Memorial rather than M. D.
Anderson Hospital in Texas (recognized as premier in radiation
therapy). Without thinking, I said the first thing that came to my
mind, "Because I don't like Texans." Laughing, John Lewis responded, "Well, you are talking to one right now."

Two weeks later, I received what I still refer to as "The Call,"
offering me the only opening on the gynecology service at Memorial, the top surgical cancer hospital in the world. I couldn't believe
it. I thought I must be dreaming. The residents, aware that such an
offer to a minority was almost unheard of, also could not believe I
had been accepted. I rushed to tell George Lewis and to thank him.
Because of the high cost of living in New York City, an arrangement
was fashioned in which Hahnemann agreed to pay $5,000 toward
my residency at Memorial. In exchange I would take the residency,
remain on staff at Hahnemann, and return (following my year at
Memorial) for two more years to train the residents and fellows at
Hahnemann in the surgical skills I would learn at Memorial. Both
Dr. George Lewis of Hahnemann and Dr. John Lewis of Memorial
voiced their pleasure that I would return to keep my original commitment to Hahnemann. As John Lewis said to me, "Money will go,
but your word will stay."

I was elated! I knew my wife would prefer to stay in the
Philadelphia area near her friends and family, but I was sure she
would be pleased for this opportunity at Memorial Sloan-Kettering.
Explaining how the training I would receive could open doors not
otherwise available to me and working with the surgeons recognized as preeminent in the field of gynecologic oncology would
guarantee placement in a prestigious hospital following my training,
I hoped my own enthusiasm would convince my wife that this was

an opportunity not to be missed. As a nurse, she would surely understand, I thought. "There is no way I am going to New York," she said. "If you want to go, it will be without me and without the babies." Disappointed but not surprised, I reluctantly told her that I must go. The lines were drawn and each of us knew that this was the beginning of the end of our marriage.

By July 1969, I was in New York City, again alone. My living in New York and supporting my family in their home near Philadelphia was a financial hardship even though my own wants were few and my tiny efficiency apartment in the hospital housing was all I needed. I tried to return to visit my family every week-end that I was not on call, using the bright blue Volkswagen that Dr. Kazem had loaned me. The relationship with my wife was strained, but my desire to see my children was stronger than my wish not to see her. Dinah visited me periodically in New York where she stayed with friends from Haiti who lived in the city. I looked forward to her visits as they helped quell my loneliness and served as a strong reminder of the commitment I had made many years ago.

"An unbelievable learning experience; extremely rewarding" is how I describe my year of study at Memorial Sloan-Kettering. The hours were long, as residents were on duty or on call from six in the morning until midnight, Monday through Friday, and until four in the afternoon on Saturday. While the work was difficult, it was exhilarating. I was thrilled to work with Dr. Alexander Brunschwig, the architect of the surgical procedure in which all pelvic organs in patients with cervical cancer are removed as a last resort, life-saving measure. A pioneer in the field, Brunschwig had an high rate of success for such a radical procedure. (With advanced technology, today's patients have an even better survival rate with this procedure.)

I assisted on the final surgery performed by Dr. Brunschwig and recall how tired he became during surgery. He died that same night and I continued the patient's post-operative care. On the day of Brunschwig's funeral, I assisted Dr. Alfred Brockunier, his closest assistant and attending physician, with a chest procedure. Brockunier had to leave in the middle of the surgery in order to attend the funeral and I was left to complete the operation. I did my best to assure the patient's family that she was receiving the same high quality care that Dr. Brockunier had provided. Because of the long recuperative period, I came to know the family well, especially the patient's daughter.

After several weeks, I sensed the daughter was becoming too dependent on me; she was calling frequently and was always in the hospital when I made rounds, even very early in the morning. This young woman expressed her gratitude again and again, and I found myself becoming embarrassed at her constant praise. I also feared her increasing fondness was inappropriate. I tried to keep our relationship strictly professional and did not return the personal interest in this young woman. I treated her as I would any member of a patient's family, and took precautions not to ever be alone with her. One day, shortly after this young woman's mother was discharged from the hospital, I received a telephone call from a delivery service telling me there was a package which I needed to pick up in person. Not expecting anything out of the ordinary, I was astonished to be handed a set of keys to a Lincoln Continental, a gift from the daughter of my patient. Of course, I could not accept such a gift, however well-intentioned.

I also clearly recall experiences with another patient whom I will never forget. She was a pleasant soul, but could never remember my name. Every time she was asked who her doctor was, she would answer, "The little brown one." I never took this as being prejudice; it was just her way of identifying me. In fact, I had to laugh, not only at her ease in marking me but also at the reaction others had to my not being upset.

Life in the hospital, dramatic as it often is, also has its quiet and personal moments. Spending long hours in surgery and on the floor of the hospital with post-operative patients often leads to close friendships among the attending physicians and between the physicians and the duty nurses. With life-and-death situations facing them every day, the medical staff usually form a professional intimacy of purpose. I very much liked the people at Memorial, but shared with only a very few of them my feelings of loneliness and my concern for my children. I was particularly fond of the nursing staff, both because they were exemplary in their patient care and also because they were understanding of the difficulty in the choice I had made in leaving my family to take the training at Memorial.

One first-year nurse in particular held my interest. She was small in stature and quiet, with a keen, dry sense of humor, the result of her acute observations of human nature. She wore a ring on her left hand and it was generally known that she was engaged to "someone from her hometown in Connecticut." I joked with her and said, on more than one occasion, "If you weren't engaged, I would ask you to the movies." She would respond in kind, "If you weren't married, I would go."

As the year of training at Memorial progressed and I realized that my occasional visits to Philadelphia to see my family would not resolve the basic problem with my marriage, I told one of the floor nurses that I would not be returning to my wife once my training at Memorial was completed. Shortly after, I sought out the nurse who had caught my eye and invited her to a movie; she accepted. Despite all my kidding with her, I still did not know her first name. I, there-fore, continued my practice of addressing her by her last name in public and, in private, I used the term of affection I used for most of the nurses, and simply called her "Dear." Near the end of the evening of our third date, she said to me, "You never call me by my name. Do you even know my name?" Momentarily flustered, I responded, "Of course." She, in turn, called my bluff and challenged me with, "Well, then, what is it? Let me hear you say my name." Embarrassed, I had to admit I did not know. Names just are not important to me. I don't think about names. What is important to me is the person. Her name is one, however, that I would never forget, as, from that time forward, she became the most important influence in my life.

While I was struggling with my personal life in New York and Philadelphia, I often thought of my homeland and wondered what would have happened had I returned to Haiti. I missed my mother and worried about her, even though she was in relatively good health during the years following her stroke. With the political situation so volatile, it was not possible for me to visit her, and the best I could do was follow the news and hope that my family in St. Marc remained out of harm's way.

After finishing my fellowship at Memorial Hospital, I returned to Hahnemann Medical College and Hospital as a senior instructor (1970–1971) in the Department of Obstetrics and Gynecology. While I was not appointed as an assistant professor and my salary was less than what others at my level were being paid, I chose not to make an issue of this inequity, but to perfect the skills I had learned at Memorial. My reward came the following year when I was promoted to Assistant Professor in the Division of Gynecologic Oncology, a new division I had helped establish.

In addition to acquiring surgical expertise in cancer treatment at Memorial, I had learned about the multi-disciplinary approach to cancer treatment and the possible contribution of basic research in the clinical management of cancer patients. Moreover, I learned much about the emotional and psychological aspects of the disease, which laid the foundation for my sensitivity to those needs of patients and for my later service as an administrator in leading others in treating patients holistically.

Still, once again, I had to prove myself to others. It may just have been coincidence, but it did seem that I was constantly having to prove myself, even to those who knew and praised my work. I preferred to take such trials in stride and can still chuckle at yet another surgical case. In a particular case we shared, Dr. B., an expert on radiation therapy, was convinced that no procedure could remove all lymph nodes in a patient's pelvis, firm in his belief that total surgical removal of cancer was an impossibility. He explained that only radiation therapy could treat all traces. I listened respectfully and did not comment, even though I was the surgeon who would be performing the operation within the hour. The following morning Dr. B. reached for the post-operative X-rays taken of the pelvic area, fully prepared to point out the lymph nodes which had not been surgically removed. I clipped the X-ray to the lighted panel so that all the physicians on the team could follow my presentation. When Dr. B.'s eyes fell upon the film, a look of disbelief overtook his posture of confidence. The X-rays revealed that the pelvic area was clear. I had successfully removed all the pelvic lymph nodes, the like of which Dr. B. had never seen before. He turned to me with the words, "Congratulations, Dr. Mortel."

This successful surgery considerably increased my credibility and, other than the petty comments I had been subjected to as a resident, I did not encounter the level of prejudice that I had been led to expect in America. Before I came to this country I had been warned of the obstacles and prejudices which might prevent me from achieving my objectives. Fortunately, I have neither encountered any obstacles nor faced any professional situation that could be claimed as prejudice. Instead, I found that, for the most part, people respected me for my knowledge and ability. I was told that I was the most respected resident at Hahnemann, even though I was the only black foreigner in a white institution. That is when I began to realize the real difference between the United States and Haiti.

In my private life, I separated from my wife, making the necessary financial arrangements to ensure our two children would be well taken care of. I continued to visit them frequently—at least until their mother remarried and chose to make it difficult for me to see Ronald and Michele. She pressed for more and more support and petitioned the court as frequently as the law allowed. Finally, family court told her that the children were being generously provided for—far beyond what was required, including the best private schools and a college education, and she was advised to discontinue her frivolous pursuit of unreasonable amounts of money. She, in turn, took her "pound of flesh" by trying to turn the children against their father. It is a sad fact that the children were grown before they understood everything I had done for them and the extent to which I care for them.

By January of 1971, the romance between Cecile Shahhein, the nurse at Memorial, and me became serious and we began talking about marriage. Many factors had to be considered before a marriage could take place—long conversations with family, and numerous intense discussions between Cecile and me as to values, religion, culture, the desire to have our own children. The fact that

both families were Catholic helped to frame our attitude and opti-
mism in making the decision to marry. As it became clear that
Cecile and I had much more in common than we had differences,
we were confident and determined that we could face any further
obstacles as a married couple.

In December of 1970 Dinah had married and moved to New
Jersey with her husband, Maurice. Nonetheless, she continued to
return to Haiti frequently to visit our parents. In 1971 I became a
naturalized American citizen, and, after the death of Duvalier, I was
able to join Dinah in visits to our family in Haiti.

Also in 1971 I was invited to join the staff at the Milton S. Hershey Medical Center in Hershey, Pennsylvania, to develop a gynecologic oncology program. It was very flattering to be sought out by
this institution, and I asked those who made the offer why they had
recruited me. I was told that the chief of neurosurgery and the chief
of pharmacology of Hershey Medical Center had contacted the
chief of gynecology at Memorial Sloan-Kettering for his best recommendation. This chief at Memorial later told me that the name
that immediately came to his mind was that of Dr. Rodrigue Mortel.

I would be the third faculty member hired in the ob/gyn department at the new Hershey Medical Center and the institution's only
gynecologic cancer surgeon. The financial incentive would double
my salary to $36,000. Following the offer from Hershey, Hahne-
mann then countered with the same salary to keep me in Philadelphia. Hershey responded with the promise of a promotion the following year, after a year of service. The opportunity to design and
develop a program in gynecologic oncology in a brand new facility
(Milton S. Hershey University Hospital had opened in 1970 and the
College of Medicine in 1967) was very tempting. I would have an
excellent opportunity for research with a possibility of starting a
gynecologic oncology division with unique characteristics by combining patient care, teaching, and basic research. My goal was clear:
the establishment of a strong gynecologic oncology division with a
fellowship program where faculty and fellows would be provided
protected time for clinical and/or basic research. With that plan and
as a new American citizen, I left Philadelphia to join the staff in the

small township of Derry, home of the Hershey bar, Hersheypark, and Penn State University's Milton S. Hershey Medical Center.

Note

1. Robert D. and Nancy Heinl, with revisions and expansion by Michael Heinl, *Written in Blood (The Story of the Haitian People)* (Lanham, MD: University Press of America, 1996), 594.

Chapter 5: The Milton S. Hershey Medical Center

Welcome to Hershey

Billboards at both the east and the west ends of Hershey offer a welcome to *Chocolate Town, U. S. A.* These signs are accompanied by the sweet smell of chocolate-in-the-making from the Hershey Factory, once located in the center of town and now perched on a large knoll on its northwest edge. Hershey, PA is distinctive both for its wafting aroma of chocolate and for its very creation. The town and much of what exists here are named for Milton S. Hershey, founder of the town which bears his name. Milton Hershey began his life as a poor farm boy and closed it as a philanthropic millionaire. From failure as a caramel maker, M. S. Hershey rose to the heights of success by building his empire on chocolate. Childless himself, Mr. Hershey devoted his personal fortune to his community and to the welfare of needy children. He is solely and personally responsible for providing jobs for the town during the Great Depression of the 1930s and for establishing a home and school for orphans.

The Hotel Hershey, the Hershey Stadium, the Milton Hershey School buildings, the Hershey Sports Arena, the Community Center, and Hershey Park (until the 1970s a small amusement park built

98

for the use of those living in the community) were all constructed during the Great Depression years in order that residents of Hershey and surrounding communities would have steady employment. The magnificent Community Center Building, dedicated in 1933, was built at a cost of $3 million, an impressive expenditure at that time. When completed in 1935, the Sports Arena was the largest mono-lithic concrete structure in the United States.[1] Today, the Hotel Hershey stands as an example of Moorish architecture and has earned its designation as a four-star hotel.

Milton Hershey's greatest legacy was his school for orphaned boys, founded in 1909 through a trust fund. The school, frequently compared to Boys' Town, provided a "common school education . . . supplemented by instruction in the useful crafts."[2] The original educational emphasis was on manual training; this is reflected in its founding name as "The Hershey Industrial School." In 1951 the name was legally changed to "Milton Hershey School" to better describe its mission as an educational institution. Milton Hershey School cares for and educates more than 1,200 disadvantaged children who live on the large, sprawling campus surrounding the community of Hershey.

Hershey Foods Corporation, central Pennsylvania's second largest industry, is headquartered in Hershey, as is Penn State's Milton S. Hershey Medical Center, the fourth largest industry, which employs more than 6,500 area residents. The original Milton S. Hershey Medical Center was founded through Mr. Hershey's trust which provides in perpetuity for the establishment and support of public educational institutions and the vocational, professional, and cultural education of residents of Derry Township (known by nearly everyone as "Hershey.")

The bulk of Mr. Hershey's estate was placed in the Milton S. Hershey School Trust and, when income from that trust reached the point of greatly exceeding the requirements of the School, it seemed fitting for the Board of Managers to consider additional uses for the funds. The Board believed that it would be the intent of Milton Hershey to commit the accrued income to a critical public need that clearly lay within the trust's charitable purposes. Thus, the Milton

S. Hershey Medical Center of the Pennsylvania State University was born.

The Medical Center's Hospital has had as its primary function the education of physicians—medical students, interns, residents, and pre-and post-doctoral fellows.[3] What was distinctive about this new College of Medicine was the philosophy that Dean George T. Harrell, Jr., MD and his pioneering colleagues instilled in it. They believed medicine is a science, but practicing medicine is an art. They further believed that physicians need to have some knowledge about their patients' values and social environments, in addition to scientific data, in order to treat or prevent illnesses. Hence, Penn State's College of Medicine became the first in the nation to have its own Department of Humanities, with courses in religion, philosophy and ethics, the history of science, and literature comprising an essential part of the medical students' curriculum so that instruction could be made relevant to the problem-solving orientation of medical students.[4]

The second innovation at this new-sprung College of Medicine relating to the human side of medicine was the emphasis given to family medicine. It was the goal of Dean Harrell to provide training in primary medical care to meet the need for family physicians in Pennsylvania's many small towns and rural areas. As there were no faculty at other institutions from which to recruit in order to establish the Department of Family and Community Medicine, Dean Harrell initially drew upon family practitioners in the Hershey area for his teaching staff. This innovative program became the model for nearly all other medical colleges to follow.

The third innovative department was Behavioral Science. Traditionally, physicians had acknowledged that many medical problems were behaviorally related, yet few medical schools made a clear distinction between aberrant behavior and mental illness, the domain of psychiatry. Dean Harrell believed that since true mental illness is not present in most medical problems that have behavioral overtones, behavioral science would be considered a basic science on the same plane as physiology or biochemistry, to be used by all clinical fields.

The Hershey Medical Center Hospital admitted its first patients in October 1970, the opening of which marked the final phase of the Medical Center complex. Such was Penn State University's College of Medicine and the Milton S. Hershey Medical Center when I arrived in Hershey in late June of 1972. Attracted by the humanistic approach in treating patients with the finest medical science combined with personal care and attention, I looked forward to being a part of Dean Harrell's new vision. That, in addition to designing and establishing a new program in gynecologic oncology, made the move to "Chocolatetown" very sweet indeed.

Upon arrival to central Pennsylvania, my first sensory impression of the small town of Hershey was its omnipresent scent of chocolate. This sweet olfactory barrage was, however, followed unexpectedly in quick succession by an assault to two additional senses—the sight and sound of a bright red fire truck cruising every street in the town, announcing through a bullhorn, "The water is now safe to drink. To all residents served by public water, the water is safe to drink. Dauphin Consolidated Water announces that the water is now safe." Such an announcement was not an auspicious greeting and my mind immediately conjured up visions of carrying potable water for my family's use back in St. Marc, and of watching the public water system of Port-au-Prince destroyed by the churning waters in the wake of Hurricane Hazel. I was aware there had been a flooding of the Susquehanna River in nearby Harrisburg a week or two prior to my arrival in Hershey, but I had not expected that disaster to have affected the small town 12 miles east of the river. I thought, "Well, I was greeted by Hurricane Hazel during my first week of Medical School in Haiti, so maybe it is fitting to be greeted by Hurricane Agnes upon my arrival at the Hershey Medical Center." I felt right at home.

My initial impression of Hershey, notwithstanding the assurance of safe water, was quite different from my first impression of Philadelphia nearly ten years earlier. Hershey was beautiful. I had been warned by friends in both Philadelphia and New York that I would not like a small town, that I would miss the cultural activities only a city can provide, and that I had better learn to play golf, for,

according to them, there would be very little work to do at a brand
new medical center that was not yet fully operational. Little did they
know I had plans that would not leave much time for recreational
activities. Nearly thirty years later, I have yet to pick up a golf club.

Hershey is like a small European town, clean and bright and
safe. I love this community. I do, however, admit to some misgivings
in 1972 as to how I would be accepted into the nearly all-white community. Further, I was concerned that Cecile and I, being a racially
mixed couple, might encounter prejudice. In a small community,
medical center or not, we would be noticed. Even though we had discussed this possibility and had reassured each other we would not be
upset by any unkind reception, I still held some concern for Cecile.
I had become accustomed to occasional adverse reactions, especially
when, with my "French-sounding name," strangers were sometimes
surprised to find a dark-skinned physician.

Prior to our arrival, I had told Cecile that I did not expect to be
at Hershey Medical Center for longer than two years. I would establish the gynecologic oncology unit, and then move on. With that in
mind, we arranged to rent an apartment, signing a year's lease. As
we had recently been married and had not yet established a household, we arrived at Briarcrest Apartments and Townhouses with
only a few belongings. We drove up to the complex with only our
suitcases. We did not see anyone in any of the yards, so we entered
the apartment, deposited our luggage, and headed for International
Furniture Rental.

Upon our return to Briarcrest, the neighbors came out to greet
us, immediately putting us at ease. They were wonderful people, so
kind and helpful telling us about the apartment complex and wel-
coming us to Hershey. The small moving van with our personal possessions did not arrive until one o'clock in the morning, yet these
neighbors, John and Nancy, came over to help us unload. Imagine,
at that hour of the night, there they were, lending us, strangers a few
hours earlier, a hand.

Cecile and I quickly settled in at 394 Briarcrest Drive, in a
three-bedroom apartment complete with sunken living room, a car-
port, and a small yard. Not long after we were settled, a family with

three children moved into the next unit. We socialized and enjoyed their children, as neither we nor the other couple in the building had children of our own. The only drawback to apartment living was that the walls were thin and any sound carried throughout the building. Our bedroom was separated from the master bedroom of the adjoining apartment by only a plasterboard wall, and I could always hear snoring.

In Hershey, even the mailman was friendly. One day the doorbell rang and I looked through the small window in the door to see who it might be. I very cautiously cracked open the door and peeked through the narrow opening. I asked the postman if I could help him and he politely told me that he had a package to deliver and needed my signature. I didn't think much more about it until seven years later when I registered to take accordion lessons at a local music store. I went to my first lesson, a bit apprehensive in anticipation of this new adventure. The teacher to whom I was assigned was the same mailman who had rapped on the door soon after our arrival in Hershey. Richard Ranaglia remembered me, most probably because I was black, and kidded me about not wanting to open the door the day we first met. I learned to play the accordion under his tutelage, but, more important, we soon became, and we remain, good friends.

One of the first medical staff I met was Alphonse E. LeureduPree, Ph.D., a member of the Department of Anatomy. He told me that when he saw my name he wondered if I were Haitian as he himself is. Dr. Leure-DuPree, however, had left Haiti at the age of two with his parents who settled in England. I enjoyed his friendship, especially that first summer when we were the only two persons of color on staff. Since that time, we have remained friends and both are now Associate Deans.

During that first summer much acclimating took place, both professionally and personally. The picnic at the home of Dr. Vincent Stenger, Chairman of Obstetrics and Gynecology, was, however, the only planned social event of the season. I thought it gracious of him to host the party, but I did miss not having more opportunities to meet the families of my colleagues. I wanted Cecile to get to know more of the staff, especially since she was a registered nurse. Once there were additional physicians on staff, we all planned more social activities so that we could expand both our professional and personal relationships. There was a sincere effort among all of us to build a Medical Center family.

Building the Obstetrics and Gynecology Department

I began my official duties on 1 July 1972, thankful that I would not be assigned emergency room duty the Fourth of July weekend as had happened my first week in Philadelphia nearly a decade earlier. The total number of faculty for the entire College of Medicine was only fifty, and until my arrival, there had been only two faculty members in the entire Department of Obstetrics and Gynecology. There were also only two residents in the department and, anticipating my arrival, they had scheduled appointments for me, so I could begin seeing patients immediately.

Being the first black physician in a very conservative community with little diversity in its population was not a concern for me; in fact, I rarely thought about it until one day I overheard the receptionist speaking to a patient. It was clear that the patient was asking to schedule an appointment with "Dr. Rodrigue Mortel." The receptionist responded to the patient, in a very matter-of-fact tone, "That is fine, Mrs. S___, but I do need to tell you that Dr. Mortel is black." Apparently out of misguided concern for preventing a possible discomfort for his patients, the department chairman had instructed the receptionist to give the patients that identifying piece of information about the Medical Center's newest cancer specialist. I immediately sought out Dr. Stenger and asked him, "Why would you tell her to say this?" Embarrassed, he apologized, saying that he thought he was just making things easier for everyone. I made it very clear that racial prejudice should not be an issue and that if a patient was dissatisfied with my services, then she could request a different doctor, but that under no circumstance was I ever again to be singled out by race. To the surprise of many, it was not long before a number of patients switched from other physicians of the department to come under my care.

I enjoy joking with patients who are comfortable with my race. For example, I remember the patient who said to me, "You have an accent. Where are you from?" My light-hearted reply to her was, "I don't have an accent. You are the one with the accent." The woman, however, persisted. "No, you have the accent. Where did you come from?" Smiling, I then challenged her to guess. "Africa," she said, with confidence. "Wrong continent," was my reply. "Cuba!" she then blurted out. "Wrong ideology," I answered. "Well, then, it must be Jamaica," said the woman. "Wrong island," I retorted with a chuckle. "What about Long Island," she then asked hopefully. "No," I responded. "Then tell me," she demanded. "Birmingham, Alabama," I offered with a broad grin. "See," she chortled triumphantly, "I knew you had an accent!"

Not all of my patients were new to me. In my move from Hahnemann to Hershey, many of my patients who lived closer to Hershey than to Philadelphia chose to continue under my personal care. In addition to already knowing some of the patients prior to my arrival at Hershey, I also was acquainted with Ruth Bernitsky, a stoma therapist nurse at Hershey, to whom I had spoken by telephone many times while at Hahnemann. She was such an asset; it was by working with Ruth that I realized what had been missing at Hahnemann. Ruth prepared the patients for what they would be facing as a result of surgery. Quietly and with great compassion taking them through the steps they would need to follow after a colostomy, she instilled in them a quiet confidence that they could manage their situation comfortably.

One of the first patients I had treated at Hahnemann was Mary W___ who, before my move to Hershey, had traveled to Philadelphia for treatment under my care. She continued her appointments at Hershey for some time before returning to the care of her family physician nearer her hometown. Periodically, however, she came to Hershey for a thorough check-up. Many years later, in the spring of 1997, twenty-seven years after I had performed an ultra radical pelvic surgery on her, Mary appeared at the new Penn State Cancer Center. She introduced herself to a nurse who had not known her before. She said to the nurse, "That doctor—your Dr. Mortel—he gave me life." To me, this was the highest compliment I could have received.

My first major surgical patient at the Hershey Medical Center was Mrs. B___, wife of an area newspaper editor. Her husband never failed to send me copies of the newspaper each time it carried an article in which I was featured or mentioned.

My first exenteration patient at the Medical Center was I___ H___. She had been referred early in the fall of 1972 in serious condition, with cancer throughout her reproductive and elimination systems. With the help of Ruth Bernitsky, Mrs. H___ became a very optimistic patient. Accepting that her surgery would result in her having to use a colostomy bag, she set about designing and making covers for this bag that would be a part of her for the rest of her life. At Christmas time she covered the bag with cheerful decorations associated with the holiday; her summer ones were brightly colored with appliqués of the sun and other symbols such as a boat and water; fall would bring bags decorated with autumn leaves or pumpkins; and the spring ones would sport various flowers in bloom. She also made these covers as gifts to other patients facing the same surgery as she had undergone. I still laugh every time I think about one bag cover in particular that was embroidered with the words, "Get well with Dr. Mortel!"

Another unforgettable patient in the early years was M___ F___ who suffered numerous complications following surgery. She spent a lot of time in the hospital for various surgical procedures. Her main incentive to regain her health was her daughter's wedding. As illness knows no bounds of time and schedules, M___ found herself still in the hospital as the day of the wedding drew near. Arrangements for the wedding, scheduled for their church, continued in the hope that M___ would be well enough to be discharged in time for the ceremony which she said was the most important event in her life. Unfortunately, she was not able to leave the hospital. Even on the morning of the wedding, she was still hoping for a miracle. Although it was not the one she expected, a miracle did occur. Since M___ could not go to the church, the church, in a sense, came to her. A member of her family arrived at the hospital to prepare her to attend the ceremony. Dressed appropriately as the mother-of-the-bride and seated in a wheelchair, she was escorted to the meditation room of the Medical Center where the wedding had been rescheduled, thanks to the hospital public relations director. To the strains of "The Wedding March," the bride and groom were escorted into the small meditation room, attended by the bridal party, the minister, and me. Thus, M___ was granted her wish to attend her daughter's wedding.

As there were only fifty new cancer patients during this first year at the Medical Center, much of my clinical schedule was taken up with benign gynecology and some obstetrical patients. I knew this would have to change if Hershey Medical Center were to be a contender in gynecologic oncology care. Well aware of what faced me, I laid the groundwork to increase our patient numbers.

Because of my prior experience at Hahnemann Hospital, I recognized what was happening at Hershey. Area physicians were wary of sending any of their patients to "the medical center" because they believed that Hershey Medical Center encouraged their patients to remain with the doctors on staff and not to return to the referring physicians in private practice. With such misunderstanding, it was easy to see why the referrals were not increasing despite the medical specialties we could offer the area physicians and their patients. Another contributing factor for the low growth rate in patients was that the medical students were being sent to Harrisburg Hospital, ten miles distance from Hershey, to gain additional experience in clinical medicine rather than being provided with that experience in the College of Medicine. This further distanced the students from the Medical Center and helped to perpetuate the myth that clinical services in gynecologic oncology were not available at the Medical Center.

As neither local physicians nor their patients understood the role of a medical center, I immediately began a campaign to establish a base of trust with the area physicians. I met personally with each one of them, sitting down to talk with them, to ask their concerns and, more importantly, to find out *their* needs by involving them in the planning of the services that would be most helpful to their own patients and to their own practices. Further, I kept them informed and involved at every step in the expansion of our services. Most of all, I reassured them that we would work with them in the best interest of their patients. I promised that once the specialty treatment at the medical center was completed, we would not only keep the primary care physician fully informed, but would suggest to the patients that they schedule alternate appointments with the division of gynecologic oncology and their own general practitioner or gynecologist. In that way, the patients would receive the care and attention of both the referring physician and the specialist.

As part of building a base of referrals, I visited smaller hospitals and physician centers in the region served by the Hershey Medical Center, explaining the work and services that could be provided by the Center's gynecologic oncology division. It was also helpful that I previously had developed a relationship with some of the physicians from central Pennsylvania who had sent their patients to Hahnemann Hospital for special cancer treatment. Because I was not embroiled in some of the political competitions among the hospitals servicing the region, I could approach each physician in turn and explain how it would be an advantage to the patients to be sent to Hershey. Within a year, just as these smaller hospitals and physician centers had once sent their patients to Hahnemann, they then began sending them to Hershey Medical Center.

These recruiting strategies worked, and soon the Medical Center saw the number of new gynecologic cancer patients increase to 150, a three-fold gain. This increased number of patients also provided clinical material for research. The Gynecologic Oncology Group (GOG), a national cooperative study group, requires an institution to have 100 new patients in order to hold full membership in the organization. As a direct result of the efforts to attract additional patients for the division, we achieved full membership in GOG.

In January of 1973, I cut myself with a scalpel during surgery. Shortly after, the surgical patient became jaundiced; subsequent testing revealed that she was infected with the hepatitis virus and soon thereafter, she died because of those complications. Days later, when I stopped at a Kentucky Fried Chicken restaurant, I suddenly became nauseated. This surprised me, as I generally can eat anything, so for me to be nauseated was very unusual. The next day I ate an avocado dish that Cecile had prepared and again became nauseous. Suspecting a connection between this nausea and my having cut myself during surgery, I went to be examined. Just as I had suspected, I was diagnosed with Hepatitis B. As hepatitis is highly contagious, I was sent home to rest for several weeks. I, of course, quickly altered this order, reducing my rest to several hours a day.

As I could not see patients, this period of enforced rest had one advantage. It allowed me time to reflect about my mission as a physician, whether I would move to another hospital as planned, or if I would extend my stay at Hershey. This period of reflection also gave me time to project some long-range goals. By the spring of 1973 John Loughead, MD called, offering to place me in consideration for the chairmanship of the Obstetrics and Gynecology Department at Hahnemann Hospital. By then, however, I had decided I was going to remain in Hershey. I told Dr. Loughead, "John, I know I said I would probably be here for only two years, but I feel now that I don't want to leave. I have been welcomed by the other physicians, by the gynecologists in the area, and by the community. This is where I want to stay."

Cecile and I had both fallen in love with the community of Hershey, and we had begun to look for a house while I was recuperating from my bout with hepatitis. Both of us liked the wooded areas surrounding Hershey and we soon found a house not far from the Medical Center. We were eager to be settled in our own home in time to greet the arrival of our first child, a daughter whom we named Denise.

When Baby Denise was only six months old, Cecile and I left her in the care of my sister Dinah while we accompanied Dr. Stenger and his wife to Haiti for a brief Christmas holiday trip. We rented a small beach house and were enjoying the wonderfully warm westerly breezes when we struck up a conversation with a group of nurses who had an afternoon free from duty at the Albert Schweitzer Hospital, which was several miles from the beach. Even though the Hospital was only ten miles from St. Marc, I had never been to the facility. The roads had been in such poor condition when I last lived in Haiti that it took at least an hour to travel that short distance and I never had had an opportunity to visit. The hospital had been in operation only five years when I had left Haiti for Canada in the early 1960s and, as a rural physician, I had had neither the time nor the means to travel anywhere other than to see my patients. Furthermore, no one from the Medical School in Port-au-Prince had been permitted to do an internship or residency there, so I had no way of making a connection with this institution which was known worldwide.

Following the afternoon at the beach, we offered to drive the nurses back to their quarters, as we were very interested in seeing the hospital firsthand. When we arrived around 3:30 p.m., we were cordially welcomed. The facility was all we had anticipated.

The Albert Schweitzer Hospital, located in the Artibonite Valley, is a tertiary care facility and serves a district of about 200,000 people. Offering the best health care delivery system in Haiti, its first level is home care with the assistance of midwives, nurses, and nutritionists. The second level care is designed so that the patient can go to one of the many dispensaries which function similarly to the rural physician clinics operated by the government. At the third level, cases are referred to the main hospital. The patients pay very little for the services, all of which are funded through the Grant Foundation established by Dr. and Mrs. William Larimer Mellon.

As we began our guided tour of the clinic, we were introduced to a resident, on rotation from Yale Medical School, whose wife was in labor. We exchanged amenities and the resident returned to the delivery room. Before long, however, it became evident that an unexpectedly difficult labor was beginning. As time passed, the labor did not progress and the patient's contractions were becoming weaker and shorter in duration. The attending general surgeon asked us, as obstetricians, for our advice, which we offered. Labor was stimulated and when there was still a failure to progress, we performed a cesarean section. Both the baby and the mother recovered well (with that baby in later years becoming a physician). We completed an abbreviated tour of the hospital and headed back to the beach house late at night, filled with stories to tell.

Little did I know at the time of our visit that I would later serve on the long-range planning committee of the hospital and be involved in its development and fund-raising. I would like to see the Schweitzer medical care system replicated throughout the nine geographical departments of Haiti. Even more so, I could not have realized that this initial visit to the Albert Schweitzer Hospital would start me on an adventure that would change my life.

A year later Cecile and I returned to Schweitzer where we donated our services to the hospital for three weeks. It was during that working visit that I became ever more personally involved in the hospital and set in motion my plans for my own personal mission for Haiti. I returned many times to Schweitzer to volunteer my services and later to assist in planning and recruiting other physicians—both Haitians and foreigners—to also give of their time and services to the hospital.

In the winter of 1974 I received a new patient who weighed well over 200 pounds and it appeared that much of that weight was in her abdomen. That area of her body was so distended that her navel was protruding. Two years earlier her own physician had examined her and found a lump directly behind and involving her navel. Through a biopsy, he diagnosed this as cancer, but did not want to operate because he felt the disease was too far advanced for surgery to be effective. He told his patient that there was nothing he could do for her and he sent her home. Two years later, she returned, as her weight had increased considerably. That time he told her that frankly he was surprised to see that she was still living, as he thought he had sent her home to die. Perplexed as to what he could suggest to his patient, he remembered that he had heard of a surgeon at the Hershey Medical Center whose specialty was gynecologic cancer and that he was known to be very successful in treating patients, particularly difficult cases. He told her, "There is a crazy cancer surgeon in Hershey that I have been hearing about; if you would like to see him, I will call to make an appointment for you."

I agreed to operate and, because of the size of the tumor in the belly of this patient, there was a long list of staff physicians, residents, and medical students who hoped to have a chance to observe this operation. On my way into surgery I offered a prayer and approached the operating table as I had many times before. Of course, I was aware of the great interest in this unusual case, but every patient is important and each surgery is significant to the person being operated on. I had tried to avoid any advance publicity about this particular case, as it was not in the best interest of the patient. Certainly this was not a typical case, but I did not want undue attention brought to the Medical Center should the surgery not be successful.

With intensity and great precision I made the first point of entry and was surprised when at the moment the surgical knife penetrated the tumor, a great gushing of fluid spilled forth, flooding the floor of the operating room. Audible cries of surprise and alarm were uttered, but I proceeded with the operation to remove an enormous growth, as attendants attempted to cover the floor with towels so that no one would slip. After three hours, the tumor had been completely removed. The weight of the tumor and its contents turned out to be approximately one hundred pounds. No one had ever seen anything like it.

The patient made a full recovery, weighing 100 pounds less than when she was admitted to the hospital. Like many of my patients, she began to send me a card on every anniversary date of her surgery. Such an unusual operation, of course, was the talk of the Medical Center, among both the surgeons and the medical students.

The culmination of this surgery, however, came in the form of humor. At the end of the final year of medical school the graduating students hold a Class Night which concludes with the "Chocolate Follies," a performance, written by the students, which spoofs teachers and events of their years in medical school. In the spring of 1974, the Chocolate Follies committee presented me with a "Weight Watchers Award" for discovering the fastest way to lose 100 pounds.

After this incident, I took a lot of good-natured kidding, including several friends who frequently asked me, "Can you also walk on water?" After hearing this several times, I told them that I had tried that when I visited the Sea of Galilee and it didn't work. I then continued, "However, I did come close to walking on water in the Dead Sea." I did not add that in the Dead Sea one cannot sink. Certainly, I did not walk on the water, but I did sit on it or *in* it, depending upon how you look at it, reading a newspaper. I personally take no credit for my medical skill; my surgical ability is a manifestation of God's will. When one of my patients told her pastor that I pray before every operation, that became the basis for his sermon using the theme, "Even scientists believe in God." I would add that God believes in scientists.

I continued to build the Division of Gynecologic Oncology and the number of patients began to increase dramatically, with referrals coming from physicians everywhere in Pennsylvania. In addition to seeing patients, I was trying to continue my research and to teach in the Medical School, as well as traveling throughout the world, performing surgery and teaching other surgeons my procedures. In fact, the Division and my own work were so successful that I ultimately found myself in a prison of my own making.

From the time of my arrival in Hershey in 1972, I had been running the entire Division without assistance; then in 1975, I was given permission to hire Dr. William Nahhas, who had trained with me at Memorial Sloan-Kettering Cancer Center, and Dr. Stephen Curry, who had trained at the M. D. Anderson Cancer Center. Both men were outstanding. When asked why I would bring in two people from such diverse philosophies of cancer treatment, I explained that by bringing the best from both approaches, we could create a synthesis and offer the best course of action to our patients. From the institutions where each of us had trained, we three could design treatment programs specifically suitable to the needs of each patient. Under this design, the Division flourished and we began to build a gynecologic oncology division to serve as a model to other departments in the country.

The three of us were known collectively as the "MCN Team." We were a seamless unit, different in temperament, but alike in our devotion to our patients and our dedication to the specialty of gynecologic oncology. Each of us had 40% protected time and I used

mine in the research laboratory addressing the "biology of endometrial carcinoma." At last I was able to fill a void in my knowledge of
biology, completing the educational goal that had eluded me from
the time I had been in medical school twenty years earlier, when
there had been no laboratories of any kind in the Medical School in
Port-au-Prince and none of the students there had received any laboratory training. From the time I finished medical school in Haiti, I
had promised myself I would some day learn to do basic research. I
firmly believed that the only way I could learn to be a good
researcher was to first learn basic laboratory techniques and protocols. I wanted to know how the research was conducted—from the
use of the instruments to the data collecting and reporting, as I
understood the necessity to thoroughly comprehend the entire
process. With Drs. Curry and Nahhas on staff, I could establish a
schedule to spend two days a week in a laboratory.

My long-term goal was to develop an academic division in
which well-balanced research would be the foundation for medical
education and patient care. I had shared these plans with Dr. Wayne
Bardin of the Rockefeller Institute who encouraged me and offered
to assist me in finding a research opportunity in the study of uterine
cancer. With this goal in mind, I intently continued for two years in
basic research, eventually publishing my findings.

One of the unique features of the Hershey Medical Center
facility was its "teaching apartments" which were situated on each
floor of the hospital. Designed by Dean Harrell, these apartments
were provided to patients who were ready to be moved from the
care required in a regular hospital room to a transition site in which
the patient could provide some of his/her own care. In addition, the
patient could be monitored by his physician or a nurse, thus allowing medical staff to observe and learn about the post-operative care
of patients. I found this hospital procedure very helpful as part of
my research on cancer patients and their post-operative care. The
results were verified when in 1975 a survey, conducted by the Medical Center, was sent to all referring physicians. These physicians
were asked to rate the level of relationship they had with the specialists at Hershey. The service rated highest was the Division of

Gynecologic Oncology. I had met the challenge I had set for myself in the fall of 1972.

Cancer Research in Paris

Early in 1978 I was granted a sabbatical leave to conduct cancer research full-time in the study of "hormone dependence of endometrial carcinoma" in the Department de Chimie Biologique at the Université de Paris XI under Professor Étienne Baulieu, the renown discoverer of RU 486, the controversial "abortion pill." Scheduled to leave for Paris in July, Cecile and I began planning in February, arranging to rent our house, determining what we needed to take with us, handling a hundred and one sundry details involved in living in Europe for an entire year.

Then in March the Chairman of the Department of Obstetrics and Gynecology resigned his position at the Medical Center, leaving vacant the Chairmanship. I was named to serve as Acting Chairman from March until my scheduled departure for Paris in July. I was encouraged to formally apply for the post of Chairman of the Department, but I declined, deciding instead to pursue my interest in laboratory research and broaden my expertise in oncology in order to improve my academic career. Nonetheless, by July a permanent Chairman still had not been appointed and I was asked to delay my departure for Paris until a chair could be named. I agreed to stay through August.

Preceded by our Volkswagen and a plethora of boxes (including a year's supply of diapers for our new daughter, Baby Renée) shipped in advance from New Jersey, our family of four arrived in the capital of France. We were also welcomed by my cousin Roger (the same Roger with whom I had collaborated in our ruse for him to leave Haiti to return to Paris during the time I was a medical student). Roger had offered to find a suitable apartment for us and to enroll Denise in kindergarten; thus, we could head immediately to our apartment on the "Place d'Italie." Cecile and I had last seen Roger in 1971 when we had taken our wedding trip (on borrowed funds) through the capitals of Europe. I also had another cousin

and numerous acquaintances from St. Marc and Port-au-Prince living in Paris. These friends and relatives made sure that we were
comfortable, taking turns showing us the sights of Paris, where to
shop, and generally how to get around in this capital city. They
even arranged a party to welcome the new Americans! Baby-sitting
services were easy to find among Haitian family and friends. I
could not help but compare this reception to the one I had received
in Philadelphia when I had first arrived in the United States, fright-
ened and friendless.

Because I had taken a full year's sabbatical leave, I received
only half-salary. That presented a challenge to Cecile who managed
the family finances. The late 1970s was also a time when the cur-
rency exchange rate between the U. S. and France was very unfa-
vorable. Cecile had learned the French custom of buying fresh food
every day for that day's needs and quickly discovered where the
open market was scheduled each day of the week. There was a system to this open market tradition, and the merchants, who remained
constant, moved each day to a different street or area of the city. In
addition, of course, were also permanent shops, such as green gro-
cers, patisseries, and butchers.

Cecile, always open to new adventures and ways to economize,
readily took to trying new recipes based on French cuisine. One of
her favorite dishes was meatballs, which she had often made in the
United States. To Cecile's satisfaction, her French meatballs were
deemed a gourmand's delight among our French and Haitian friends.
The meat was lean and the flavor rich—absolutely mouth-watering.
We served this at every gathering, regardless of what else was on
the menu for the evening, because everyone loved Cecile's home-
made meatballs.

Cecile and I enjoyed entertaining, and had been in Paris only a
month before we hosted a party for my research colleagues. Even
though entertaining had to be kept to a small scale given our modest income, parties were a drawing card. I paid no attention to anyone's political leanings and we invited people we liked. Because
politics dominates every aspect of life in Haiti, most of the guests
were not accustomed to socializing with persons who did not share

their political beliefs. Later, many of the guests thanked us for "bringing us all together as Haitians," especially with people they otherwise would never have met.

These social events also provided a warm reception for various members of our family who visited us during our year's stay in France. Cecile's sisters, Dinah and her husband, and my older children, Ronald and Michele, all enjoyed time in Paris. Topics of conversation ranged from the newest exhibit at Le Louvre to medical research, from where to find a bargain to where were the best butcher shops. Cecile picked up many tips on shopping and learned even more about what made French cooking uniquely French. As often occurs at social gatherings, one evening the conversation turned to the cultural differences in food preferences. The discussion ranged from caviar to snails and from countries in which dog is a delicacy to France in which horses are raised for consumption much as beef is in England and the United States. One thing that surprised us is that there are butcher shops in France, which sell only horsemeat.

One day Cecile called me at work with the following revelation, "You won't believe what I just discovered. I went shopping today to our favorite butcher shop. I had never thought about the sign above the shop. Do you remember it?" I did not, as my trips to the butchers were infrequent at best. "Well," continued Cecile, "painted on the sign is the head of a horse. Do you know what that means? That wonderful beef with which I was making my *boulette de viandes*— the meatballs you so love—is horse meat!" Needless to say, that was the end of the meatballs.

I loved my work in the laboratory at the University de Paris, although I was unusual in that I was a clinician conducting research. In France, nearly all medical doctors then were *either* clinical physicians *or* researchers, but not both. Members of the Parisian medical community were intrigued that I was a surgeon who also was a researcher.

Life in Paris was wonderful. The work was exciting and challenging. I have never felt so empowered as I did in the laboratory. I have always believed that the real answers to treating cancer would be found through research and I wanted to be a part of this. That was difficult for some of my colleagues to understand. They knew me as a successful surgeon on the cutting edge of new techniques, in life-saving operations. I guess they saw surgery as more glamorous or closer to where the real action was happening. In my view, however, there is no mystery to surgery. It is based on skill and knowledge, not magic. Laboratory research, on the other hand, is the real magic. While I love performing surgery, a surgeon changes the life of only one person. A researcher can discover something that will benefit all of mankind.

One of the patterns I found difficult to adjust to, however, was the workday schedule. In Paris, I arose, took Denise to school, returned home to have breakfast with Cecile, and arrived at the laboratory at nine o'clock, three hours later than my day had begun at the Hershey Medical Center. At the Chimie Biologique, however, even at nine o'clock I was always the first to arrive. Others began arriving around 9:30 and socializing would continue until ten o'clock when work would begin in earnest. At 11:30 there would be a break for an aperitif. Lunch would start at noon, and work would resume at about 2:00 p.m. At 4:30 p.m. tea was served, then the researchers would return to work by 5:00 p.m. and continue working until seven or seven-thirty. I also was surprised the first week-end when I went to the laboratory on Saturday morning and discovered that "everything was locked up tight." I could not get into the laboratory on Saturday—quite a change from my schedule in the United States.

The year in Paris doing research was the best year of my life. It marked the beginning of a completely new direction for me as teacher, clinician, and researcher. My research focus was on the way hormones affect cancer, and how some cancers are hormonally responsive. These studies became the basis for proposing a new form of treatment for endometrial cancer, and the experience as a researcher further honed the skills I would later use as Director of the Penn State Cancer Center.

After several months in Paris, Cecile and I began to think seriously about remaining in France, particularly after March 1979 when near the end of the month we were in our apartment viewing the world news. We watched the screen in disbelief as we saw scenes very recognizable to us. Then we heard the familiar names of "Harrisburg, Hershey, Middletown, and Three Mile Island." We listened with great concern as the newscasters, accompanied by video footage, described the evacuation of persons living in the area of the nuclear reactors at Three Mile Island (TMI). We watched the live press conferences with Pennsylvania Governor Richard Thornburg as well as the spokesman for GPU, the power company that operated TMI. Mesmerized with what we could hardly believe we were seeing, we listened as residents in the area of TMI were told that the cooling towers were in danger of a "melt-down." Persons living downwind from the nuclear power plant, built on an island of approximately three miles in length in the middle of the Susquehanna River, were advised to leave their homes, while all other residents in the surrounding areas were to make their own choices about evacuating. Schools and government offices closed, while 100,000 people wrestled with the decision of whether to leave or stay. Cecile and I looked at each other and said, "We are not going back." Within two weeks the contaminated cooling tower was shut down and the area was declared "safe." How safe remains to be seen. Nonetheless, most of the residents returned to their homes and by mid-May Cecile and I again began talking about going home to Hershey.

Shortly thereafter I was approached and asked if I would design, develop, and establish a special program for the University of Paris, one that would incorporate basic research and patient care as well as the standard medical curriculum. The program was planned to begin two years later, after I had fulfilled my sabbatical obligation, and would be underwritten by the Foundation de France where I would be made a full professor. Before I left Paris, however, I was summoned by John Lewis, Chief of Gynecology Service at Memorial Sloan-Kettering, to fly to New York. Dr. Lewis offered me a new position in research and clinical practice in which I would combine the services of four institutions: Sloan-Kettering Institute, Memorial Hospital, Cornell University, and Rockefeller University.

I would receive an academic appointment as a full professor at Cornell as well as an attending surgeon at Sloan-Kettering, coordinating clinical gynecologic oncology research between Memorial and Cornell with a laboratory at Rockefeller University. In addition, I would be given three slots for the recruitment of a full-time biochemist and technicians. In other words, I could write my own ticket and build the entire clinical research program. This was the proverbial "chance of a lifetime." The proposition was very appealing because it would give me the opportunity to do all of the things I most enjoyed doing: research, clinical work, surgery, and administration. This position was available, however, only if I could accept it immediately.

There were two obstacles to overcome before I could accept: (1) the offer from the University of Paris to establish the special program they wanted by which I would combine research and clinics and (2) my commitment to Penn State and the time I owed the Medical Center for my current sabbatical. I returned to Paris, my head full of plans and dilemmas.

For the moment, however, I had obligations to fulfill right there in Paris in planning a major symposium on "Research on Cancer of the Endometrium." Held in Paris in 1980, after I had returned to the United States, the symposium attracted the best-known names in cancer research and treatment from throughout the world. The proceedings from this momentous convocation became the basis for a book, *The Endometrium, Hormonal Impacts*, published in 1981 by Plenum Publishers. The three editors included Jean Pierre Gautray, who specialized in gynecology; Jean de Brux, a specialist in pathology; and me, with my specialty in endometrial cancer. I also joined with Étienne Baulieu and Paul Robel in publishing several articles for medical journals and chapters in books.

At the same time I was weighing my options, the Curie Institute invited me to interview for a Directorship to expand the clinical and basic research program of the Institute. The Board of Directors asked for a ten-year commitment to develop a model of combining clinical practice and research, the program they had wanted me to build previously. While very interested in accepting this offer, I could commit to only five years. This was not acceptable to the Board and the matter was dropped.

In August I returned to Hershey where I met with the Chairman of the Department. "What do you envision yourself doing here, after your experience in Paris?" the Chairman inquired. I responded that I wanted funding for a research laboratory and approval to recruit a Ph.D. as well as a research technician; I also told him of the offer from Memorial Sloan-Kettering. The Chairman promised to seek financial support for me to remain at Hershey; however, even with that support, I thought there were more advantages to accepting the position at Memorial Sloan-Kettering. I made several more trips to New York, meeting with the administrators who assured me that their institution likely would reimburse Hershey Medical Center for the sabbatical time I owed Hershey.

While these meetings were occurring, Cecile and I continued to discuss the advantages and disadvantages of each offer. We loved Hershey, yet we both also found the New York City environs appealing. I could continue my research in New York, Paris, or Hershey; the difference would be the degree to which I could do everything I saw as being essential to improving the survival rate of current and future cancer patients.

Ultimately I determined that the best professional opportunity would be to accept the offer in New York City—but only if there could be a fair and amicable resolution of my sabbatical obligation to Hershey Medical Center. Following discussion with the Dean and weighing all factors, I made my choice. Cecile and I bid on a house in Rye, NY outside New York City, and prepared to enroll Denise in school.

Eagerly looking forward to working with Dr. Bardin in research at the then Rockefeller Institute, I told Memorial Sloan-Kettering I would accept their offer. I then made an appointment with Memorial's President, Dr. Lewis Thomas, to resolve the dilemma of the sabbatical time ($35,000 to "buy back" the time) still owed to Hershey. To my great surprise, the President would not pay for the sabbatical time that would honorably discharge me from my obligation to Hershey. Rather, he suggested to me that I should ignore the commitment, as it was unlikely that the Medical Center would take any action against me if I left. I protested, "But I *signed. I gave my word.*" Regrettably, we could not resolve the dilemma and I was unable to accept Memorial's offer.

Establishing a Research Laboratory at Hershey

The following fall (1980) upon my return to Hershey, I requested the institution's commitment to support me in conducting basic research and to provide adequate research space, a well-equipped biochemistry laboratory, slots to recruit technicians and a full-time basic scientist, as well as start-up funds for equipment and supplies. In return, I promised that the laboratory would be self-supporting in two years. The chairman found the funding and I opened the laboratory in one of the three wings of the medical center. This initial research lab was the first step in what eventually became a successful gynecologic oncology research program, one that would become the model for many other gynecologic oncology divisions in the country.

The new laboratory housed Dr. Swaroop, a biochemist; Dr. Zaino, a gynecologic pathologist; and me, a gynecologic oncologist, as principal researchers. Before long our research began to yield very positive results and for an entire decade our laboratory dominated basic research in endometrial carcinoma in this country. We presented at every society meeting where we had submitted abstracts, and, through grants, within three years, our laboratory became totally self-supporting.

Our gynecologic oncology division became one of the best in the country and the fellowship we offered in gynecologic oncology was very much sought after. Drs. Curry and Nahhas were instrumental in instituting many new programs. Eventually we had the largest patient volume in the Department and we were performing surgery for both benign and malignant conditions. The crowning touch, which we still laugh about, occurred when our colleagues in the Department of Obstetrics and Gynecology began to refer to us good-naturedly as the "Department" of Gynecologic Oncology in the "Division" of Obstetrics and Gynecology.

Both physicians and patients in central Pennsylvania held our Division of Gynecologic Oncology in high regard. During the entire time that Curry, Nahhas and I were together in Hershey, I can recall only two instances where we had a prejudicial encounter with patients. In one instance, a patient was referred to us but refused to be seen by anyone who was a foreigner, a black, or a Catholic. Obviously she had to be referred elsewhere since Dr. Curry is Catholic, Dr. Nahhas a foreigner, and I am all three! Another case involved a woman who did not want to be examined by either a foreigner or a black; she was assigned to Dr. Curry. While we did not mind agreeing to patients' preferences where we three were concerned, we were not so tolerant of patients who made demands about the students and residents assigned to their care. Those few patients who expressed the desire not to be seen by students and residents were invited to seek medical care elsewhere. Otherwise, the thousands and thousands of patients we attended were quite pleased at the competency of the Hershey team and were appreciative of the care they received. Referring physicians expressed their satisfaction with our division, and students and residents noted the hardworking conditions in gynecologic oncology while voicing gratitude for the effectiveness of our teaching. It is refreshing to know that for the 28 years of my association with the Division of Gynecologic Oncology, none of us has been cited in any malpractice litigation.

In the spring of 1982 my family and I were preparing to return to Paris to continue my work with the Ligue Nationale Francaise Contre le Cancer where I would have the responsibility for continuing my own research while also involving clinicians of the University of Paris in laboratory research. I was very excited at the prospect of once again working with Étienne Baulieu who had encouraged my return to Paris.

Cecile's task was to convince Denise, now age eight, and Renée, age four, that Paris would be wonderful, that it would be fun and a new experience full of opportunities. Denise in particular was the age at which she absolutely did not want to leave her friends and all that was familiar to her; she also did her best to convince her sister to agree with her. Even today, I commend Cecile for her skill in talking the children into going to Paris willingly. It wasn't easy, but Cecile managed to coax the girls to the point they were actually looking forward to going. By May most of our belongings were packed; the furniture was in storage; and boxes of household items, clothing, books, and toys were in New Jersey ready to be loaded on the transport ship. We had paid the tuition to enroll the children in Parisian private schools. In addition, we had rented our house to a newly hired pathologist.

In June, upon my return from Haiti where I had gone to see my parents before my leaving for Paris, I was summoned by the Dean. He ordered me to cancel my travel plans. "You can't go to Paris. You cannot leave the Medical Center at this time. The chairman of your department has just resigned and I need you here until a replacement can be found." This announcement took me completely by surprise. Without hesitation I blurted out, "But we are all packed, our flight is booked, our furniture is in storage, and our car is on a ship. The people who are renting our home are sitting in a motel waiting for us to leave so they can move into the house. Paris is waiting." "I am sorry, Rod," said the Dean. "I understand how upsetting this must be for you, but I have no choice and you have no choice. You are the senior member of the department and as such, you must stay here. Not only are we without a chairman, we would be severely short-staffed if I should let you go. Look at it this way: it is better to hear this today than tomorrow or, worse yet, next week when you would have had to re-pack everything and fly back." I tried to keep my sense of humor as I responded with what I hoped was a smile, "We probably would not have come back!"

As always, duty took precedence over preference, and I asked only that I be able to go to Paris in person to explain the emergency of this situation. The Dean agreed and sent me to Paris to request a six-month delay in starting work for the Foundation. I met with Dr. Baulieu who consented to hold the position open for me. I must admit I was very disappointed that I had to return to Hershey. I wanted to be in Paris with my family and I did not want to be a candidate for the chairmanship. I was excited about the work I was to do at the Foundation, establishing a model program of clinicians providing patient care as well as performing laboratory research, as such a program did not exist in France at that time. I was looking forward to helping the University of Paris make a shift in their thinking and in their system. In addition, being in Paris was going to provide time to spend as a family, something we had been nearly deprived of during the seven-year period while the Division of Gynecologic Oncology was being built. Furthermore, my research was going well, my career was on the right track, and I simply did not want to change that course by assuming the duties of acting chairman. Morale in the Department was low, many of the faculty had no career goals beyond where they were at present, and the department was not perceived as being strong. Frankly, I had been looking forward to getting away from the negativism.

Two months into serving as Acting Department Chairman, I received a call from the Chairman of the Search Committee, asking if I would be interested in the permanent position of Chairman of the Department. I answered, "No. I really would like to fulfill my obligation to the Institute in Paris. We began plans for this laboratory two years ago and I would like to see it completed." The search for a department chairman continued. Later, I was told that the more frequently persons both outside and inside the institution at Hershey were asked for nominations for the position of Chairman of the Department of Obstetrics and Gynecology, the more the name of Rodrigue Mortel was suggested. The Search Committee was being told that they already had the best candidate within their own ranks and that they need look no further.

In October the Search Committee asked me to formally announce my interest and submit a CV. Although our children were too young to be involved in the discussion, Cecile and I spent days and sleepless nights discerning what would be best for the family and my long-term career goals. The choice was difficult. What the department needed was not me, but the person known to all who was born 2,000 years ago. I asked myself, "Do you want to risk losing your own reputation in the process of trying to rebuild this department?" Yet, even though I wanted to do the research in Paris, I realized I had a good program going at Hershey, the envy of many other institutions. I was concerned that a new chairman might not favor the growth of the Gynecologic Oncology Division and the attention it was receiving. Thus, I reluctantly complied with the request to throw my hat in the ring.

On 22 December, following a national search, I was offered the position as Chairman of the Department effective 1 January 1983. I then traveled to Paris to inform Dr. Baulieu of the new development and to propose an alternative as to how the model program he wanted could still be initiated. I proposed to send a biochemist from my own laboratory to spend four months in Paris to set up the new laboratory there. I would then agree to spend a week to ten days every three months in Paris. Dr. Baulieu agreed with these words, "Well, I guess part of you is better than none of you."

For the next two years I traveled to Paris every three months, just as we had agreed in early January of 1983. While the travel was tiring and time-consuming, I am convinced the result of the work was worth it. The research program gained recognition among the medical community and we presented our findings at two international meetings between 1983 and 1985. In addition, our research discoveries led us to a novel treatment, which underwent national clinical testing conducted by the Gynecology Oncology Group, sponsored and funded by the National Cancer Institute. This treatment has been shown to be more effective in some cases than the treatment previously being used.

Trying to rebuild an academic department was quite a challenge, and many persons did not expect me to succeed where two predecessors, both highly intelligent and from reputable universities, had failed. Of course, I became more determined than ever to succeed, for the Dean, for my race, for Haiti, and for myself. What I faced was a department that had, in short, fallen apart (some would go so far as to term it "dysfunctional") during the previous two years. There had been a revolving door of physicians, and, as many people commented, the department numbers had been decimated. I decided to give myself no more than ten years to make the department what it should be. I told the Dean, "If I can't make the kinds of changes that need to be made within ten years, then I won't be able to make them at all, and I *should* leave. If I am successful, then it will be time in ten years to move to a new challenge." With that in mind, I set priorities, with the first task being to demonstrate to everyone that there would be an entirely new department with a new mission and a new direction.

I was certain that the department needed a marketing plan and a public relations campaign to regain the confidence of our patients and to attract potential clients. With the help of the Marketing and Public Relations Departments, I launched an advertising promotion. Introducing a slogan—"For every woman, at every stage of life"— through print media, television, and radio spots, the new Department of Obstetrics and Gynecology found itself placed in the public eye. Many chairmen of the other departments were critical of this move, as they claimed that advertising was unbecoming to the medical profession. I now like to remind them that these were ideas ahead of their time, since advertising has since become an important part of the medical profession.

In retrospect, I can see that perhaps I was ten years before my time on this plan, and I will admit that there are some things I would have done differently. Why? Because our promotional campaign failed. We had met with success in the short-term, but in the long-term, the program was a failure. Shortly after the advertising had begun, we experienced a surge in the number of obstetric and gynecology patients. However, we had not anticipated such a large number of patient responses, and we did not have the *staff* to handle the increase. We should have made sure we had a guarantee from the institution for additional staff, space, and services to accommodate the increased interest and number of patients, but we had not. Further, we should have had in place a better recruitment plan to attract specialists in obstetrics and gynecology to be ready for the additional patients our program would attract.

Another obstacle facing us was that many members of our own department believed that as a department we sometimes were not "fully understood." Those not in the specialty don't always realize that the Department of Obstetrics and Gynecology requires more resources than some other departments; for example, every patient must be provided with a chaperone/female staff so that she is not alone in the room with the physician. Because of a spate of lawsuits nationally against gynecology specialists, it is now a rule in most medical centers and in many private practices that a woman cannot be alone with her physician because of the nature of the specialty. The workload for obstetricians is also heavier, as they are on call twenty-four hours a day. In addition, there was the issue of medical students; many pregnant women were uncomfortable being examined by (and potentially entrusting an unborn life to) students with unfamiliar and very young faces.

I next set out to make the changes needed if the department were to (1) regain its reputation for excellence; (2) attract new specialists as well as residents; (3) retain the good people in the department; and (4) attract new patients, particularly those who were considering private clinics rather than the Medical Center. I knew the kind of department we needed to build and I began a master plan, including (1) hiring physicians who were willing to be truly "attending to" the special needs of women; (2) establishing services for high-risk pregnancies, including *in vitro* fertilization; and (3) becoming even more selective in the hiring of new residents.

An external review of our Department in 1987 indicated we were on a successful track; the only criticism centered on my managerial style. Some junior faculty felt that I was too dictatorial. No doubt I was, as I felt it essential to have firm control with a strong emphasis on faculty development. Because of this review, however, I recruited a few senior faculty in mid-career who provided a good liaison between the junior faculty and the Chairman.

One of the initial steps I took in this recruitment plan was to meet with Dr. David Halbert, a former colleague who had come to the Medical Center within a year of my own arrival. Known as a caring and compassionate obstetrician, David Halbert had become unhappy with the rigidity of the promotion and tenure criteria in an institutional setting. As a result, he had resigned his position and left the Department to open a private practice in the community of Hershey. A few years later, he built an office less than a mile from the

Medical Center. Yet, even with that close proximity, Dr. Halbert sent his patients elsewhere for hospital care.

In the early 1990s Dr. Halbert was finally recruited back to the Medical Center as a full-time faculty member in the Department. We leased the building that had housed his clinical practice and the Department continued to provide the kind of specialized services desired by his established clientele. At that time, Medical Center patients referred to this particular clinic were those who preferred not to be attended by residents and medical students. Now, all ob/gyn patients are seen in the new Women's Health Center.

Shortly after the return of Dr. Halbert to the Department, we began to make the progress for which we had planned. The number of obstetrics patients skyrocketed, the number of obstetric deliveries nearly doubled, and the number of gynecologic procedures increased significantly. In addition, there was renewed interest among a large number of medical students from the College of Medicine to choose obstetrics and gynecology as a specialty; our institution soon had a number higher than the national average of medical students selecting a specialty in obstetrics and gynecology.

With the influx of this new talent, the Department remains the regional center for high-risk pregnancies. Assisted reproductive technologies such as *in vitro* fertilization give new hope to couples who previously have been unsuccessful in conceiving.

The Department also began to attract more of our medical students to our residency program. An average of 50 percent of the residents in our Department now come from our own College of Medicine. Within only a few years, the Medical Center's Ob/Gyn Department regained its status, with a much sought-after residency program both within the institution and without. Its gynecologic fellowship program is one of only thirty programs in this country approved by the American Board of Obstetrics and Gynecology.

In 1994 the Penn State University Hospital was cited by *U.S. News & World Report* as one of the best gynecology hospitals in the nation, according to its Guide, "1994 America's Best Hospitals," which appeared in the 18 July issue. Of the forty hospitals ranked for gynecology service, Penn State's Department of Obstetrics and Gynecology was ranked 37th.[5]

I personally have been honored several times by *Good Housekeeping* magazine, first as a leading obstetrician and gynecologist in 1988. In 1992's "The Best Cancer Specialists in the U.S.," *Good Housekeeping* (October 1992), my name again appears in the list of Gynecologic Cancer Surgeons. According to the magazine, "*Good Housekeeping* interviewed more than 350 department chairmen and sections chiefs at 110 major hospitals and comprehensive cancer centers nationwide . . . The list contains the 419 surgeons and medical and radiation oncologists named most often."[6]

In 1994 my name was among those cited as "the best doctors in America," obstetrics and gynecology, for gynecologic oncology. *The Best Doctors in America*, published by Woodward/White, Inc. of Aiken, SC, is a highly selective directory of physicians chosen for the publication based on an extensive nationwide survey of thousands of medical specialists. Slightly more than two percent of the nation's 350,000 practicing physicians were listed in the 1994 directory.[7]

Again in 1997 Hershey Medical Center was cited by *U.S. News & World Report* in their 28 July issue as one of the best hospitals in the nation in four categories, according to its eighth annual rankings, "America's Best Hospitals," including 38th for cancer treatment. This listing assessed care for 17 specialties based on reputation and various medical data. "Any institution listed among the top 42 medical centers in any specialty should be considered a leading center," according to *U.S. News*. The Hershey Medical Center was also ranked in the top 100 in 11 specialties in *U.S. News & World Report's Survey of America's Best Hospitals* for the three-year period, 1993–95.[8]

I am told that most of the honors garnered by the specialty of cancer treatment and by those individual physicians named as "best in the nation" from the Hershey Medical Center can be attributed to my leadership. That is very humbling, as when I am asked about my leadership style, I reply that I just do what I think needs to be done. It never occurred to me that there might be those who could not see the overall goal right from the start. I have always tried to meet the expectations set for me by the institution or by my own goals and, in turn, I hold the same high expectations for those in my charge, without giving directives. The confidence placed in me as Department Chairman was all the incentive I needed to move the Department forward.

Notes

1. Richard Russell Klotz, *The Rise and Demise of the Hershey Junior College* (Hershey, PA: The Hershey Educational and Cultural Center, 1973), 15.

2. Ibid., 20.

3. Ellie Aurand, "Pennsylvania's New University Hospital Opens, *Penn State Journal*, vol. 3, no. 7 (October 1970, 1.)

4. Michael Bezilla, *Penn State: an illustrated history* (University Park: The Pennsylvania State University Press, 1985), 341.

5. "Department of Ob-Gyn Achieves *U.S. News & World Report* Ranking, *Vital Signs*, Milton S. Hershey Medical Center, circa August 1994, 2.

6. Maxine Abrams, "The Best Cancer Specialists in the U.S.," *Good Housekeeping*, October 1992, 135+.

7. "Seventeen Medical Canter Doctors Named "Best in America," *Vital Signs*, Milton S. Hershey Medical Center, February 1994, 3.

8. "Hershey and Geisinger Ranked by *U.S. News & World Report*, *Vital Signs*, Penn State Geisinger Health System, August 1997, 1.

Chapter 6: The Penn State Cancer Center

Nearly every morning as I approach Penn State University's College of Medicine at the Milton S. Hershey Medical Center, I think of my mother. "Well. Manman," I often say aloud, "I am now going to school for both of us. You didn't know when you insisted I attend The Brothers that I would be spending the rest of my life in school, did you?" And I wonder how she could have known the critical importance of sending me to school? The closest she ever got there was delivering forgotten books to the classroom of the children in whose household she worked. Whatever gave her the insight to see what a difference education could make?

As I walk from the parking lot to the office, I also think back to 1972, when the Hospital and College of Medicine were in their infancy. I can't help comparing the simpler structure the Medical Center was then to the behemoth the Center had become by 1995, the year the Penn State Cancer Center formally opened. I also frequently recall how earnestly I had accepted the challenge to mold the brighter tomorrow I believed would be in store. One thing was for sure, the vision I had for the Cancer Center most appropriately suited the slogan I had borrowed from Ronald Reagan's presidential campaign, "You ain't seen nothin' yet!"

The First Hershey Medical Center Cancer Center

In the early 1970s the Milton S. Hershey Medical Center had been the recipient of a specialized cancer research grant (funded by the National Cancer Institute [NCI]) to build the cancer research wing of the Medical Center and to support basic research, shared resources, and developmental programs. This early cancer center was very productive through this funding and the grant was renewed for several years. What prevented the center from becoming a bona fide cancer center, however, was a clinical component. Aware of this lack, during the last year of grant funding the hospital brought in a consulting firm to assess clinical cancer services and to make recommendations for improvement. Unfortunately that assessment study was not strong enough to satisfy the continuance of NCI funding and, following the departure of the principal investigator at the cancer center, the Medical Center lost the NCI funding and it ceased to exist as a program.

Nonetheless, the assessment report was helpful in that it noted the Medical Center had a strong research program even though the clinical services were reported as not patient-oriented. Specifically, the report noted that (1) the increase in the number of new patients over the years was minimal; (2) there were no marketing strategies for the cancer programs at the institution; (3) the number of medical oncologists in the surrounding geographic area continued to expand and offer clinical services that competed with those offered at the Medical Center; (4) the major cancer centers in Philadelphia, Maryland, and Ohio had begun an aggressive marketing campaign to target surrounding community hospitals; (5) there were numerous entrepreneurial interests in developing freestanding cancer care facilities; and (6) economic incentives offered from these facilities to community physicians led to the delay or avoidance of referring cancer patients to tertiary care centers such as the Medical Center. The report concluded, ". . . unless Hershey Medical Center commits the resources necessary for a competitive growth-oriented marketing strategy for its cancer program, the institution's relative position and influence are likely to erode in the face of competitive environmental forces."[1]

We had to face the facts. Even though cancer care and treatment at the Hershey Medical Center were regarded as outstanding, the problem was that the services were not as widely used as population studies projected they should be. Between 1987 and 1995, the Medical Center had reached out to more than 130,601 cancer program participants, allocating both staff and financial resources to community educational and cancer screening programs in the central Pennsylvania region. Yet the services were not attracting the number of patients we were fully capable of treating.

Others shared my belief that a refocused cancer center would address this concern by furthering the Medical Center's community outreach program to provide cancer screening and education through a network of primary care physicians and community organizations. In addition, the location of the Hershey Medical Center placed it in a prime position to be of service to central Pennsylvania, an area which still lacked an authentic "Cancer Center," with all the components necessary for NCI designation.

With Philadelphia to the east and Pittsburgh to the west, both ends of the state had access to comprehensive cancer care. Nonetheless, patients living in central Pennsylvania had to travel two to five hours each way to receive high technology cancer treatment in either of the two largest cities of the Commonwealth. Meeting the need for comprehensive cancer care in the middle of the state seemed to be a logical move. A new cancer center, designed as part of Penn State's Milton S. Hershey Medical Center, would offer all the benefits of an academic health center, as well as excellent patient-oriented care and cancer management.

However, the concept of a cancer center, as both an academic health center and an inherent part of a teaching hospital, was unfamiliar to many Pennsylvanians. Except for those living near Philadelphia or Pittsburgh, the idea of patient treatment through a multidisciplinary team (which is the core premise in an academic health center) was foreign. Most central Pennsylvania patients were accustomed to being treated solely by a single physician (or in a group practice). Many patients had not experienced the kind of service in which treatment would originate from the physician/special-

ist, with continuing care handled by a nurse coordinator who would do the scheduling, supervise the care, and arrange for any additional services ordered by the attending physician. We would need to educate potential clients as to what we meant by and what we could offer in a *comprehensive* approach to treatment.

Further, we would have to address the fact that the public-at-large had no skills by which to evaluate the increasing number of local cancer treatment clinics that were advertising "high dose radiation treatment" and other novel approaches to treatment. Many of these "quick-fix" clinics used high dose radiation and other atypical treatments as if such treatments were simply "more of a good thing" rather than being what most oncology specialists regarded them— scientifically unproven approaches to treatment of the disease. In addition, many of the physicians in these independent cancer treatment clinics were not aware of the new clinical research being conducted in the major cancer centers across the nation. They did not have the latest information on treatment because they were not a part of the established professional associations and information-sharing groups.

Moreover, some of these independent cancer treatment clinics were potentially harmful to patients in that many of the physicians offering services did not fully understand that they could work with a cancer specialist and still play a very important role in the care of their own patients. Primary care physicians needed to be shown that they could provide better service to their patients through being affiliated with professional organizations, information-sharing groups, and, most importantly, tertiary care providers such as the Cancer Center established by the Hershey Medical Center.

Finally, a plan would have to address the abundance of private practice oncologists in Dauphin County and the shortage of cancer specialists in Schuylkill County, a rural area viewed as a demographically "underserved" area of the state. Therefore, a two-pronged plan was needed both to (1) broaden the scope and services of the Hershey Medical Center to compete with the large number of oncologists in private practice and (2) expand the geographical area Hershey Medical Center could serve in order to address the needs of

Schuylkill County in addition to its primary service area of Dauphin County.

The new Dean of the College of Medicine, C. McCollister Evarts, MD, brought in external consultants on two occasions and also charged an internal task force to make recommendations for the delivery of clinical cancer services to regain the cancer center grant. For whatever reasons, however, the recommendations were never followed.

Then, in 1994 to my great surprise, Dean Evarts handed me the report of a second task force and asked me to accept a new position which would entail planning and establishing a cancer center to match the overall high quality of the Hershey Medical Center. This offer came one week before I was scheduled to fly to Rome to attend the ceremonies surrounding the elevation of my friend Archbishop William Keeler of Baltimore to Cardinal. I told the Dean that I would like some time to think about this offer and promised him, "I'll have an answer for you within a month."

I went home to my family where we immediately held a meeting to consider the offer. We agreed that we would pray together in Rome for God's guidance in our decision. A few days later, during the high mass in St. Peter's Basilica, which was packed with thousands of worshippers, I glanced up following a prayer and noticed a priest signaling me from about a hundred yards distance from where I was standing. I looked at him quizzically and he nodded. I pointed to myself and signaled, "Me?" Again he nodded. I then quickly wended my way through the crowd to reach him. He then asked me, "What language? English, French, Italian, or Spanish.?" I responded, "Any of them." He then asked me, in English, if I would like to carry the gifts to the Holy Father during the mass. "You must be kidding," I said. "No," he replied. "You can even take your wife with you," he continued. I couldn't believe my ears, but managed to gulp a reply, "I would be honored." Elated at being selected for this high privilege, I followed the priest behind the altar and took part in the rehearsal. During the mass as I walked toward the altar, I passed by Archbishop Keeler, seated among the many being elevated to Cardinal. Because of my focus on my task and the nature of the service, I did not try to make eye contact with him. Later Cardinal Keeler told me he could not believe his eyes when he saw me, one of his guests, carrying the gift to His Holiness. After presenting the gift to the Holy Father, I was honored by his holding a brief conversation with me. I knew my prayers had been answered.

Upon my return to Hershey I told the Dean I would be interested in his offer. I believed the reasons to establish a Penn State Cancer Center were clear and compelling: (1) a need had been demonstrated; (2) numerous successful cancer treatment programs were already in place; (3) cancer research in general was producing promising results; (4) the Medical Center had space in which to expand; (5) a multidisciplinary approach to treatment was increasingly being broadened; and (6) our internal medical personnel were excited at the prospect of the Cancer Center. To bring this together, all we needed was a *vision*. That I could supply.

Serendipitously, in late 1994 and early 1995 while we were developing plans for the Penn State Cancer Center, *US News and World Report* reviewed cancer programs throughout the United States. In its July 1995 issue, at about the same time we were preparing to publicly launch the Penn State Cancer Center, the magazine ranked the Penn State cancer *program* as the 38th best in the nation. Likewise, 17 Hershey Medical Center physicians were honored in the second edition of Woodward/White's *The Best Doctors in America*, a highly selective directory of approximately 7,200 physicians in more than 350 medical specialties. Several of those honored from Hershey were cancer specialists. This distinction helped to underscore the direction we were taking to promote the Penn State Cancer Center. All studies, committees, task forces, and teams arrived at the same conclusion: Hershey Medical Center needed and could support something beyond its acknowledged excellent, but not quite comprehensive, cancer programs.

Essentially I was given *carte blanche* to develop the Cancer Center. The first thing I did was to make it very clear to all that for any cancer center to be nationally recognized, the essential criterion is a strong research base. A center can have exemplary clinicians,

totally satisfied patients, state-of-the-art equipment, modern facilities, a contented staff, and outstanding administrators, but if it is not
research-based, it cannot expect to achieve national stature. My firm
conviction was based on the experience I had gained through my
year of service on the NCI Cancer Center Advisory Board and as a
member of various teams which participated in the site visit of
numerous NCI-designated Cancer Centers. Therefore, my priority
for the Penn State University Cancer Center was preordained. I
would direct the Cancer Center through the design of a comprehensive program which ultimately would lead to research—translating
what is learned from the laboratory into the clinic, and taking what
is learned in the clinic back to the bench.

My Earlier Preparation

Without realizing the full significance at the time, I later realized I
had spent much of my professional life preparing for a position such
as Director of the Penn State Cancer Center. True, I had not specifically set my course to be the Director, but thinking back over all of
the events since I had arrived in Hershey, most of my training and
initiatives had been focused on a comprehensive cancer program.
For twenty-five years I had made opportunities to learn any skill I
thought would make me better prepared as a physician and as a person. Early in my career I well knew the area for which I most lacked
training was research and as soon as I could arrange it, I took steps
to remedy that deficiency. Because I fervently believed that the
bench (lab) and the bedside (clinic) had to work together in the
interest of the patient, I knew it was imperative for me to train and
then to actually conduct research.

In 1970, by my own choice I began an intensive reading schedule in biochemistry, microbiology, and physiology. I then had the
opportunity to work with George Lewis, MD as an assistant in investigating the role of hormones in endometrial cancer. After being
named Chief of the Division of Gynecologic Oncology at Hershey
Medical Center, I began my own research on this question: "Is there
a way by which one can predict which patients with endometrial

cancer are likely to respond successfully to hormonal treatment and be spared the side effects of chemotherapy?" Cancer specialists knew that 30 to 35 percent of patients with advanced endometrial cancer respond to hormone treatment, but none of us knew which individual patients would respond and which would not. We wanted to find a way to predict which patients would benefit.

Seeking an answer to this question prompted me to spend one day a week in basic research. Because I wanted to learn the step-by-step process of doing basic research, I began my self-training by observing laboratory technicians where I learned the proper research techniques through observation, asking questions, and engaging in "hands-on" research.

By 1974 I was well-grounded in both "textbooks and techniques," and I began to formulate a specific research question on endometrial cancer, a question that could be investigated in the laboratory. Through conducting a review of the literature, I found studies showing that in women with advanced or disseminated endometrial cancer, some tumors respond to hormone therapy and some do not. Studies also showed those tumors that do not respond must be treated by chemotherapy. Because with chemotherapy the patient usually suffers from side effects, I was interested in identifying those who could first be treated successfully through hormone therapy, thus reducing their time (and its side effects) in chemotherapy.

Based on earlier findings which indicated that (1) chemotherapy can be delayed if hormone treatment is used (in those for whom hormone treatment is effective) and (2) hormone treatment may decrease the size of the tumor, I designed the following preliminary research questions:

1. Is there a way to predict those patients who are likely to respond to hormone therapy?
2. Can the duration of positive response to hormone therapy be extended?
3. Is there a way to increase the number of patients likely to respond to hormone therapy?

It was at this time that I began to work with Dr. Wayne Bardin to investigate the basic premises of hormonal action. When our studies provided clear indication that hormone treatment for endometrial cancer would not be effective unless there was a receptor in the (cancer) cell, we then focused on a process to determine if the cancer cell (of a given patient) has this necessary receptor. Since not all cancer tissues have receptors, I was initially interested in identifying the characteristics of cancers that do have receptors.

I spent approximately a year in developing the assay (test) for measuring receptors, using samples of tumors taken from both humans and rabbits. All experiments, of course, were subject to permission from the Institutional Review Board, a requirement in every research institution.

Shortly thereafter, Dr. William Mann, MD, a resident in obstetrics and gynecology who had taken a year's leave from his residency program to conduct research, joined the Cancer Center. When by 1975 I had recruited additional physicians for the clinical work in the Ob/Gyn Department, I then could devote two days a week, rather than one, to laboratory research. By 1978, I realized that the only solution to moving the research forward was to take time away from my duties as Department Chairman. I applied for a full-year sabbatical leave and that fall joined Professor Étienne Baulieu at the Department de Chimie Biologique at the Université de Paris XI where I could concentrate full-time on endometrial research studies.

At the research university in Paris the biochemical department researchers were conducting studies using a variety of animals; however, they were not including animals with tumors. Rather, they were investigating only normal endometrium (including that of humans), studying the physiology of "how things work and how human functions operate in normal circumstances under normal conditions." Fortunately for my purposes, the biochemists were amenable to my desire to take their basic research in receptors a step further by including laboratory animals with tumors in the study. My hope was to progress from these studies to advanced research in endometrial cancer. I had also contacted Jean-Pierre Wolfe, Chief of

Gynecology at the Institute of Gustave Roussy, from whom I could obtain human cancer tissue.

Thus, I was able to conduct parallel studies, using both normal and malignant endometrium, in research which heretofore had not been attempted. Having already demonstrated that some tumors contain receptors and some do not, my challenge was to determine how the receptors are regulated. Our team believed that if the tumor contains progesterone receptors, it should respond to progesterone treatment. We would treat the tumor with progesterone and attempt to show that the presence of a receptor is necessary to assure the success of treatment with progesterone.

What we needed, however, was a large enough human population from which to draw a sample. Our study required a sizeable number of women with advanced endometrial cancer whom we could treat with progesterone. Unfortunately, the Institute itself did not have a large population of patients with cancer at the stage needed for the study, and my remaining time in Paris was not sufficient to establish a collaborative with other research or teaching institutions in order to obtain the needed number of subjects. While this was very disappointing, I knew I would continue the research but, for the time being, it would be confined to the laboratory.

The problem facing cancer clinicians was that treating endometrial cancer with progesterone could not continue for an extended duration, as the effectiveness of that treatment decreased over time. What was happening, shown by the studies conducted by the researchers in the Paris laboratory and confirmed through studies in Finland, was that progesterone was having a negative effect on its own receptors, consuming them over a period of time. Thus, clinicians needed "something" that would increase the effectiveness of the treatment so that the receptors would not be expended.

Researchers, meanwhile, were finding that there are a finite number of receptors in each cell of cancerous tissue. When those receptors were filled, they discovered, the cell could not accept more progesterone. The researchers' goal then was to (1) find that "something" that would increase the cell's receptivity to the progesterone and (2) increase the number of receptors so that the cell could absorb more progesterone.

A breakthrough for the Paris researchers came with the synthesizing of tamoxifen as a non-steroidal anti-estrogen. This successful creation of tamoxifen made it possible to design a study to determine if that compound would increase the number of endometrial cell receptors available to receive progesterone. If the number of receptors could be increased, continued treatment with progesterone might then further reduce the tumor size.

When additional studies showed that tamoxifen increased the concentration of receptors, these results became the core for all studies to follow in the use of tamoxifen in increasing the number and effectiveness of receptors. We believed that if we combined tamoxifen with progesterone on patients who had tumors with receptors, not only would they respond positively to treatment, but the duration of the treatment could be extended. This hypothesis became the basis for the studies conducted at the Hershey Medical Center.

Hershey Medical Center Cancer Research

When I returned to Hershey I began testing *in vitro* (in the test tube) the research hypothesis and theory originally formulated in Paris. However, there were difficulties testing the hypothesis only *in vitro*; what was needed were studies *in vivo* (in living tissue).

Meanwhile, there was high interest in the potential capabilities of tamoxifen. A number of us saw the possibilities in this compound for the treatment of cancer. We presumed that if estrogen is a factor in building a tumor, then an anti-estrogen should have a reverse effect. Using a tissue sample, we found that by using tamoxifen we could increase the number of receptors in the cells of cancerous tissue. The implications of this finding indicated that by increasing the number of receptors, progesterone effectiveness could be prolonged in patients with endometrial cancer.

What was exciting, yet somewhat puzzling, is that these results indicated a contrary effect in the treatment of endometrial cancer compared to treatment used in breast cancer. Tamoxifen, which acts as an *antiestrogen* in breast cancer, appeared to serve as a weak *estrogen* in endometrial cancer. Therefore, the treatment for breast cancer could not be extrapolated to treatment of endometrial cancer. Further, these findings indicated a need to recognize and either counter or minimize the side effects of using tamoxifen in treating patients with endometrial cancer.

In 1980, I organized a research team at the Medical Center to work together on the problem of endometrial cancer. Propelled by what we believed to be sound theory, we still were faced with the same problem I had found in Paris—not having a population from which to draw a sample. While we were able to use human tissue taken from hysterectomy specimens removed as part of the treatment for endometrial adenocarcinoma, we could not use humans in the study because of tumor and tissue heterogeneity. Thus, our only choice was to develop an animal model.

Following nearly two years of developing a model using nude mice, we grafted human tumors onto the mice. Fulfilling all protocols and conditions for the experiment, we continued using these research procedures on mice.

In 1982, by the time we had completed the development of a validated model and were ready to begin the actual testing of the hypothesis, I was preparing to return to Paris. I had been appointed Visiting Professor at the University of Paris and Professor "Endocrinologie de la Reproduction" at the Foundation de France where it was anticipated that I would set up a laboratory and establish a program combining research and clinical practice. It was at this time that the Hershey Medical Center reneged on their earlier agreement to release me to accept the year's appointment in France. Because I was needed to serve as Acting Chairman of the Department of Obstetrics and Gynecology, I had no choice but to remain at the Medical Center. This unsought appointment as chairman left me with little time to remain active on the Hershey Medical Center research team and no available time to actively participate in the research laboratory in France. Nonetheless, I was so committed to the research in which I was involved that I was able to negotiate with Dean Prystowsky to make periodic trips to Paris to establish the laboratory the Foundation de France wanted and to supervise the researcher I had appointed in my stead.

Once the Paris laboratory was established, I was able to oversee the actual research trials of the study at the Hershey Medical Center. This study continued for thirteen years. While the results were very encouraging in the nude mice models, a clinical testing with human subjects was needed. In anticipation of that clinical testing, a dosage and treatment schedule (one that could be used with human subjects) was first established in the model. That preliminary data became the background for a pilot study conducted by the Gynecologic Oncology Group (GOG), a national clinical cooperative group that includes most academic centers in this country. In late 1989, GOG presented a formal protocol to NCI for evaluation.

By spring 1990, the National Institutes of Health had approved the request for human trials of this new hormonal treatment for endometrial cancer. The data-collecting part of the research with human subjects then continued for several years. However, the research was limited by the fact that while endometrial cancer is the most common cancer in women, it is usually discovered and diagnosed in its early stages. While this is very heartening for the patients, it slows down the accession rate of subjects into the trial, as the treatment using tamoxifen is designed for more advanced or disseminated stages of endometrial cancer. Regardless of the seemingly slow pace, our research discoveries led us to a novel treatment which has been shown to be more effective in some cases than the treatment previously being used.

A New Penn State Cancer Center: My Vision

By becoming the Director of the Penn State Cancer Center, I was expected to take an administrative rather than research role; however, it was a given that research would have an equal place with the clinic and education. My first charge was to design and establish a program to meet the future needs of central Pennsylvania cancer patients. After consulting with many individuals from within and outside the institution, I presented my master plan to the Dean in mid-December. The concept was "a cancer center without walls," in which all elements would *work* together but not necessarily be *housed* together. Dean Evarts accepted my recommendations without change and in January 1995 I was formally appointed Associate Dean and Director of the Penn State University Cancer Center. "As the Medical Center moves forward to meet the challenges of managed care within the current healthcare environment," said Dean Evarts, in an interview for *Penn State Medicine*, "It is critical that we develop a preeminence in the diagnosis and management of cancer. We already have a significant amount of research directed toward solving the problems associated with cancer, and a focus is needed upon the overall management of cancer. For this extremely important task, I have asked Rod Mortel to provide the leadership to develop a modern cancer center."[2]

The new Penn State Cancer Center did not require construction of a new facility, but it did call for a reorganization of existing programs and personnel in order to bring everyone involved under a single, administrative umbrella. I proposed this new organizational structure to provide a more inclusive approach to patient care, expansion of existing services, and addition of new programs such as a patient support group and a patient advisory committee. The center's clinical services would consist of oncology outpatient practice sites and an infusion center, as well as a pain management and palliative care program, with clinical nurse coordinators overseeing care that was to be compassionate and patient-centered. The Adult Oncology Practice Site and Infusion Center would serve all medical oncology, hematology, gynecologic oncology, and comprehensive care patients. The community service component of the Cancer Center would be two-fold; first, it would focus on screening and educating the public, in cooperation with the Central Pennsylvania Oncology Group and the American Cancer Society, and second, it would offer continuing education programs for physicians, nurses, and allied health professionals.

Shortly following the announcement of my appointment, I was interviewed as to my plans for the Cancer Center. I responded, "We are fortunate to have at this Medical Center many talented individuals dedicated to cancer research as well as cancer diagnosis and treatment. I am looking forward to coordinating all cancer-related activities in the institution and to assisting in making our Medical Center the site for the delivery of state-of-the-art, total, and compassionate care to cancer patients in central Pennsylvania."[3]

My "Vision for the Future" was, like everything else I did as a physician, centered on the welfare of patients:

> "Penn State University Cancer Center provides a multidisciplinary, comprehensive, and integrated approach to cancer prevention, education, diagnosis, treatment, and follow-up care for children and adults. The Center serves as the point of convergence for the collaboration of cancer research activities and offers centralized coordination of national and regional cancer research with clinical trials and protocols. The Center serves as a resource for community-based physicians to foster collaboration in treatment efforts and coordination of care for patients in their communities.
>
> All who are a part of our program strive for excellence and share a commitment to the Cancer Center's mission of cancer research, education, diagnosis, and treatment. I am proud to be part of this passion to succeed."[4]

My self-imposed mandate as Director of the Cancer Center was multifaceted: (1) obtain financial support; (2) build trust; (3) form links among all stakeholders; (4) attract the best physicians and other medical and staff personnel; (5) increase the number of patients choosing the services of the Penn State Cancer Center; and (6) form alliances with all other organizations who deliver services to patients, physicians, hospitals, and outreach programs. Beyond that formidable challenge, the major personal goal I set was for the Penn State Cancer Center to be recognized, within three years, by the NCI as an officially designated Cancer Center.

With already more than 75 cancer-related clinical and research projects underway at the Medical Center, my responsibility was to take all of the constitutive elements and use them as the building blocks for a comprehensive program directed through a single conduit: the Penn State Cancer Center. In the laboratories, basic research scientists were partnering with physicians to develop a greater understanding of the genetics of cancer, and more than 200 researchers and physicians were collaborating on investigative teams. In the clinics, basic research efforts were being translated into treatment applications with specially trained staff helping patients adjust to and manage new treatment strategies.

Research funding for the Cancer Center totaled only $6.5 million, supported by public and private organizations. I, therefore, immediately began to search for additional sources of funding. I also investigated the "sharing" of both fiscal and human resources, such as access to the media and common protocols for treatment, with other areas of the Medical Center. In addition, I reviewed demographic information from the ten counties surrounding the Medical Center, including projections of the impact on medical services by the elderly population in Pennsylvania.

By November 1995, with the help of Mark Reisinger, Director of Governmental Health Relations for Hershey Medical Center, I had designed a strategy to approach the Pennsylvania Legislature. Mark and I met individually with every House Republican in central Pennsylvania and presented our case on the need for a bona fide Cancer Center in central Pennsylvania, one prominent enough to be designated by the NCI. This would require financial support from the state legislature as a line item.

Buoyed by the warm reception and positive response these legislators offered, I met with Bruce Smith, Chairman of the Central Pennsylvania Republican Caucus of the House of Representatives. While I had known Representative Smith prior to this time, I had never before had an official agenda to discuss or a cause to promote with the entire Caucus. Mr. Smith was very cordial and receptive to my request for support for the Penn State Cancer Center; in fact, his response was so favorable that he called a full meeting of the Caucus, a body that usually communicates by phone and which Smith admitted had not ever met as a committee of the whole. After meeting and reviewing my proposal, the Caucus members voted to make the Cancer Center their top priority. Every member signed the letter of support which, in turn, was sent to the Republican leadership of the House of Representatives who took it to the full House. There, the House of Representatives unanimously supported the Penn State Cancer Center. I next visited every Central Pennsylvania State Senator, the result of which was their overall commitment to support of the Center with a grant effective July 1996.

During the second year of operation, a breakfast meeting of the Republican Caucus was held and I delivered a "progress report" as to how the Cancer Center had utilized the appropriation and how much additional funding we would need to achieve our goal. This meeting was well attended, and the support of the members of the Caucus was vocal. I was later told that our request for support of the Cancer Center had given the Caucus a common cause all members could champion. I directly attribute my experience as a Robert Wood Johnson Fellow in our nation's capital for the training I received in understanding how to use the political path for a positive objective. This breakfast meeting with the legislators became an annual event.

The state legislature's support substantially increased the credibility of the Cancer Center and served as a catalyst for the few oppositionists to the Cancer Center to become more allied with our mission. Therefore, we could move forward with far fewer impediments. A benchmark report in September 1995 reflects the speed with which changes to the cancer program were implemented. The Penn State Cancer Center's accomplishments included the establishment of the organization's structure and administrative office; transition of cancer-related disciplines into the existing hematology/oncology clinic site; expansion of the clinic site staff to serve additional patients and physicians in clinic; appointments of five master's level clinical program coordinators; additional faculty appointments; expansion of marketing and public relations: a toll-free number; patient advisory group, display board in the hospital rotunda; and community outreach efforts in collaboration with the

American Health and Education Center and the American Cancer Society.[5]

Denise: A Study in Courage

In the midst of all of this growth, during the fall of 1995 I enrolled in a Spanish II course. I was preparing myself in anticipation of a trip to the Dominican Republic, Haiti's island-sharing, Spanish-speaking neighbor, and I wanted to increase my fluency in the language. As I was the only Spanish II student that semester, the teacher for Spanish III invited me to join her class. In such a small group it became easy to socialize with nearly everyone, although not to share much personal information. I became casually acquainted with Denise Moffatt, a young woman in her early twenties. She was a good student of the language, having spent some time in Mexico. An attractive brunette, she wore her hair short and curly. I recall thinking at the time that I thought of her only as a pleasant, typical American student, who was helpful to several of us struggling with the language.

I thought no more of Denise until the following summer of 1996 when the Penn State Cancer Center sponsored the Cancer Survival Rally. Friday evening of the weekend rally, I attended the late night candlelight vigil. I remember thinking how dark it was there at the high school track in Middletown. Around 10:00 p.m. people began to congregate in an area where a young woman was addressing the group. A gentleman, who later was identified as the woman's father, held a large candle to provide light by which the speaker could read her prepared remarks. I knew we were about to hear a survivor's tale, although I was not standing close enough to recognize the speaker as anyone I might know. As she began her story, people were respectfully attentive; as her narrative unfolded, a stillness pervaded the listeners; and as she concluded, there was not a dry eye among us.

During a routine breast self-examination while she was in Mexico, Denise had discovered what she thought to be a lump on her breast. She immediately sought medical attention. However, the physician who examined her assured her that it was not a cancerous lump, but simply a fibrocystic disease. Upon her return to the United States, Denise was reexamined and again reassured that there was nothing to be concerned about. Several months later, still not satisfied with what she had been told, Denise made an appointment with a surgeon. Three days before her date of graduation from college, the surgeon confirmed Denise's worst fears: she had advanced stage breast cancer. There was no time to delay. Her surgery was scheduled immediately and rather than marching in a college commencement, Denise was undergoing a mastectomy. The surgery was followed by chemotherapy treatment and a peripheral stem cell transplant. Denise drew the audience to her as she told of her four-week hospitalization at Johns Hopkins Medical Center, the longest and most frightening weeks of her life.

Like many cancer patients, Denise found support and encouragement in a group of women who befriended her. During one of her hospital stays this support group sent letters to everyone they could think of and, as a result, Denise received more than 800 cards, including one from Mother Teresa. Another form of support came when a favorite professor of hers from Albright College would stop her class at the specific time Denise was undergoing intense chemotherapy and would ask the class to concentrate on positive thoughts or prayers for Denise.

Concluding her story, Denise told of the overflow of love and prayers she had been given, "I am very glad that I shared my story. From giving a little information about myself I received an outpouring of support. My aunt and uncle held a benefit for me and 200 people came, 85 percent of whom I did not know. . . . This experience taught me how very easy it is to reach out to people. I received a lot of support from my family, but the strangers who helped me showed me that there is a lot of love in this world where so many people see only violence."[6]

I was particularly impressed with the speaker's joy in living: "I was going through a very rough time, but I was full of joy. I have since figured out what my secret is. . . . what I know is something that everybody knows. I know that I am going to die. Not necessarily today, tomorrow, or the next day. And not necessarily of cancer. I just know that someday, I am going to die. I used to know this in my intellectual mind, but I now know it in my heart and in my soul. I now know how truly beautiful life is and how lucky I am to have each moment, no matter what my state of health. I now understand what a gift the *present* time really is."[7]

At six o'clock the next morning, after the rally at which Denise (although I had not recognized her) spoke, I returned to the track where I was scheduled to participate in a "run for survival." As I approached, I saw someone I recognized. It was Denise, the girl from my Spanish classes. I greeted her and asked her what she was doing there so early in the morning. She responded that she had been there all night. I then asked her, "Did you hear the young woman who spoke last night?" She grinned and told me that she was the speaker. I was astonished. I told her how moved I had been by her account, then asked her why she had never mentioned her struggle during the time we were taking classes. "Well," she replied, "this is not something one says to the person sitting next to her in a class."

Even though I have had close familiarity with numerous cancer patients of all ages, I was particularly moved by Denise's story. Perhaps it was her youth, combined with her demeanor of fragility steeled against adversity that touched me. Or it may be that she reminded me of my own daughters, young women close in age to Denise. Or maybe it was simply her courage and calm delivery in the telling of the event that had turned her world upside down.

Later that same morning I met Denise's parents and discussed with them the possibility of Denise's talking with high school junior and senior girls as part of the Penn State Cancer Center's educational programs. Denise agreed to help, as long as she could work around her classes at Loyola where she was studying for a master's degree in psychology. She wanted to tell the girls that, "Yes, if this happened to me, it can happen to you as well." I scheduled her to speak as part of the outreach program. Her message is profound, and every person hearing her is moved by her closing remarks, "I imagine that each of you has had your life touched by cancer in some way. It is my hope that each of you will know that you are alive, in your hearts and in your souls, not just in your minds. Life is precious. Take good care of that life, as you have only one."[8] Denise continued serving as a spokeswoman on survival, and although she faced recurrence of her cancer, she was married five years later in a wedding ceremony that received wide press coverage.

Penn State Cancer Center: The Reality

On 9 November 1995 the Penn State Cancer Center celebrated its opening by hosting an Inaugural Symposium, with leading cancer researchers from across the country participating in the symposium, "From Bench to Clinic." The theme of this and each successive annual symposium has focused on both cancer research and clinical applications, solidly affirming the core foundational beliefs of its Director. Noted researchers and specialists from Johns Hopkins Oncology Center, Harvard Medical School, University of Virginia Cancer Center, Fox Chase Cancer Center, and the National Cancer Institute were among the speakers during the day-long symposium which drew more than 200 participants. Subjects of the papers ranged from genetics to estrogen implications. In speaking to the press during that inaugural event, I announced that the goal of the new center was to "provide a multidisciplinary, comprehensive approach to cancer prevention, education, diagnosis, treatment and follow-up care for children and adults, as well as research into its causes and cures."[9] I further stated that I believed the need for the center is "obvious, considering the fact that three out of four families experience some form of cancer in a family member and that the American Cancer Society estimates about one third of all Americans will develop cancer in their lifetimes."[10]

In December the Cancer Center announced the establishment of monthly interdisciplinary conferences with the intent of bringing together Medical Center clinical faculty and basic scientists in an interdisciplinary forum where discussions could be broad-based or focus on disease-specific body systems and sites. Also in December the Cancer Center began to receive support specific to the Center itself. This support increased when we were honored with funding by the Foreman Foundation, a newly designated endowment in support of melanoma cancer research. Established by Philip Foreman of the Foreman Group, during their first year the foundation raised approximately $50,000 through their initial (thence to be annual) golf tournament. Additional funding came from (1) the Elizabethtown Rotary's cancer endowment fund to be used for basic clinical research and patient care; (2) trust accounts for various cancer-related projects, including the creation of a cancer education and resource library; and (3) numerous contributions and memorials maintained in a Cancer Center gift fund. Not to be overlooked was the $250,000 appropriation from the Pennsylvania State Legislature.

The Penn State Cancer Center very quickly became an active partner in the Central Pennsylvania Oncology Group (CPOG), a multidisciplinary group of more than 150 oncologists, hematologists, pathologists, radiation therapists, surgeons, and nurses from a 34-county area of central Pennsylvania. CPOG meets regularly to provide professional education programs related to cancer treatment and care. It correspondingly produces a number of publications for cancer patients and caregivers, including the *Cancer Home Care Guide* and *Helping People Cope*. Through a speakers' bureau, workshops, and support groups, CPOG reaches out to the community with presentations on cancer awareness and prevention. It has become the central corridor for the sharing of cancer care information and resources in central Pennsylvania.

In addition to our affiliation with CPOG, I sought collaboration between the Cancer Center and the Pennsylvania Department of Health (PDH), which fosters programs that are comprehensive while CPOG focuses on those that are specialized. I was particularly interested in PDH's distinctive strategic plan and the centering of its $4.7 million budget on a tumor registry and cancer control. Further, I met with the Pennsylvania Cancer Advisory Board (PCAB) which approves funding for cancer research projects.

Another player important to the success of the Penn State Cancer Center is the American Health Education Center (AHEC). This organization was initiated by the United States Congress (following

the Carnegie Commission's Report on Higher Education and the
Nation's Health in 1970) as a mechanism for alleviating the shortage and disproportionate distribution of health-care providers.
AHECs are regional, not-for-profit organizations formed through
the cooperation of schools of medicine, dentistry, nursing, public
health, pharmacy, and allied health professions with local community health-care systems. The AHEC centers work to support existing primary care practitioners and to remediate the shortage of primary health-care professionals in underserved areas.[11] The Penn
State Cancer Center works closely with AHEC in programs with a
common mission to underserved areas of central Pennsylvania.

After only one year of operation, the Penn State Cancer Center
began to position itself in the central Pennsylvania area. More importantly, it had high visibility. The philosophy of a multidisciplinary
team approach in the management of cancer patients produced divi-
dends as shown by patient satisfaction surveys. The exchange
between surgeons and medical oncologists working side-by-side in
the Cancer Center, the continuity of care assured by the nurse coordinators, and the continuous presence of the social workers made a
visible difference in the manner in which care was delivered to
patients. There was a significant increase in the utilization of the
infusion area. The annual symposium, the monthly interdisciplinary
conferences, and the quarterly newsletters were bridging basic scientists and clinicians interested in the problem of cancer. The Cancer Center was approved for affiliate membership in the Eastern
Cooperative Oncology Group, and discussion continued with community oncologists for their active participation in nationally approved protocol studies.

With the health administration and marketing background of
my administrative aide, Mary Dewey, and her enthusiasm in the creation of a new entity within the Medical Center, we moved quickly.
After only one year the Cancer Center had progressed beyond
expectations. The recruitment of Dr. Robert Gordon, the guidance
of the Policy Committee, and the educational program of Dr. Harold
Harvey brought high visibility within the institution. Importantly,
the operation of the Cancer Center had instilled in the faculty a

sense of purpose, changed the manner in which care is delivered to cancer patients, and provided support to oncologists in the communities surrounding the Medical Center. We were elated.

In September 1996, only one year following the opening of the Penn State Cancer Center, the Hershey Medical Center proudly announced that it had achieved notable status. Dean Evarts wrote, " . . . it is clear that great strides have been made in the Cancer Center under your leadership. They have occurred in patient care, outreach, education, and research. If we continue this early momentum, we will move the Cancer Center towards a position of importance in central Pennsylvania and beyond."[12]

Strategies to reach that position included the following for the Center's second year: continued development of oncology clinical pathways; further development of a cancer network; expansion of clinical trials efforts; and identification of further academic opportunities for students, residents, and fellows in the Cancer Center. While there were to be many future quests, the major objective remained achieving National Cancer Institute designation.

The Annual Report for Fiscal Year 1995/96 noted the Cancer Center's strong commitment to scientific research, evidenced by more than $9.9 million in grant-funded, cancer-related research from more than 80 cancer-related research awards. This represented more than 22 percent of the total funding base for the Center. More than 200 researchers and physicians collaborated on investigative teams to develop a greater understanding of the genetics of cancer: carcinogenesis, hormones and growth factors, and tumor virology. Most notably, these research projects offered leading-edge hope to patients for whom other methods had failed. It also opened the doors to successful new treatments for cancer victims of the future.

The second Annual Symposium, held in October 1996, had as its theme, "Cancer Prevention, Cancer Risk: Basic Principles and Clinical Applications." Guest faculty included national specialists, medical schools, cancer centers, and, again, the National Cancer Institute. Topics included, among others, the role of surgery, ornithine decarboxylase, chemo-prevention, and oncogenes.

In November 1996 the first bone marrow transplantation was

performed at our facility, and a total of thirty-two transplantations were performed during our second year. In the spring of 1997 the Cancer Center established a clinical trials office. Short-term goals of that office included ongoing networking with medical and nursing staff members to identify and seek approval for appropriate protocols; streamlining submission of protocols to the institutional review board; recruiting eligible patients to enter these protocols; prompt communication to physicians when new protocols became available; and continual update of the web page for timely access to clinical trials detail and eligibility criteria. If anyone had any doubts about the success of the Penn State Cancer Center, these timely accomplishments quickly dispelled any concern.

In February 1997 came the announcement that Penn State's Milton S. Hershey Medical Center was merging with Geisinger Medical Center. All who knew the work of the Penn State Cancer Center, whether directly or indirectly, were concerned. Would the Center be no more? Would it be absorbed by another unit? Or would it continue as its own entity? One thing I knew for certain—I had not spent time and energy to throw both away without doing everything in my power to continue the progress we had made.

By this point, the Penn State Cancer Center had been gaining recognition for its cancer research, essential to reaching the goal of a NCI designation. We were very gratified, as the designation was of primary concern to all who had invested in the research program—funders, administrators, and researchers alike. NCI designation (or lack thereof) would have a significant impact on the future of the Cancer Center as well as the College of Medicine. To those involved either directly or peripherally, the conviction was the same: Penn State Cancer Center, as a research center, must remain intact.

We strongly believed that the state legislature should continue to contribute to the effort of placing the only central Pennsylvania academic institution on parity with those in Pittsburgh and Philadelphia. As those cancer centers had been receiving financial assistance for their programs, it seemed only fair to seek the same assistance for the Penn State Cancer Center. In addition, by bringing high technology to Hershey, patients could be treated close to home and the community oncologists would have access to NCI approved treatment protocols. Furthermore, a NCI designation would bring more federal dollars to the center of the state.

By June 1997 the Cancer Center again reported an increase in visits to the practice site over the previous fiscal year. Clinical visits had risen by nine percent while the chemotherapy/infusion room visits had increased by 23 percent. In addition, a total of 60 bone marrow transplants had been performed since the first successful one in November 1996.

The Director's Message in the *Annual Report for Fiscal Year 1996/97* makes note of four major achievements in the area of patient care, education, and research: (1) the bone marrow transplantation program was developed beyond expectations; (2) the Cancer Clinical Trial Office provided support to physicians in entering patients in the National Cancer Institute approved clinical studies; (3) eight awards, totaling $110,000, were granted by the Cancer Center; and (4) the Cancer Center financed a tumor bank designed to provide long-term storage of both normal and malignant tissue for research studies.

All who reviewed this report had to agree that the accomplishments of this two-year-old Cancer Center were remarkable. And all agreed that the Cancer Center must remain as a proud heritage and active entity and should be given the opportunity to expand and achieve even more. The only remaining decision to be agreed upon was the form the Cancer Center would take.

October 1997 saw the Third Annual Symposium with guest faculty representing the Universities of California and Chicago, University of Virginia School of Medicine, University of Pittsburgh Cancer Institute, The University of Texas Southwestern Medical Center, and the National Cancer Institute. A representative sampling of presentations included interferons, unique tumor antigens, t-cell epitope based cancer vaccines, and dendritic cell-based therapy.

In the fall of 1997, I was once again named by *Good Housekeeping Magazine* in its "401 Best Doctors for Women, 1997." The doctors in the list were nominated by more than 260 department chairs and section chiefs in obstetrics and gynecology at major medical centers across the country. From the more than 1,500 named, 401 names were culled from those most cited.[13] This award brought additional recognition to the Center and augured well for its future. I was so pleased to see my long-standing friend Stephen Curry included in the category of General Obstetrician/Gynecologists.[14]

However, there was no time for resting on laurels. Once it was determined that Geisinger Medical Center and Health Systems was interested in supporting only the clinical area of a cancer center, the Hershey Medical Center efforts went into expanding the research-based and education aspects of the Penn State Cancer Center. With renewed determination, we focused our research objective on identifying research programs that could lead to the prevention of cancer. To date we have identified five suitable programs to support: 1. cell biology; 2. viral carcinogenesis; 3. chemical carcinogenesis; 4. tumor immunology; and 5. drug discovery.

After five very successful years as the Director of the Cancer Center, I believed that my job was to begin the steps leading to national recognition. I organized a small delegation from the Center to meet with the NCI staff to acquire a better understanding of the guidelines and to be assigned a contact person to work with us during the entire process. We then invited three consultants from other Cancer Centers to assess our program, make recommendations as to the readiness of our institution, and advise us on the best way to package the information in the application. The suggestions of the consultants came as no surprise. In summary, the following recommendations were made:

- The Penn State Cancer Center is a potentially viable and desirable venture.
- There are four viable programs which can be the basis of the proposed Cancer Center grant.
- The proposed shared services, appearing to be of high quality, could be improved by support of an approved core grant.
- The Center Director must have (1) the authority to review and prioritize cancer related clinical trial protocols, (2) an adequate budget for administrative staff and faculty, (3)

authority to raise funds for the Cancer Center from grateful patients and donors, and (4) more space, particularly laboratory, assigned to the Cancer Center.

• While commendations are given to Dr. Mortel and the dedicated senior members of the Center, and noting that Penn State has the intellectual resources and personnel to support a first rate program, the consultants believe very strongly that the Penn State Cancer Center must have a much stronger institutional commitment to be successful in competing for the core grant funding.[15]

Notes

1. "Penn State University Cancer Center," benchmark report, September 1995, unpaginated.

2. "Mortel Named Associate Dean and Cancer Center Director," *Penn State Medicine*, March 1995, 9.

3. Ibid.

4. *A Vision for the Future: A Case Statement*. Penn State University Cancer Center, May 1995, 1.

5. "Penn State University Cancer Center," Ibid.

6. Ibid., 5–7.

7. Ibid., 8.

8. Ibid., 9.

9. Rob Marquette, "Hershey Medical Center Dedicates New Cancer Center," *The Sun*, November 15, 1995, 9.

10. Ibid.

11. "To Make a Difference," Pennsylvania Statewide AHEC Program, np, nd, 3.

12. C. McCollister Evarts, MD, Dean, College of Medicine, Milton S. Hershey Medical Center, quoted in "Director's Message," *Annual Report 1995/96*, Penn State University Cancer Center, September 1996, 1.

13. Maxine Abrams, "The Best Doctors for Women," *Good Housekeeping*, August 1997, 53–72.

14. Ibid., 72.

15. Report of the Cancer Center Advisory Committee, "Penn State University Cancer Center," July 2000.

Chapter 7: Gynecologic Oncology Organizations

In 1994 during the time I was asked by the Dean to establish the Penn State Cancer Center, the Department of Obstetrics and Gynecology was "running on autopilot," having reached all the goals I had set for it. We had an excellent staff, had established good procedures, and were offering the best services possible. We had regained our reputation for excellence; attracted new specialists; retained top professionals; interested new patients; hired the foremost physicians committed to women's health; established services for high-risk pregnancies; utilized the finest technology in reproduction problems; and honed our selection process for attracting the best residents. In a word, we had done it!

At the same time, I was being commended by the gynecologic oncology community for creating the successful Gynecologic Cancer Foundation (GCF), which had been nearly ten years in the making and involved many others in the initial stages. The seeds for a society initially had been planted at the organizational meeting at the Key Biscayne Hotel in 1970, the meeting to which I had been invited to present a paper to the Society members, then a group of fifty-seven physicians. During these three packed days of speeches and paper presentations, the founding members established very rigid membership criteria, by-laws, and officers for the new society.

Because I was serving as a Fellow at Memorial Sloan-Kettering under John L. Lewis (in-coming president of SGO) and had previously completed my residency at Hahneman under George Lewis (immediate past-president), I was very pleased to be in the company of both my mentors at this initial meeting and hoped someday to be invited to become a member. The meeting ended with the establishing of the Society of Gynecologic Oncologists.

Eleven months after the organization of the Society (and perhaps because of that move), the American Board of Obstetrics and Gynecology (ABOG) hosted a conference on the subspecialization of obstetrics and gynecology. One month later that Board established an ad hoc committee on Gynecologic Oncology, thus raising the status of the subspecialty. The charge to this committee, under the chairmanship of John L. Lewis, was to define the training programs and the requirements of certification for special competence in gynecologic oncology. Not unexpectedly, gynecologic oncologists were not all in agreement on what should constitute board certification and who should grant it, so discussion continued for several years before agreement could be reached. It was not until 1974 that certification examinations were in place for gynecologic oncology, and I was among those who received board certification the year it was first made available.

In 1976 I was elected into full membership of SGO. Soon after, I served a three-year term as a council member. I became a familiar figure in the Society when in 1980 I first presented progress reports on my research.

The Research and Education Foundation

In the early 1980s SGO began to plan how it could encourage and award young investigators who were conducting promising research. Because of my own interest in research, I was an early advocate of establishing a foundation that would provide funding to researchers and was pleased when the membership voted to form a committee to explore the feasibility of a foundation program. This committee's recommendation was for SGO to pledge $5,000–

$10,000 annually to fund awards, because to assume responsibility for anything more extensive would be cost prohibitive. Known as the Research and Education Foundation Award, the grant would be solely for the purpose of supporting researchers with materials and supplies and would be awarded directly to individuals and not to their institutions. While the intent of the award was noble and generous, it was thought by many not to be very successful, as there was too little money offered and, therefore, too few applicants.

In 1989, following my election as vice-president for 1990, I became chairman of the Foundation Committee and was asked to submit a proposal to redesign its operation. I had for years believed that research and clinical care could not be viewed separately and that neither research nor clinical care could work as effectively standing alone as they could together. Because of my conviction that the Society could be the vehicle to change the face of gynecologic oncology, I developed a proposal that would completely alter our course, would provide a new platform, and would stretch our thinking and our purpose beyond what most of the membership had ever considered.

A New Foundation Concept

Ardently committed to research, clinical practice, and teaching as the three elements that compose the triad of academic medicine, I have consistently said, "Research is the *foundation* of all we do; clinical practice is *what* we do, and teaching is the showing others *how* we do it."[1] Because neither clinical nor basic science research is taught in the Medical School of Port-au-Prince in Haiti, I had not had the opportunity to develop a taste or technique for basic research until my post-graduate work at Memorial Sloan-Kettering Cancer Center nearly ten years after finishing medical school. It was only then that I saw how important research is and, with every successive appointment, I made sure I could be involved in research, either in the laboratory or by securing funding so that research in my field could be expanded by others. For the past twenty years I have encouraged both basic and clinical research and have devoted my efforts to the support of laboratory study.

In the mid-1970s I had devised a plan to learn basic research methods and in 1978 was granted a sabbatical leave by Penn State University to devote an entire academic year to the study of the biology of endometrial carcinoma at the University of Paris under the direction of Professor Étienne Baulieu, best-known for his discovery of RU486. When it became evident that the biology of endometrial cancer could not be adequately studied unless the experiments were conducted with pure cancer samples, my stake in research stopped being an interest and became a passion. Through my presentations at the yearly scientific sessions of the Society, interest was stimulated in other members to expose and encourage their young faculty and Fellows to pursue basic gynecologic oncology research. This increased attention to basic research led to stronger programs in many medical schools.

While clear in the direction needed to develop a proposal for creating a strong and effective Foundation, my vision for the Society went far beyond creating a Foundation to support research. First, I had realized for years that the subspecialty of gynecologic oncology was not widely known; second, the subspecialty was misunderstood even by those who knew of its existence; and third, it was this subspecialty that could become the breakthrough in patient care. Research and clinical care can not be viewed separately; further, neither can they work as effectively standing alone as they can together.

My excitement increased as to the possibilities an authenticated foundation could provide. I had seen the determination of the Foundation de France (the institution that had invited me to set up a laboratory where the clinicians would play a fundamental role in conducting research), and I remembered very clearly my commitment to that project in which I spent a grueling year rebuilding the Obstetrics and Gynecology Department at the Hershey Medical Center while traveling bimonthly to France to supervise the work there.

While not everyone agreed with the global perspective I was promoting, I was determined not to allow opposing viewpoints to deter me. I believed that when others saw how effective a multidisciplinary approach could be to the broad spectrum of treating cancer, they, too, would become believers. Every now and again I would remind myself that maybe I did look at things differently. "Why are you doing this?" my colleagues kept asking. "Because it needs to be done," was my unfailing reply.

From the moment many years ago in Haiti when I had determined that I would go to Medical School, I realized I had the ability to visualize a plan from inception to completion. Such thinking was second nature to me. I could map out each move and know in advance what step would lead where.

While the course may have been clear to me, the road was not always smooth. The example that came to my mind at that time was the struggle I had been experiencing as Chairman of Obstetrics and Gynecology. There, I had come face-to-face with conflicting points of view when I began to rebuild the department. I had insisted on a research laboratory as a condition for accepting the chairmanship and had subsequently taken the lead in the Department's metamorphosis into a very successful gynecologic oncology research program. Much of the Department's success could be directly attributed to the multidisciplinary approach I had fostered—a community outreach program of cancer screening and education through a network of primary care physicians and community organizations, as well as a multidisciplinary approach to patient care through coordination of all services for each individual.

I viewed all of those components not only as necessary to the creation of a successful department but also as essential to the success of the Society and its Foundation. I was determined to replicate the process by instilling those same components into building a master strategy for creating a Foundation. All that remained to be done was to convince everyone else of the value of this plan.

National Cancer Institute: the Other Side of the Foundation

While developing a clear and compelling proposal for the Foundation was my primary task, this was not the only goal. As I saw it, the Foundation would serve as the cornerstone of a new era for the

Society. It was this vision of what needed to be and "what *could* be" that enabled me to take this concept forward.

By 1989 the Society of Gynecologic Oncology was a highly respected medical society, but still remained an organization not widely known outside the umbrella of "gynecology." The Society easily could have stayed in its safe and successful niche, holding annual meetings and providing a forum for its members. It could have continued to award small prizes for research and scientific papers and it could have continued to serve as a network for its members. It would have survived on this track for many years, content in its fellowship and the advancement of its mission to support the best in gynecologic oncology care. Or, it could take a new direction, break ground, take risks, make connections, and change its destiny forever.

We were definitely at a crossroads, one of those times in the history of any organization when faced with choosing between a smoothly running status quo or breaking out of the mold into uncharted territory. Because I had been asked to prepare a proposal to re-establish the Foundation, I returned to the membership with a complete change of direction, an opportunity for the Society to take a new stand, to stretch beyond what any of them had ever done. I was seeking a transformation in the organizational culture and mission to change the very essence of not only the Society but also the subspecialty of gynecologic oncology. I was asking the membership to trust me, and to entrust to me the future of the Society.

Among themselves some members were making comments such as, "There is no need for us to change. We are strong. We are good. We are recognized as the premier society for our subspecialty. We are on the cutting edge of cancer care and treatment. Every day we learn new techniques and procedures. And we are willing to think about funding a Foundation. That's enough. Don't also ask us to change who we are and what the Society is." But that is exactly what I did. I changed who we were and what we did.

My goal was to convince the Society to establish both (1) a Foundation and (2) a National Cancer Institute Gynecologic Oncology Section. Further, my report included a plan for funding the

Foundation. It began, "As the only professional medical organization dedicated solely to the care of women with malignant disease,
the Society of Gynecologic Oncologists (SGO) recognizes its special responsibility to the women, families, and economic well-being
of our nation. To meet that responsibility, the Society's leadership
has created the Gynecologic Cancer Foundation. Its mission is to
foster, nourish, and sustain research and education for succeeding
generations of gynecologic oncologists and their patients, and to
ensure that both the medical profession and the public at large have
access to the most up-to-date information relating to the prevention,
detection, and treatment of cancer in women."[2]

The first objective of the Foundation would be to support
research through a series of awards to both new and established
clinical investigators working in the field of gynecologic oncology.
Four distinct research awards would be offered:

- Innovative Study Award—$50,000 per year to commission
  specific scientific research by a qualified individual or organization specifically when federal funding has not been
  made available.
- Career Development Award—$75,000 per year to provide
  financial assistance each year for up to five years to an SGO
  member conducting research at the NCI/NIH (National
  Institutes of Health), or another well-renowned academic
  institution.
- Senior Faculty Award—$60,000 per year for two years to
  provide funding for an independent investigator conducting
  gynecologic oncology research at the NCI/NIH.
- Faculty Development Award—$35,000 per year to support
  research projects conducted by a junior faculty member
  who has demonstrated potential for becoming an independent investigator with emphasis on research encompassing
  any aspect of gynecologic malignancy.

Second, the Foundation would be committed to (1) providing
opportunities for ongoing professional education and training to

refresh and update practitioners' skills and knowledge and (2) encouraging young practitioners to pursue an academic career. The former would provide a series of seminars addressing areas such as advances in chemotherapy and radiobiology, the latest surgical procedures and techniques, cryotherapy, electrocoagulation, and hormone treatment. The latter would provide incentive grants for training in the laboratory of a renowned scientist to acquire essential knowledge in such areas as molecular biology.

Third, the Foundation would identify public information, education, and outreach as one of its top priorities. An annual commitment of $125,000 would be made to maintain a significant variety of programs designed to reach hundreds of thousands of women across the country. These would include a speakers' bureau; production and distribution of videos, brochures, and other educational materials; a mass market distribution of printed informational materials; a newsletter; and an annual workshop for medical writers and other media.

At the February 1991 Annual Meeting in Orlando, Florida, I presented "The SGO Research and Education Foundation Report to SGO Membership." I began by requesting the support of the membership to move ahead with the organization of the Foundation: "We are speaking of a defined, tax-exempt legal entity, which will offer to the Society the opportunity to attract an expanded constituency and financial resources. . . ." I explained that the new Foundation would serve as an excellent opportunity for (medical) suppliers to expand their involvement through funding research. Further, I made the point that the Foundation should be regarded as "a mechanism which will provide funds for the Society to carry out its goals and objectives."[3]

A major concern of the Society was the lack of visibility of gynecologic oncology at the national level. We were hampered by the general perception that obstetricians and gynecologists lacked interest in research. It was up to us to change that. "It is our duty," I emphasized, "to take the lead in this. We have an obligation to promote research in our own subspecialty. If we truly believe that research is valuable to the treatment, and perhaps cure, of gynecologic cancer, then we *must* establish a major Foundation, one that will gain the attention of funders, researchers, and the National Institutes of Health. More importantly, we ourselves must pledge the seed money. Corporations are not going to put their money in an organization unless that organization—we, the Society—shows that we first put our own money into an endowment. In addition, the Foundation must be a separate entity. It is only by standing independently from the Society that it can attract the kind of big money that is needed to support research."[4]

My report and added comments were greeted by cheers as well as some grumbling. A number of members were very upset at the thought of separating the Foundation from the Society. They expressed their objections, in some cases quite vocally. I had expected this mix of reactions and looked at my fellow members of the Council, smiling as if to say, "I know why you wanted me to do this." Then turning to the larger group, I urged my colleagues to ". . . take off our personal and institutional hats, put on our 'societal hats,' pull together, further build and enhance our great Society, develop our image in the medical community and the public, and move ahead. We have now gathered sufficient momentum to launch some major initiatives, initiatives likely to broaden our scope and enhance our influence as the authoritative voice in all women's health care issues, particularly in matters related to cancer in women. Politically, the timing is right."[5]

I next called for a mobilization of the Society membership in working toward the establishment of a Gynecologic Oncology Section of NCI. I explained that if the Society were serious about its subspecialty, then it was urgent for us to be more vocal. I reminded my colleagues that only through a broader name recognition could the subspecialty gain the standing of other research programs. Stature, I reminded them, is what provides the seeding for funding which in turn allows for research essential to new treatments and eventual cures for cancer.

I laid out the two-fold Mission Statement of the Foundation:

1. Develop an aggressive educational program in order to disseminate information on current trends, techniques and

other aspects of prevention, detection, and treatment of cancer in women.

2. Raise the level of academic activity in women's health care programs by developing a cadre of clinical investigators.

The Gynecologic Cancer Foundation

Following extended discussion, the majority of the members voted to proceed with the Foundation. Later, Dr. C. Paul Morrow's Presidential speech praised the work that had gone into establishing the Foundation by complimenting me, " . . . Rod Mortel who almost single-handedly brought the SGO Foundation into existence."[6] The SGO's *Newsletter* of April 1991 reported the proceedings:

> SGO membership approved plans for the development of a research and educational Foundation at their annual business meeting.
>
> The Foundation, slated to be inaugurated this summer, would assist in raising the level of academia within gynecologic oncology, help disseminate information on current trends, techniques, and other aspects to the medical community and the general public, and promote and initiate research in the field.[7]

In April 1991 I was featured in the *SGO Newsletter* in an article titled "SGO Profile." This is not a regular feature of the publication, but most likely was written to honor my work in establishing the Foundation. The profile begins with the acknowledgement that I "made an indelible mark on the gynecologic oncology field by being named the first black, foreign-educated individual to chair one of the nation's 127 medical school-based obstetrics and gynecology departments. . . . rose from the ranks of impoverished Haiti to become one of today's leading experts in gynecologic oncology."[8] After highlighting my medical career, the profile concludes, "Dr. Mortel is a member of numerous medical associations including SGO where he has served as its vice president as well as a member of both the Scientific Program and Research and Educational

Foundation Committees. Dr. Mortel was instrumental in establishing a Foundation for the Society of Gynecologic Oncologists recently approved at SGO's 1991 Annual Meeting."[9]

By the fall of that first year the Society's newsletter began to carry a banner of support, "The SGO leadership believes that a new, separate entity, dedicated to promoting the importance of gynecologic oncology as a major factor in the national health agenda, would enable members of the health professions, related corporations, and interested individuals to join together to (a) concentrate their energies on identifying and funding research and education projects of long-range importance to the prevention, detection, and treatment of gynecologic cancers, and (b) secure necessary financial resources dedicated to supporting these initiatives."[10] The findings confirmed the recommendations that the Foundation would succeed only if it "is clearly supported by a well-informed, dedicated SGO Council and committed volunteer leadership; establishes its credibility as a separate organization from SGO; is receptive to the needs of the discipline and the medical community; and targets all projects ultimately to provide a public service."[11]

While establishing the Foundation was certainly at the forefront of the Society's agenda, other issues were also being addressed. In 1991, spurred on by a new confidence in their growing power, the membership took a stand, speaking out against the stalling tactics taken by the federal legislators concerning women's health issues. They were particularly outspoken against the legislators' negative stance on a bill that would have provided an additional $100 million for research into diseases that strike women. Taking this stand in promoting research gave many members the sense of empowerment they needed to commit to the Foundation and a Gynecologic Oncology Section of NCI.

During the first year of the Foundation I was active in its initial funding. Our organizational consultant would have preferred a single funder with a donation of $1 million, but I was satisfied with the quarter million dollars pledged by the members themselves during year one. As is typical, during the first year the Foundation spent more than it took in. This upset some of the members, particularly those who had been early critics of the Foundation. Through all the usual rumblings I tried to keep my good humor. My supporters were concerned with "the heat" I was taking. However, I just laughed and responded, "I can take the heat because I am used to it. Don't forget, I was born in the heat of Haiti!"

To offset the criticism, there was greater praise. The 1992 Presidential Speech of the Annual Meeting of the Society included the following compliment: *"the Foundation . . . may well be the most important thing we have done as a Society."*[12]

Gynecologic Oncology Section at NCI

Behind the scenes, I continued the drive to establish a Gynecologic Oncology Section in the Surgery Branch of the Division of Cancer Treatment at the NCI. In its fifty-five years of existence, many attempts had been made to establish new sections, but for a variety of reasons, efforts had failed. Because of my experience in Washington, I was able to devise the best strategy with the right people at the right time. All of the elements fell into place, creating the framework needed to establish this new gynecologic oncology section. Moreover, I was able to integrate the drive for a Gynecologic Oncology Section at NCI through the establishment of the Gynecologic Cancer Foundation. In addition, by moving toward establishing the new section, I had created an additional research environment for the Fellows being funded by the Foundation, and the creation of the Foundation guaranteed the funding by which research Fellows could be supported in their work at NCI.

With the added prestige of our link to NCI, the Foundation began to thrive and, during the second year of the fundraising drive, donations greatly increased with several companies pledging $50,000 a year for two years or more. With this considerable amount of pledged funding, the future of the Foundation was secured.

By the fall of 1992 the Foundation had attracted five major sponsors. In addition, we had appointments with three major healthcare industry suppliers and several more pharmaceutical companies. President J. Taylor Wharton, MD, complimented the

work, "When SGO examined the feasibility of creating a Foundation to expand and intensify research and education efforts specifically impacting gynecologic oncology, membership response was
overwhelmingly in favor of the idea. We all agreed, back in July
1991, that the Foundation warranted our full attention and support
because it is dedicated to our patients and to the benefit of women
in general. Since the official unveiling of GCF by Rodrigue Mortel, MD, at the 1992 Annual Meeting, we have maintained a steady
pace at gathering support from our membership. Thanks to both the
membership and some very significant corporate support, GCF is
moving forward."[13]

The Foundation was well on its way to creating a permanent
endowment which would generate, in perpetuity, interest income of
at least $240,000 annually. This was quite an increase from the first
Foundation efforts ten years earlier. There are now more than 26
organizations who have pledged their financial support totaling
more than $1.2 million. The expressed feeling among most of the
members of the Society echoed the earlier words of Wesley Fowler
that ". . . this is the best thing that ever happened to the Society."

Buoyed by ever-increasing interest and corporate pledges to
the Foundation, I called on the NCI and asked for matching funds.
They agreed, making a commitment to co-support two Fellows at
the Institute. Further, I helped forge a contract between NCI and the
Foundation that would continue the partnership beyond personal
tenures of office.

In November of 1992 the Gynecologic Oncology Program
received its designation as the newest Section in the Surgery Branch
of the Division of Cancer Treatment at the NCI. According to the
news releases, the NIH established the new section in an effort to
focus research on gynecologic cancer. In announcing the establishment of the section to the scientific community, Dr. Bruce Chabner,
Division Director, said that NIH planned to build a significant
research team to strengthen research and training, and to establish
clinical protocols in gynecologic oncology. According to Dr. Chabner, ". . . Mortel has played a major role in this achievement as a
member of NCI's Division of Cancer Treatment advisory board."[14]

When asked for my reaction, I replied, "This is an area that I have long felt deserved more attention. It is gratifying that we have been successful. SGO has been concerned for many years with the absence of a program specifically dedicated to gynecologic malignancies. This is the one area in oncology where the specialist cares for the patient from beginning to end of the treatment."[15]

By the February 1993 Annual Meeting the Foundation was completely operational, with Society membership committed to two goals: (1) maintaining the GCF as an important funding source for researchers, and (2) assuring that the Society would retain its newly found professional standing. Corporate sponsors had demonstrated their support of the Society's mission, and their pledges reflected the seriousness of that commitment. In addition, the NCI had established three research positions specifically dedicated to gynecologic oncology.

While gratified by these successes, I cautioned the membership that, even with the excellent start, there were still many formidable tasks facing the Foundation: "Our education goals present an even greater challenge. *We are unknown.* Yes, my friends, we—the leaders in our field, surgical specialists, cancer care providers, patient care advocates—have an image problem."[16] I went on to explain that not only are many corporations unaware of who we are and what we do as gynecologic oncologists, but, even worse, we are not widely known by women and their families. I explained that women must be informed of the need for a gynecologic oncologist in the reproductive healthcare process so that they are not afraid to insist that this specialist be involved in the care they receive when they are told of their risks or diagnosis of malignant disease.

I announced two educational programs to address this lack of public awareness. The first was a brochure outlining the role of a gynecologic oncologist in women's health care; the brochure, "Beating the Odds of Gynecologic Cancer," would be made available to private practitioners to provide to their patients and to academicians for use in educational material displays. By the beginning of 1999 more than 10,000 copies had been distributed, along with 10,000 copies of "Active Prevention," 75,000 copies of "Maintain

Your Gynecologic Health," and 75,000 copies of the "Ovarian Cancer National Resource List."

The second program was a long-range plan targeted at developing media outreach. The Foundation would be taking our mission "to the pages of women's magazines, newspapers, and radio and television stations nationwide to share information about the prevention, detection, and treatment of female cancers—and how critical we are in that process."[17]

I concluded my report by saying, "At last year's annual meeting, we listened to outgoing SGO president Wesley Fowler speak to us about paradigm shifts. GCF is, in fact, a paradigm shift—a change in the way this Society and our subspecialty will make itself known to the scientific, medical, and patient communities. And, just like any paradigm shift, it will challenge us to think in ways we have never thought before—to stay ahead, to take risks, to enhance our futures, and to enrich the level of expertise and care we can provide our patients."[18]

Rodrigue Mortel, MD, President of SGO

In 1993 I was voted President-elect of the Society in recognition of my efforts towards the newly established NCI section, the Gynecologic Cancer Foundation, and many other scientific contributions I had made to the specialty of gynecologic oncology. Shortly following my nomination, I was called to the podium by Dr. John Lewis, in-coming president of the Foundation, where I was presented with a plaque honoring me for my leadership in the formation of the Foundation. The plaque is engraved with the following:

To Rodrigue Mortel, MD
In recognition and with sincere appreciation
for his dedication to the creation and success
of the Gynecologic Cancer Foundation, 1990–1994.

This written tribute was followed by a standing ovation. I took office in 1994, our Silver Anniversary Year, and "hit the ground running" with an agenda to match. My first action was to institute a standing Committee for Education that would offer courses to members throughout the year. Once those courses were established, I turned my attention to the three major areas of the Society which I believed required some tending to: (1) unity of the membership, (2) diversity in the ranks, and (3) accountability.

My first goal, unity of membership, was aimed at (a) averting a schism between the younger members, who had begun their own informal cadre, and the older members, who were entrenched in their own hierarchy; (b) closing the gap between those in private clinical practice and those in academic medicine; and (c) laying the groundwork for a worldwide federation of gynecologic oncologists to work together on common concerns in the field. These issues, I felt, could be addressed by bringing people together to talk. It has always amazed me that when people have a chance to be heard and to discuss their differences in an atmosphere of respect, they usually find they have much more in common than their differences might suggest.

My second goal addressed the issue of diversity by (a) placing more women on the SGO committees, (b) encouraging more women medical students to enter the subspecialty, and (c) forming an advisory board of women "consumers." We need the vision and the voices of women, we need women in leadership roles, and we need them in the forefront as advocates for this Society. Secondly, I called for the membership to welcome all eligible gynecologic oncologists into the Society, as we need to include rather than exclude. Further, I urged the Society to set a long-range goal to become a branch, rather than remain a section, of NCI. Gratified as we were to be recognized as a section, we should not sit back, secure in our own success, and expect the NCI to beat a path to our door. The final issue of diversity was the need to expand and extend the interests of the Society by developing industry partnerships.

The third goal, the question of accountability, became a much larger issue than I had anticipated, one that stirred the entire Society, even though the membership had been grumbling for several years about "high overhead costs." I thought that the best tactic would be an internal fiscal review to put everyone's concerns to rest. It is simply good business to investigate an issue when members or staff of any organization are openly complaining. I suggested that we get to the source of the concerns and we did.

Following this fiscal review we recommended that all committee chairmen submit reports to the Executive Committee to be summarized and published for the general membership. Because of my multilingual background I am keenly aware of the nuance of words and how easily messages can be misinterpreted. Long ago I learned that it is vital to communicate clearly, and I have found that an informed organization is a more effective organization.

It was most gratifying—and a tribute to the entire Society—that to a large degree we were able to accomplish the three goals of unity, diversity, and accountability. Even those which were met by some initial discomfort were openly discussed and steps were taken to initiate action toward solutions.

At the end of my tenure, I left the presidency with a challenge to the membership that they consider very seriously their responsibility as members of the Society and as members of the most respected profession in modern civilization. I urged them to create the vision for the next twenty-five years and to develop an action plan for what we as an organization and as individuals can contribute to humanity. In concluding my remarks as outgoing president in 1995, I reminded them ". . . as it is the physician's skill which saves lives, and the physician's art which heals, so it is the physician's passion which will improve the lot of humanity."[19]

I do not seek acclaim for the accomplishments of SGO or any other organization to which I try to contribute. To have brought people together for a common good cause has always been reward enough. Nonetheless, I have received my share of accolades. Among those many words of praise, perhaps the ones that mean the most to me were spoken by Stephen L. Curry, MD in his SGO Presidential Address in 1996: "Now you would think that after having been exposed to such great people I would be fully prepared to practice gynecologic oncology; but the person who taught me the most and showed me the best system of care was Rod Mortel. I am forever in his debt," Dr. Curry stated. He smiled at me, his mentor, and continued, "I remember my very first day at Penn State. I was scheduled to have a two-hour meeting with Dr. Mortel first thing in the morning. I expected that since he had trained at Memorial and I was going to work for him he would tell me how things were to be done and I would follow. Instead, this is what he said: 'Steve, you trained in one system and I in the other. Let's put the best of each together into *our* system. Over the next two hours we are going to negotiate each major area.' When I became interested in home care and terminal care, it was Rod Mortel who pushed me to do research and to write when others were indicating that these were frivolous areas for gynecologic oncology surgeons."[20]

In 1997 the 28th Annual Meeting of the Society of Gynecologic Oncologists received record coverage from the media when televised stories featuring the best research studies appeared on CNN Early Edition and Headline News, ABC News This Morning, Good Morning America, and CBS This Morning. Print stories were run in the *Washington Post, Boston Globe, San Diego Union-Tribune, Chicago Sun-Times*, and *Orange Count Register*, to name a few. The meeting was picked up by both Associated Press and Reuters National Wire Services and more than 21 million people were able to hear, read, or see news and information emanating from the meeting.

International Gynecologic Cancer Society

Part of my original plan for unity in the vision for SGO was a major external initiative. I strongly believed that unity within the Society of Gynecologic Oncologists would provide the strength and energy to reach out and assist colleagues outside the United States in organizing gynecologic oncologists in their own countries and thus have a major impact on the care of gynecologic oncology patients throughout the world. I envisioned a federation of societies from Asia, the Middle East, Africa, Europe, and the Americas. I further believed the formation of a Gynecologic Oncology Federation would provide a more collegial relationship for both scholarship and the working together on common concerns in the field. Unfortunately, my idea was met by resistance from SGO as well as the International Gynecologic Cancer Society (IGCS) who believed they were already providing the service I was suggesting.

Realizing that the membership of these organizations did not fully understand the magnitude of my vision for a global unification to provide training and assistance to gynecologic oncologists in developing countries, I decided to do what I do best: bring people together. I invited the leadership of the SGO, IGCS, and the Federation International of Gynecologic Obstetrics (FIGO) to meet with me. I asked for their suggestions as to how the goals of a Federation could best be accomplished. Following a two-hour brainstorming, the discussants came to these conclusions:

1. FIGO, a well-respected international organization, would be the best vehicle through which to propose standards for the subspecialty of gynecologic oncology;
2. SGO, highly respected and well-established, would best be utilized to assist in the area of continuing education in gynecologic oncology; and
3. IGCS, as an interdisciplinary society, would place strong emphasis in the future on multidisciplinary aspects of gynecologic education, as well as providing training opportunities for physicians in developing countries.

As a result of this meeting, SGO accepted my proposal for establishing and chairing its international committee, while IGCS requested me to chair their committee on education. What we believed was that through such a joint effort the mission of global unity proposed by the Federation could be accomplished.

Under my leadership as Chairman, the Education Committee of IGCS agreed upon a comprehensive mission statement which provides great latitude: "The Education Committee of the IGCS will strive to meet the continuing educational needs of its members."[21] Through a multidisciplinary approach to the management of patients with gynecologic cancer, the Committee agreed that its major efforts would include the following:

- Bi-annual scientific sessions.
- Postgraduate courses offered during the two days preceding the first scientific session.
- Awards for excellent presentations at the scientific sessions to increase the number and quality of abstracts, audiovisual aids, clarity of presentation, and participation of young investigators and Fellows.
- Print material with information about the IGCS, its philosophy and benefits to members for the purpose of increased interest and membership in the Society.
- Travel scholarships averaging $2,000 each to support individuals from developing countries to attend the scientific sessions and postgraduate courses.
- Training scholarships to enable gynecologists from developing countries to spend six to twelve months in institutions capable of teaching and providing special skills in the management of gynecologic cancer patients.
- A practical handbook for ob/gyn generalists, general surgeons, or family physicians in developing countries and in some regions of industrialized nations to use as a quick reference.

As a large number of industrialized nations and most developing countries have not been able to bridge the various oncologic disciplines, the Education Committee's work was driven by the following question: "What role can the IGCS play to positively affect the care of gynecologic oncology patients in developing countries?" To approach this question, the Committee designed a program, "First Gynecologic Oncology Conference Targeting Developing Countries," to which 400 physicians from various countries expressed an interest in attending. Fifty were selected to attend the conference in Rome in 1999 with all expenses except lodging covered by the Society. A total of 44 attendees represented 26 countries of various geographic regions, the majority coming from the eastern European block. This conference in Rome was so successful that a similar one is scheduled for Buenos Aires in October 2000 to target Central America, South America, Mexico, and the Caribbean countries. In 2002 this global training will be repeated in Seoul, Korea and Edinburgh, Scotland in 2004. The IGCS has also arranged for three physicians from developing countries to receive scholarships for six months training: one each in Germany, England, and Australia. While funding has come from various sources, the Education Committee itself received a $10,000 prize from SmithKline Beecham pharmaceuticals for its innovative and humanitarian work in establishing this global outreach.

Growth of The Gynecologic Cancer Foundation

Parallel to the momentum generated by IGCS, the GCF also was expanding its sphere of influence. Today the GCF supports a toll-free number that consumers can call for information about gynecologic malignancies. This information line has been an integral part of the Foundation's effort to provide information to thousands of people interested in finding out more about gynecologic cancers and the specialists who treat them. By 1999 this line had logged over 55,000 calls. Another project is the Women's Cancer Network, an interactive website which over 400,000 women signed on to in the first year. The site has received four top awards and was highlighted in a letter sent to all members of the US Congress. Reuters News Service constantly updates the site with the latest in women's health and cancer research. Included in the site are facts on treatment options, such as the availability of innovative or experimental therapies, as well as information regarding gynecologic oncology and methods of accessing appropriate care.

The work of the Foundation has also been widely covered in the media, including a full hour on *Larry King Live* dedicated to ovarian cancer. The information hotline response that was promoted on this program generated 5,000 calls when it first aired. In addition, the Department of Health and Human Services and the NCI produced a program on ovarian cancer for the Discovery Channel and created two magazine ads that have appeared in publications such as *People, Prevention, Southern Living, Cooking Light, Weight Watchers,* and others. Further, the Public Service Announcement was aired on television three times more than most announcements. Featuring singer/actress Cher, and endorsed by the Ad Council, the announcement aired almost 150 times, more than half the airings occurring in the top 20 television markets, such as Los Angeles, New York, and Boston. Further, a newly expanded patient-education brochure, *Maintaining Your Gynecologic Health With Education and Early Detection,* was published in 1997. In addition, since GCF launched its program to publicize the newsworthy findings featured in *Gynecologic Oncology,* more than 15 scientific papers have been highlighted and more than 50 reporter inquiries and/or interviews have been held.

With this national exposure the Foundation is receiving support from diverse endowments and charities. Permanent Charities of the Entertainment Industries provided a grant of $10,000 to support the printing and distribution of the GCF patient brochure on the basis of the brochure's "powerful impact" on public education.[22]

Between 1992 and 1999 GCF has awarded more than $500,000 in research grants. The first jointly appointed GCF /NCI Research Project was awarded in 1995. This two-year position provides $50,000 annually to conduct research in a laboratory in any division of NCI. The Karin Smith/GCF Research Project in Ovarian Cancer is awarded for one year at $50,000 and is open to established investigators. Another major research grant award is the GCF Research Project in Surgery, supported by a grant from Ethicon Endo-Surgery; it, too, offers a one year grant of $50,000. In 1997 GCF added the following awards to its laurels: Florence and Marshall Schwid/Gynecologic Cancer Foundation Project in Ovarian Cancer ($50,000), Eva Metzger/GCF Research Project in Ovarian Cancer ($50,000), and GCF Fellow Award ($1,000).

The number of individual financial donors has increased steadily and, as of January 1999, 116 women have had their lives honored through the financial donations of family and friends, now totaling over $50,000. In addition, more than $550,000 has been donated by SGO members themselves to support the GCF, and through the Charitable Gift Program, bequests totaling nearly $1.5 have been received. I have never stopped working toward increasing the funding and influence of the GCF. I have assisted every step of the way as the Foundation expanded its services, and I am proud of the research the Foundation is able to support. When asked, "Whoever would have thought a small society of gynecologic oncologists could have such an impact on cancer research, education, and treatment," I have no trouble answering.

GCF was also instrumental in having September 1999 declared the first annual Gynecologic Cancer Awareness Month. Sponsored by Ortho Biotech, the Foundation is now able to promote health awareness in a variety of ways, including additional media announcements, regional seminars to bring women and cancer specialists together, re-releasing the public service announcements, and posting additional information to GCF's website and linking it to other sites involved in the same issues. As the recognized Founder and Chairman of GCF, 1991–1994, I am pleased and humbled at the words appearing above my photo in the winter/spring GCF Bulletin, "With Our Sincerest Thanks."

All of the efforts I made as an individual also provided greater visibility to the Hershey Medical Center and the Department of Obstetrics and Gynecology, as again in 1997 Hershey Medical Center was cited by *U.S. News & World Report* in their July 28 issue as one of the best hospitals in the nation in four categories, including cancer treatment, according to its eighth annual rankings, "America's Best Hospitals."[23] The Hershey Medical Center was also ranked in the top 100 in 11 specialties in *U.S. News & World Report's Survey of America's Best Hospitals* for the three-year period, 1993–95.[24]

At that point in my life I could have rested on my laurels. As chairman of a medical college department, I had reached the top of the academic ladder; as president of the Society of Gynecologic Oncologists, I had received the highest recognition of excellence by my peers; as one of the "Best 401 Doctors in the United States" (*Good Housekeeping*), I had been recognized by peers and patients for my expertise in the care of women; as a committee chair in SGO, I had led the successful effort in establishing the Gynecologic Oncology Section at NCI. Further, the creation and success of the Foundation clearly affirmed the importance of academic gynecologic oncology and provided a clear vision of how to fund research in the future. Having achieved those goals, I was ready to retire from academic medicine and continue my work in Haiti.

Notes

1. Rodrigue Mortel, "the Impact of Sabbatical Leave on a Clinical Discipline," the Dean's Lecture Series, Fall 1994, Milton S. Hershey Medical School.

2. Rodrigue Mortel, "Prospectus," the Gynecological Cancer Foundation, 1990.

3. Rodrigue Mortel, "SGO Research and Education Foundation Report to SGO Membership—February, 1991."

4. Ibid.

5. Ibid.

6. C. Paul Morrow, MD, "'Who Are We?' A Paean to Gynecologic Oncology," Presidential Address, Society of Gynecologic Oncologists, Orlando, FL, February 19, 1991.

7. (SGO) *Newsletter*, April 1991, 3.

8. "SGO Profile," (SGO) *Newsletter*, April 1991, 3.

9. Ibid.

10. "Foundation Feasibility Study Moves into Phase II," *SGO Issues*, (Fall 1991) Vol. 10, n. 2, 1.

11. Ibid.

12. Wesley Fowler, Presidential Address, Annual Meeting, SGO, San Antonio, Texas, February 1992.

13. *SGO Issues*, (Fall 1992) Vol. 11, n. 4, 2.

14. "Mortel Success in Establishing New NCI Section," *Vital Signs* (February 1993), 3.

15. Ibid.

16. Rodrigue Mortel, "Report to the Membership: Gynecologic Cancer Foundation," Palm Desert, CA, February 1993.

17. Ibid.

18. Ibid.

19. Rodrigue Mortel, MD, "Quo Vadis: The Vision Triumvirate (The Next Twenty-five Years)," Presidential Address, Society of Gynecologic Oncologists, February 1995.

20. Stephen L. Curry, MD, "For Whom We Care," Presidential Address, Society of Gynecologic Oncologists, February 1996.

21. Report from the Education Committee, International Gynecologic Cancer Society, n.d.

22. "Permanent Charities Provides Grant," *GCF Bulletin*, V. I, no. 2 (Spring 1997), 2.

23. "Hershey and Geisinger Ranked by *U.S. News & World Report*, *Vital Signs*, Penn State Geisinger Health System, August 1997, 1.

24. Ibid.

Chapter 8: Honors

I am very flattered at the many honors and awards that have come my way during my professional career and I continue to marvel at the opportunities I have had to serve both my homeland and other countries in need. It is most gratifying to see the results of my small contributions to others who may not have had the same good fortune that I have had in America. Whether sending supplies to Haiti and hospital beds to Romania or working to provide ways in which physicians from developing countries can receive specialized training in industrialized nations, I have continued to remember how much a helping hand can mean to a person's life. Providing these opportunities never fails to touch my own heart and remind me of the many times I was the first to open doors that had previously been locked.

In early 1983 when I became the first foreign educated black to chair an obstetrics and gynecology department in one of the 126 medical schools in the United States, the appointment reverberated throughout the scientific community, both locally and nationally. Shortly after my appointment, the Dean hosted a reception and dinner to welcome Cecile and me as new members of the "family of chairmen." At that time, my personal background was not widely known among my colleagues. While most of my acquaintances knew that I had been born and educated in Haiti, few knew the circumstances under which I had lived.

During this dinner in my honor and hosted by Dr. Harry Prystowsky, Dean of the College of Medicine, his wife, Rhalda, who was seated next to me, asked about my background, particularly my education and family. I responded by telling her of my birth in the poorest country in this hemisphere. Prompted by her interest, I began my story and soon those seated at the table stopped in the midst of their dinners to listen. While most of the guests sat in silence, one asked the question I had come to expect when people heard my tale: "How can this be? How is it possible to have come from such poverty to reach such an acclaimed position in life?"

"It was my mother," I said. "Even though she was completely illiterate, my mother was one of the most intelligent people I have ever known. If she had had the opportunity, she probably would have ended up where I did. She knew the importance of an education. Because she had never recovered from her own disappointment over a broken promise of being sent to school by the family with whom she lived in St. Marc, she spent many years of her life making sure that my opportunity for an education would not be denied. My mother was the greatest influence on my life. Without her, I very likely would not have left St. Marc, let alone Haiti. I can hardly imagine what my life would have been without her sacrifice."

I told the dinner guests that my mother, my faith, and my determination are the three elements that framed my life. I explained, "The pivotal point for me was being evicted into the streets at age eleven with nowhere to go. We lived in the streets for almost a week, sleeping on the porch of a friend's house and being allowed inside only to wash up. After that long and frightful week of being homeless, we moved into a room in the home of my father's cousin. For days I watched my mother crying and my father looking helpless throughout the entire ordeal; even at my young age I could feel his shame that he could not provide for us."

Urged by Mrs. Prystowsky to continue my tale, I told of leaving home at seventeen to attend the lycée in Port-au-Prince, and of later earning one of the coveted forty places in the Medical School.

I described the obstacles I had faced during my two years as a rural physician for 10,000 people, and of my frustration over the lack of both medicine and facilities for medical treatment. When I mentioned that I had arrived in the United States, after a year in Montreal, with a single suitcase and $50, Mrs. Prystowsky responded, "I had no idea of these hardships. What an extraordinary person you are." "Not extraordinary," I replied, "just lucky."

Horatio Alger Award

The following day, although unknown to me at the time, Dr. Prystowsky suggested that his wife discuss my story with Dr. John O. Hershey, former president of Milton Hershey School. During that meeting, John Hershey listened intently to Mrs. Prystowsky's retelling the dinner party conversation. At the conclusion Dr. Hershey said, "This is a Horatio Alger story." John Hershey should know—he himself is a member of the Horatio Alger Association of Distinguished Americans. Dr. Hershey had told Mrs. Prystowsky he would guess that there is not another person in the United States who began life in such poverty and achieved what I have achieved. He continued, "If ever there was a Horatio Alger story, this one is it. The struggles many of us rose above are nothing compared to what this man experienced. We at least were born in a land of opportunity. He was born in a country that has been described as 'without hope.' Just imagine growing up with absolutely *nothing*, with parents who owned nothing, in a country that could offer nothing. How did he do it? You are right—this is an unbelievable story and needs to be told."

The following week, Dr. Hershey and Mrs. Prystowsky worked with Cecile to prepare a detailed summary of my life. They asked her, "Do you think you can do this without letting Rodrigue know? Nominees are not to be told that they are being considered for the award, so we must do this quietly." Cecile said she would get as much pertinent information as possible by finding opportunities to ask me details about my childhood. In order not to arouse suspicion, Cecile had to devise ways to ask me questions that would seem only of casual interest. I remained completely unaware of her intent; I thought she was asking me for more particulars of my life because the dinner conversation had raised questions in her own mind.

Nearly two years passed before John Hershey invited me to lunch. During the course of the meal, he began to recount the history of the Horatio Alger Association. He told me that Horatio Alger was an American author whose novels featured the meteoric rise from "rags to riches" of boys who were "honest, loyal, industrious, and with religious principles."[1] Born in 1832, Alger was a sickly child, but became an honor student at Harvard College, followed by a successful life as an editor, a poet, a minister, and a teacher. The fictional heroes in his stories influenced an entire generation of youth and his books were read "by virtually every boy and many girls who were growing up in America."[2] I allowed that I had heard the phrase, "a Horatio Alger hero," but knew only that it referred to someone who rose above adversity.

Dr. Hershey continued with further information about the Horatio Alger Association, a non-profit service organization dedicated to motivating and educating young people to the economic opportunities afforded them under the American free enterprise system. I listened attentively, expecting Dr. Hershey to ask me to sponsor someone worthy of this honor. Instead, he said to me, "You have been selected as one of this year's award recipients. Congratulations!" I was astonished, as I had had no idea of the investigation about my life, even in my own household! "I am flattered, but totally surprised, John," I stated honestly. "Why me? What have I done to deserve this honor?" John Hershey replied, "Because, my dear fellow, you exemplify—in large measure, I might add—the ideals of the award."

Even though Dr. Hershey had provided me with the background, I did not realize the significance of my selection as only one of ten persons from the entire country to be so honored. Soon after I had met with him, however, I began to read about the Association and was astonished to learn of the intense competition, high standard of selection, and the illustrious circle I soon would be joining. Still, however, the magnitude of this honor did not fully hit me until mid-March when the award was announced publicly. I was soon caught up in a flurry of activity, enveloped by newspaper interviews, telephone calls, notes of congratulation, and requests for speaking engagements. I also began to receive congratulatory letters from high profile persons such as Norman Vincent Peale and the Governor of Pennsylvania, among others. Print articles also began to appear in a range of publications, from in-house newsletters to the international *Medical World News*, which stated, "The association will present the awards, which honor people who have triumphed over adverse circumstances to achieve tremendous success."[3] My fellow inductees for 1985 included Norman Brinker, Chairman and CEO of Chili's, Inc.; John C. Crean, Chairman and CEO of Fleetwood Enterprises, Inc.; Mario M. Cuomo, Governor of the State of New York; Leonard L. Farber, Chairman of the Board, Leonard L. Farber, Inc.; Henry A. Johnson, President and CEO, Spiegel, Inc.; Allen E. Paulson, Chairman and CEO, Gulfstream Aerospace Corporation; Jack D. Sparks, Chairman and CEO, Whirlpool Corporation; Fred C. Trump, Chairman of the Board, The Trump Organization; and Hicks B. Waldron, Chair and CEO, Avon Products, Inc. Other notable past recipients of the Award included Ronald Reagan, Bernard Baruch, Pearl Buck, Ralph Bunche, James Doolittle, Dwight D. Eisenhower, Conrad Hilton, Art Linkletter, Clare Booth Luce, Thurgood Marshall, and Norman Vincent Peale, among many others of similar distinction.

As an admirer of Ronald Reagan, I looked forward to the possibility of meeting him at the award ceremony scheduled for 10 May 1985. I identified with the slogan being used by the Republican Party in Reagan's re-election campaign and I planned to use those words in the acceptance speech I would be delivering. My own attitude so well suited the idea of "You ain't seen nothin' yet" that I wanted to incorporate that notion in the rendition of my own story. Thus, I began my first draft, late at night, at my desk under a single light, much as I had studied by lamplight many years ago.

> It has been a long road. From a one room shack where we were born to a comfortable house where we now live; from studying with light provided by a kerosene lamp to receiving this award today. . . .

Thus began my acceptance speech; I continued to refine it, alone in the quiet hours, as I wanted everyone to hear it for the first time the night I would deliver it. This, like my struggle for an education, I had to do by myself.

On 7 May eight members of my family traveled to New York City for the Award Festivities. The four-day activities began with an informal "Welcome to Horatio Alger" reception at Rockefeller Center (the Association headquarters at that time) and culminated with the 38th Annual Awards Dinner at the Waldorf Astoria on 10 May. Attending the $250/plate induction dinner was a large delegation from Penn State, including, among others,

President of Penn State University, Dr. Bryce Jordan; The Most Reverend (later Cardinal) William H. Keeler, my good friend and Bishop of the Harrisburg Diocese; Dr. Harry Prystowsky, the Dean of the College of Medicine; Dr. Stephen Curry, good friend and formerly a member of the faculty at the College of Medicine; and Dr. Vincent Stenger, former Chairman of the Obstetrics and Gynecology Department. The Hershey Foods table included many other acquaintances and friends, including Dr. John Hershey and William Dearden, both former Horatio Alger Awardees. Still other friends, such as Dr. Alberto Manetta, a faculty colleague at the Hershey Medical Center, were situated at various tables throughout the ballroom. Cecile and I were seated on the West Dais, along with other honorees. Usually at ease with people, that night I felt just a bit overwhelmed—not so much for myself, but for my mother. I wondered what she must be thinking, sitting out there in the midst of the splendor and the famous, such as Art Linkletter, Norman Vincent Peale, Tom Landry, Arthur Ochs Sulzberger, Ed McMahon, David Merrick, Bill Bradley, Alfonse D'Amato, Gerald Ford, Donald Trump, and Richard Blackwell, to name only a few.

The evening's program opened with remarks from the Master of Ceremonies, Art Linkletter, followed by a processional led by Dean W. Jeffers, Chairman of the Board of Directors. Dr. Peale offered the invocation preceding the Pledge of Allegiance and the National Anthem. After a stirring message from the president of the association, R. David Thomas, scholarships were presented to win-ning students. Throughout the dinner, between each course, a member of the Association introduced two of the new Horatio Alger Awardees, each individually. I was introduced by Dr. Benjy F. Brooks who read the profile of "Dr. Rodrigue Mortel." A hush fell over the audience as my story unfolded. Dr. Brooks told of my impoverished background, one that was beyond the comprehension of most of those seven hundred assembled for this ceremony. As Dr. Brooks finished his introduction and presentation, I was greeted with applause. As I began my acceptance speech, all eyes were upon me. I noticed how still the room was; I could even hear the hum of the air conditioning. There was no rustling of programs and no clatter of tableware. I had the complete attention of this audience:

Mr. Chairman, Dr. Brown, Members, and Guests:

I am accepting this award with mixed emotions. I am thrilled to be selected for such a high honor and I am equally fearful that after such an award, a downhill course might follow. I hope, however, that the flame that leads us to fame continues to burn and to turn mountains into molehills and rivers into streams.

It has been a long road. From a one room shack where we were born to a comfortable house where we now live; from studying with light provided by a kerosene lamp to receiving this award today under the chandeliers of the Waldorf Astoria; from never being exposed to clinical or laboratory research in our medical school to providing today what our peers consider to be significant contributions to the understanding and treatment of gynecologic cancer; from a rural doctor in the most underdeveloped country in the Western Hemisphere to Chairman of a clinical department of one of the most prestigious universities of the world's most advanced nation; the road was indeed long. It has been rough at times, but all the obstacles were only stimuli to succeed. Such success could not be achieved anywhere but in the United States of America. However, I say to you this evening—as a great American did just one year ago, "You ain't seen nothin' yet!"

Laughter and spontaneous applause burst forth from every table as they recognized President Reagan's campaign slogan. I grinned and looked into the faces of those smiling in return, resuming my prepared speech,

> . . . I have just been handed a torch to brighten my way and to help me touch more effectively the hopeless of Haiti and the unbelievers of America.

Again, applause broke out. I paused briefly, and then continued. Thunderous clapping of hands could be heard as I finished the next sentence. I acknowledged their warm response and went on,

> . . . Although many people need to be credited for my being here this evening, time will allow me to mention just a few. (My gaze fell upon my mother, as Dinah whispered to her that I was thanking her in front of this great assembly.) First, to my mother who deprived herself of everything to provide me with food, clothing, and education, I am indebted forever.

Every eye turned to Lamercie and Dinah while hands applauded their son and brother. As I spoke my next sentence, tears began to form in the eyes of many of the audience when I looked directly at Dinah and said in a hushed tone, trying to keep my voice steady,

> To my sister who dropped out of school in order for me to go on, I am very grateful.

A broad smile then spread over my face as I turned to Cecile, sitting by my side.

> To my lovely wife and our two beautiful children who spend days and nights without me, and who have supported me all the way through, I pledge love forever.

Yet again, I had to stop because of the tumultuous clapping of hands. The applause continued almost non-stop. Nearing the end of my speech, I went on, by now beaming,

To all my friends and co-workers who have contributed one
way or another to my ascension to this podium, I simply say,
"Thank you." To America the beautiful, I say, "He who does
not know you, knows nothing about opportunity and free enterprise." Finally, to all other nations in the world, I raise my voice
to say, "Look at America and let the bells of freedom ring on
your land and for all your people." Thank you.

By acclamation, the entire room rose in thunderous applause.

Later, Jerry Kobrin, columnist for the *Orange County Register*,
recounted that event in a column he wrote on 10 April in urging his
readers to meet me if they ever had the opportunity,

> Trust me, this doctor can make you feel better. You may
> not recognize his name, but a remarkable man is currently
> visiting our province. If you're offered an opportunity to meet
> Dr. Rodrigue Mortel during his five-day stay, grab it. You'll
> thank me.
>
> I heard Mortel speak 11 months ago in New York City,
> when he was among those being honored with the Horatio
> Alger Award, and he was given the banquet's greatest ovation.
> That's no small feat, considering that he shared the dais with
> such heavyweight orators as New York Governor Mario
> Cuomo, Art Linkletter, and Dr. Norman Vincent Peale.
>
> Mortel is not a professional speaker. A professor at Penn-
> sylvania State University, he's chairman of the school's depart-
> ment of obstetrics and gynecology, and has gained renown in
> his field.
>
> What brought a sophisticated audience to its feet in the
> Waldorf Astoria ballroom was the story he had to tell—and
> how he told it . . . .
>
> If at all possible, friends, listen to this doctor. Believe me,
> you'll feel better. Also, there's a good chance that you'll stop
> feeling sorry for yourself.[4]

Following all of the Horatio Alger presentations, well-wishers
who invited me to address gatherings of political and religious orga-

nizations across the country, as well as to appear on radio and television, surrounded me. John Crean, also a 1985 honoree, invited me
to be a guest in his home the following spring to speak at the California Lutheran College in Thousand Oaks.

During the coming year, the requests for speaking engagements increased. Mr. John (Mac) Aichele, Chairman of the Board of
Managers of the Milton Hershey School, and William Fisher, then
President of the School, as well as a graduate, approached me, saying I absolutely had to speak at graduation the following spring. Dr.
Bryce Jordan, President of Penn State University, requested me to
speak at the 1986 Spring Commencement at University Park.
(Because of a conflict in scheduling, I was unavailable on that date,
but agreed to speak at the Winter Graduation in January.) Everywhere I spoke, the audiences cheered.

I also received an invitation from Tom Fuentes, chairman of
the Orange County Republican 400 Club, asking me to speak to the
membership of the Pro-Life Action Committee. I combined this
request with John Crean's invitation.

According to columnist Jerry Kobrin,

> A standing-room-only crowd welcomed Haitian-born Dr.
> Rodrigue Mortel to Orangeshire the other night when he
> addressed the Republicans' 400 Club at Countryside Inn, and
> he responded by offering the audience a choice of two
> speeches.
>
> As a 1985 recipient of the Horatio Alger Award, he said
> he could talk about "My Feelings Toward America, The Beau-
> tiful Land of Opportunity." Or, as a world-renown professor
> based at Penn State University, he said he could deliver a dis-
> course titled, "Photo Affinity Techniques for Progesterone
> Receptor in the Human Endometrial Carcinoma Grafted in
> Nude Mice." With eyes twinkling, he asked for a show of
> hands. It was no contest. America won.[5]

My speech at the Club was well received. I began, with obvious
emotion,

I love America. I love what America stands for. I love the principles at work here—I love the leadership position that America occupies in the world. I love the direction in which our present leader is taking America. But you cannot understand the depth and extent of my feelings unless you have an idea of my background and the road that I have traveled over the past 40 years. . . .

Only in America, can a farmer become a Senator, and an actor a President. Only in America can a rural doctor from a foreign country become Chairman of an academic department. Only in America can each human being have a goal and the hope to reach it. Only in America can each person define his or her own truth and have a private quest . . . Only in America can every human being give a meaning to his or her life, and this is the only place in the world where human rights are protected and freedom of all kinds guaranteed . . .

The next day I spoke at the Preus-Brandt Forum of the California Lutheran University on the topic "Secrets to Achievement and Success." I told the audience how I had vowed as a child that those I loved would not live forever in poverty: . . . "I watched my mother cry for days and my father live through that ordeal, and I thought to myself there must be a better way." I told the audience I discovered that way in the United States.[6]

On the following day at a breakfast meeting arranged by Tom Fuentes, I addressed the Pro-Life Political Action Committee of Orange County at the Irvine Marriott. And, again, the audience was generous in their praise.

Culminating this whirlwind tour, I accepted an invitation from the Reverend Robert Schuller and addressed the Sunday service, the "Hour of Power" Television Program at the Crystal Cathedral in Garden Grove. John Crean accompanied me, as he was active in the promotion of the Cathedral, having donated the first $1 million for the building of the church. I began my delivery by recounting a visit to Haiti with my wife's family,

Cecile's sister was sitting on the second story balcony of my mother's house when she stood up and looked around the neighborhood. Her gaze fell upon horses, people milling about, a woman cooking on a charcoal stove in the street directly in front of our house, and persons carrying water in open containers through the heat and dust of St. Marc. She sighed, took a deep breath, and asked, "How in the world did you ever get out of here?" Her question was asked with sincerity and such incredulity in her voice that it led me to pause before answering her. She then rephrased her question, "How does anyone ever get out of here?" I had no answer for her.

Continuing, I told the congregation of my humble beginnings in unimaginable poverty, my mother's sacrifice, my determination to succeed, and, most of all, my desire to assist others to have a better life. I urged my listeners to convert their obstacles to opportunities, to be positive in their thinking, and to build upon what America provides—power, free enterprise, and strong spiritual values. As I finished, the applause resounded in the magnificent crystal house of worship. Ten years later, Robert Schuller still remembered the impact I had had that Sunday morning, and he invited me for a return engagement. He said to me, "Rodrigue, you held that congregation in the palm of your hand; if ever you tire of medicine you could become an evangelist."

Shortly after my return to Pennsylvania, I was invited to speak at the induction ceremony of the National Honor Society of Hershey High School on 12 May, and on 12 June I served as the Commencement Speaker at the Milton Hershey School graduation.

I have been somewhat apprehensive since the day I accepted your invitation to this happy and unique occasion. My apprehension stemmed from my inexperience in delivering a speech that is not medically related. .

Following a low chuckle from the audience, I continued with a wide smile,

The students pointed out clearly that many of you share with me a similar background. Milton Hershey School provided you with all that is necessary for education, and it is the Hershey Medical Center that provided me with all the opportunities necessary to reach the top in academic medicine. Therefore, as a big brother, I feel obligated to share with you the fact that achievement and success are two entirely different entities.

I originally came from Haiti, the most densely populated country in the Caribbean Basin, located only 1500 miles from New York City. [7]

As I began my story, a hush fell over the magnificent auditorium of Founders Hall. Many in the audience had known hardship and poverty, but none could come close to the kind of life that my story reflected:

> . . . my family lived in a small town and were housed in a damp wooden shack with dirt floors, without electricity or sanitary facilities . . . . For most Haitians, mere survival was a full-time pursuit. I remember my mother spending a whole day doing the laundry. It would take her hours just to walk to the stream, wash the clothes, and walk back home. As children, we, too, walked—to neighbors or to the water source, filling our buckets and carrying the precious burden back home. . . .
>
> Believe me, ladies and gentlemen, the only place a radical change can occur, the only country which allows for realization of a dream is the United States of America. Only in America, can one go from the farm to the United States capital. . . . Only in America can a son of two Mennonites become a multimillionaire after experimenting with new ways of making chocolate. . . . Only America gives to the world a spirit based on personal growth and the integrity of the individual. Only in America can every one of us give meaning to our life, and this is the only place in the world where human rights are protected and freedom of all kinds guaranteed. . . .

I then turned to the graduating class, and spoke directly to them.

Class of 1986,
When the Egyptians of the old kingdom built 79 royal tombs
called pyramids, with blocks of granite two to three tons each
encased in one another without glue or cement; when they built
the obelisks, monolithic blocks where they engraved hiero-
glyphic characters, which defy even today's scientists, they
demonstrated to us the power of intelligence. When Isaac New-
ton wrote his theory of universal gravitation, and when
Descartes put forth his postulate "Cogito, ergo sum" which
means, "I think, therefore, I am," this was to magnify the power
of men through intelligence and dignify the significance and
the value of knowledge.
        . . . you will face difficulties, obstacles, hesitation, uncer-
tainty. However, the drive and determination that bring you
where you are today, will also push you to the top of the next
mountain. I invite you to climb it as a doctor if you are bothered by human sufferings, if you can help the sick, alleviate the
pain, console the incurable. Consider climbing it as an engi-
neer, architect, or plumber, if you have the sophisticated tech-
nical skills, which will be needed in the 21st century. Climb it
as an administrator or a businessman, if your individual initiative and creativity can stimulate the ability or the potential to
work as a team. If you can, bring something new to the trade
and help improve life for your customers. Climb it as an attor-
ney, if you have the ability to defend someone who is right,
even if he is poor and to condemn the criminal even if he is a
millionaire. Climb it as a teacher, if you have the ability to
draw from students potential that they did not know they had.
Climb it as a scientist, if you have the ability to place your scientific resources to the service of mankind. Climb it as a minister, if you have the ability to promote justice, love, honesty
and to preach against discrimination and dehumanization. Yes,
there is here a common denominator. This is human compassion and that is the key to success.

Human compassion pushed Mr. Hershey to say, "Why not let other boys have the experience I had living on a farm. It is the happiest and best life there is." Human compassion led Mr. Hershey to leave his entire fortune to the school. If knowledge, ambition, determination, and hard work are essential for someone to become an achiever, being successful is doing something that one loves, something that matters; it means helping someone achieve a goal. It means helping a community solve its problems. It means playing a song, helping others feel better about themselves and about being alive. It means funding a productive business or discovering a cure for a deadly disease. It means being elected to office in order to improve life in general. It means the realization that every human has dignity and every human has a right to succeed.

A good life well lived is not enough. Each of us must bring another along. It is an important part of a successful life to know that it was not lived alone. There is no satisfaction as great as helping another to share a decent and productive life. If every one of us can manage to touch and bring happiness to at least one other person, each one of us will be able to say one day that life was worth living. I would like to close with a quotation attributed to Stephen Grellet. "I shall pass through this world but once; any good thing, therefore, I can do, or any kindness I can show to any human being, let me do it now; let me not defer it or neglect it, because I shall not pass this way again."

At the conclusion of this address, the audience rose in a standing ovation, the first time (I was later told) a speaker had so moved a graduation assemblage at Milton Hershey School.

Celebration in St. Marc

In 1987 the City of St. Marc bestowed upon me an honor that meant more to my mother than any other award I have received. With that honor, I disproved the adage that a prophet goes unsung in his own country when I returned to St. Marc for a celebration held by the city. I recall with fondness, boyhood pride, and adult humility the reception I received from the townspeople, many of whom remembered me as a child and many of whom had not only followed my career but also took note of my generosity to the city. I was particularly pleased that my mother was there to bask in the celebration. She had seen me lauded in the United States, she had observed my leadership role in the Hershey Medical Center, and now she could share in the honor given me by the people of our city. How she enjoyed it all! "*Ti ro ro*," she kiddingly liked to call me. "Commander of the whites," as she addressed me, was now being feted on the same street where more than forty years before we had been homeless.

Penn State University Faculty Scholar

Parallel to the information being collected for the Horatio Alger Award, a compilation of my scientific achievements was being prepared in support of my nomination for the Faculty Scholar medal, presented by Penn State University for outstanding accomplishments in life sciences. It was honor enough to be nominated and I did not expect to be selected as the winner, yet one year following the Horatio Alger Award I traveled to University Park to receive the medal "presented in recognition of a single contribution or series of related contributions in arts and humanities, life and health sciences, physical sciences and engineering, or social and behavioral sciences." According to President Bryce Jordan, "Dr. Mortel's reputation, both national and international, is evidence that he is a leader in his field. He is a great source of pride to Penn State and we are grateful for his contributions to the academic community." I responded with the following, "One will succeed by learning from the past, living fully in the present, and repeatedly setting higher goals for the future."[8] I considered this award the epitome of academic recognition, as it honored what I considered the core of my academic career—making a contribution to research that would benefit mankind.

Robert Wood Johnson Health Policy Fellow

During the following two years I concentrated my activities on the future of the Department of Obstetrics and Gynecology and the role it should play at the national level in a time of a complex medical environment and governmental regulations. I found myself increasingly being drawn toward matters of health policy, becoming progressively more disenchanted with the grip of the federal government on physicians and hospitals.

As a Department Chairman, I received an enormous amount of mail, and by 1987 I began to comment on the ever-growing number of laws and regulations that crossed my desk. While part of me knew that medical laws and regulations are very necessary in order for the profession to operate smoothly and for the well-being of all concerned, I felt more and more that many of these laws and regulations were stultifying. I believed that they reflected decisions that were not always well-thought-out or in the best interests of medicine—for either the patients or the physicians. More than once I said to whoever was within earshot, "I can't believe all these regulations in medicine. This is stupid. How can we prevent it from continuing?" That line of thinking led me to wonder how I could become more involved in the law-making process. I wanted to know more about how laws are made and how legislation is influenced.

I remembered that when I had returned from Paris, Dr. John Burnside was spending a sabbatical as a Robert Wood Johnson Fellow, something to do with working with legislators in Washington, DC. I telephoned Dr. Burnside in Texas to ask him about his experience. "It was wonderful. One of the best experiences in my life," John told me. "If you are interested, I'll send you an application." He did, and after discussion with Cecile, I applied for a sabbatical leave from Penn State and a Robert Wood Johnson Health Policy Fellowship from the National Academy of Sciences' Institute of Medicine. These fellowships are intended to provide opportunities for mid-career professional people working in academic settings to gain an understanding of major health policy issues and how these issues are addressed in our political system.

To my delight, I competed successfully for a spot in the program and was named a Fellow. The day the announcement was delivered by mail, the only one of us at home was Denise, then a freshman at Lebanon Catholic High School. I was attending a conference and Cecile was out walking. Denise had been hoping that I would not be selected, as she did not want to leave her friends and have to move to Washington. Denise never wanted to go anywhere. She fought change. She would cry and say she wouldn't go with us, whether it was a move to Paris or simply across town. When Denise saw the mail, she opened it, praying it would not be the news her father was hoping for. She read the contents of the letter, then got on her bicycle to track down her mother. By the time she found Cecile, Denise was crying. When Cecile asked her what was the matter, Denise, sobbing through her tears, blurted out, "Daddy's going to Washington."

Everyone in the family, of course, went to Washington. In the fall of 1988 we rented an apartment in Rockville, within commuting distance of the capital. The girls were enrolled in a parochial school to which they very quickly adapted. In fact, Denise, as Cecile and I knew would happen, loved her school and her friends in Rockville and, following our year's stay, did not want to leave. In fact, she was so upset at the thought of leaving Rockville, that a day before we were to return to Hershey she got up in the middle of the night and took the car. She had had no experience driving on the street, as I had only just begun to take her out to the campus of the National Institutes of Health to teach her the basics of driving. By the time Cecile and I arose around daybreak, Denise was just returning home and navigating the car into the driveway.

Denise was not the only one who loved Washington. I thrived in the atmosphere of the fellowship program. Robert Wood Johnson Policy Fellows all have professional backgrounds in the health field and I was one of three physicians in my class of six Fellows. My selection also marked the first time a foreign-born American had been chosen since the inception of the program 15 years earlier.[9] As reported in an interview, "For three months, beginning this September, Mortel and the five other Fellows will eat, sleep and breathe the political side of health care. They will become pseudo-legislators in helping federal officials mold this country's approach to health issues."[10]

We six initially went through a three-month orientation and training period where we met with key White House advisers, including officials of the Office of Management and Budget; top administrators of agencies responsible for health activities; Congressional committee staff members; and representatives of health interest groups—the people who influence and help formulate health policy. We spent a great deal of time at the Centers for Disease Control and the Federal Drug Administration. In addition, we met with the Justices of the Supreme Court and their assistants. These exciting three months of study were a comprehensive and compressed course in the how, why, and by whom the government operates.

The remaining nine months of the fellowship were to be spent either assisting as a committee staff member in Congress or in the executive branch of the government. During the month of December we each interviewed in an area of interest; all positions, of course, would be served in health policy. Because of the secrecy and issues of confidentiality found in the executive branch of the government, most of the Fellows sought positions in the legislative offices. It was clear to most of us that the Congressional staff were more open than the executive offices could be and that a Fellow could have the opportunity to learn and do much more in the legislative than the executive branch.

I elected to accept an offer from Congressman Sander Levin, a Democrat from the 17th District of Michigan, who was a member of the Health Subcommittee of the House Ways and Means Committee that held jurisdiction over the Medicare legislation in which I was very interested. It was my job to respond to constituents. I first researched each inquiry and contacted the appropriate agency necessary to solve the problem. This not only gave me the satisfaction of helping someone, but it also taught me the ropes so that when I returned to the university, I would know my way around the federal bureaucracy and would be able to solve similar problems for my academic and medical colleagues.[11]

Representative Levin had been Director of the Agency on International Development in Jimmy Carter's administration and he had visited Haiti many times. One could tell he was a friend to Haiti and very interested in helping that country in its post-Duvalier era when the nation was going through considerable political turmoil. At the time I was assisting in his office, one of his sons was working in Haiti as a member of a group investigating human rights abuses.

During the nine months I served as a Legislative Health Aide I learned much about politics, negotiations, and compromises. With the help of Levin's office, I assisted in getting two bills on the Medicare Reconciliation Act through the U. S. Congress. I learned how to work with government agencies and became keenly aware of the checks and balances in the U. S. political system. I particularly enjoyed the mark-up sessions where the public and the press are not invited and deals are worked out between the executive and legislative branches. It was reassuring to observe the two branches negotiate in good faith during these sessions, and I left Washington with increased confidence in the government.

In the evaluation report following my service as a Fellow, I clearly indicated my high regard of the fellowship program:

> The experience I have had this year in Washington could not have been possible anywhere else. To follow the health policy legislation from beginning to end in the House, to see how politics and the budget affect sessions, to witness the behind-the-scenes interaction between the administration and the committee was indeed a unique experience. It was difficult in the beginning to understand how the system could work effectively with the three branches of government being totally independent, but I believe that the system works partly because people there negotiate and compromise. I am convinced more than ever that as health care providers we need to develop a partnership with Congress in setting up health policy. The curriculum for undergraduate medical education needs to be modified to affect physicians' behavior. Graduate medical education needs to fit

the needs of the country. Physicians need to be educated in health economics and health policy issues. Members of Congress need to be invited to hospitals and office settings and become familiar with problems related to patient demands and family expectations.

I loved what I saw and I enjoyed what I did. No longer will I be satisfied if making and formulating health policy is not part of the job. No longer can I teach medical students and residents without considering the economic and policy aspects. No longer can I remain isolated and keep the faculty away from what is happening or may be happening in Washington in health policy. This year will significantly impact on my career, and steps have already been taken for the expansion of my activities to include health policy related projects.[12]

Further, I learned much about Haiti through the documents I had access to while in Congress. I had never really understood the policy of the United States toward Haiti over the past century until I became acquainted with the many reports written by various groups involved in the policy-making section of the U. S. government. That year in Washington (1989) was clouded only by the death of my mother and of Cecile's father occurring within two months of each other.

I am convinced that my year in Paris and the year in Washington laid the foundation for my later political successes, most especially (1) with the National Cancer Institute in establishing a Gynecologic Oncology Section in the Surgery Branch of the Division of Cancer Treatment, (2) with the Society of Gynecologic Oncologists in establishing the Gynecologic Cancer Foundation, and (3) in becoming the first foreigner and foreign-educated black president of the elite Society of Gynecologic Oncologists.

Upon my return to Hershey, I maintained close contact with and continued to visit Rep. Levin's office in Washington. I wrote health policy articles with Dr. Danner Clouser, nationally known medical ethicist and a professor at Hershey Medical Center, and with Dr. Joseph Trautlein, Professor of Medicine and later Medical

Director of HealthAmerica. I soon found myself the political watch-
dog for the Society of Gynecologic Oncologists. I had left Washington totally convinced that doctors should make themselves available to Congress for advice and opinions, and numerous times I
have testified before Congress on behalf of the Society of Gynecologic Oncologists and cancer patients.

Church Missions

The year in Washington also helped lay the groundwork for my
soon-to-be leadership involvement with the Church. Cecile and I
decided that our year's stay in Washington presented the best time-
frame in which to receive training in the Leaders in Ministry Program, sponsored by the Diocese of Harrisburg. With a letter of support from our pastor, we enrolled in the program being held one
Saturday a month. We traveled home to Hershey for some of the
sessions held in Harrisburg and commuted from Washington to participate in small group sessions held in Gettysburg. Following two
years training, I became a member, then the chair of the Liturgy
Committee of St. Joan of Arc Church. Never one to be content with
the status quo, I proposed a retreat during which a number of
changes were adopted in the manner in which the Liturgy Committee would function in the future.

My contacts at the Hershey Medical Center have given an
enormous boost to my medical mission to Haiti which began in
1973 when I had first visited the Albert Schweitzer Hospital and
became aware of how I could lend my services to the Hospital, caring for patients in the Artibonite Valley. Every year since, I have
returned to Haiti to donate time and supplies. With the assistance of
numerous pharmaceutical companies and the generosity of several
services at the Medical Center, I was able to provide surgical supplies and radiological equipment, as well as antibiotics and numerous other medications to the various health facilities in Haiti. Surgical services and medical supplies were desperately needed in St.
Marc, and with the generosity of my own institution and other medical resources, I collected so many supplies and pieces of equipment

that the only problem I faced was finding the financial resources for their transport to Haiti.

Fortunately, friends who knew of my commitment to Haiti connected me with Christian Aid Ministries, a Mennonite organization with missions in various parts of the world, including Haiti. This organization volunteered to transport all supplies and equipment I could gather. The leadership later invited me to travel to Romania to assess the medical needs of the region where their mission was located and to assist in meeting the needs of the people there. At that time the hospitals in the Romanian region had no IV fluids, no X-ray equipment, and no suture material. Because of these shortages, surgery could not be performed in the hospital. There was no radiographic equipment and the pharmacies had no drugs. In addition, the orphanages were full of children, both normal as well as mentally retarded, living in totally inhumane conditions. I was able to organize a campaign and collect IV fluids, suture material, and radiographic equipment—all for Romania. Since that time, I have continued to help both Haiti and Romania.

Some time later, Hershey Medical Center purchased all new beds for the hospital. I asked the supplier if I could have the old beds, each costing $5,000 when new. I was given the beds, provided I did not use them in the United States. These beds were a godsend, and Christian Aid Ministries helped to arrange for their transport to three hospitals: one in St. Marc to replace all their antiquated hospital beds, the second in Port-au-Prince, and the third one in Romania. With the publicity generated in the United States by this philanthropic effort, many nursing homes generously offered used beds as they replaced them with new ones. All of these beds were sent to hospitals and orphanages in Romania. Four years later, the Hershey Medical Center changed all the hospital mattresses; I was asked if I wanted them, and those, too, were sent to both Haiti and Romania.

One notable contribution was made when the director of the laundry service asked if I could find a use for new surgical "scrubs" that had been packed away in the laundry storage area three years earlier. The surgical gowns had never been distributed because the pockets had not been attached at the right place; this flaw made the scrubs unsuitable for the hospital operating teams. Christian Aid Ministries picked up the gowns and shipped them in equal parts to Haiti, Romania, and Bulgaria. Through my various contacts with interested individuals and organizations, other distressed regions also have received aid. No item is too insignificant to be collected, carted, and sent to countries in need.

Through my friendship with Cardinal Keeler, I was able to facilitate adoption of the Diocese of Gonaives by the Archdiocese of Baltimore, the adoption of the Tarasse Chapel by St. Joan of Arc Parish in Hershey and, more recently, the Parish of St. Marc by St. Paul Parish in Annville. In addition to the spiritual interaction brought by these adoptions, financial assistance has also been provided to build and support schools, drill new wells, and assist in farming.

One memorable visit in conjunction with these parish adoptions occurred in 1988 when two priests from the Hershey area accompanied our family to Tarasse to attend the festivities celebrating the opening of a new school. Following a full-day inaugural event, the priests went to St. Marc where they visited my mother and concelebrated mass in her own home. Nothing could have meant more to her. She thought she was in heaven. It was the most spiritually gratifying event of her life and one I shall never forget.

During a subsequent visit specifically arranged to form a church partnership in the parish of St. Marc, I discovered a small community whose congregation was meeting for worship under a mango tree. Because the worshippers could not afford a building, the peasant landowner on whose property the congregants met had graciously allowed them to use his land and had offered this site for a church, if ever possible. The assemblage had been trying for some time to obtain funding to build a hangar, under which they could meet, at least to provide them shelter from the rain and intense sun. Moved by the devotion of these people, I decided to build a church on this site in memory of my mother who had died six years prior to that visit to Haiti. The church itself has a capacity for 100 parishioners.

While I personally cannot provide complete financial support to operate a church or a hospital or a school, what I can do is introduce people, host them in my home, tell them who else might be interested in the same endeavor, and basically just help everyone make the necessary connections to collaborate their efforts. I strongly believe in the precept of the Church that whatever we can do to help others will come back to reward us in some manner. I have seen that happen for myself as well as for others. I give what I can—money, skills, friendship—and, always, my life is enhanced because of it. I learned long ago that if I just put people together, in touch with each other, they then see the need for and importance of their contributions. They usually find a way to work together.

For what was deemed contributions to humanity, I was honored by the Religious Heritage of America, a non-profit, interfaith organization founded in 1951. The group attempts to establish role models by recognizing men, women, and youngsters who apply their faith daily and affirm the vitality of America's Judeo-Christian heritage.[13] Barbara Eichhorst, administrative vice-president of the group, said its selection is based on the nominees' "contributions to their community and congregation and their professional accomplishments."[14]

I particularly cherish this national Churchman of the Year Award because it focuses attention on how I have touched the lives of other people.[15] Judith Patton reported that despite a medical career that includes many awards and special honors for research and contributions to the medical community, I treasure this award because it focuses attention on the needs of others. It shows to me that some people recognize my work and that I am on the right track. The joy of helping others is my goal and that is the reason I went into medicine and the reason why I'm involved in community service. This is meaningful because I have touched the lives of other people. The more I practice medicine and the more I take care of patients, the more my faith strengthens me.[16]

Giving has been a way of life for me. By nature, Haitians are generous of spirit and are known for their warm hospitality. They are reared to give back—to help younger brothers or sisters, to help their parents, and to help any relative, friend, or even fellow citizen. From the time of my birth, I was expected to share of my time, talents, and whatever meagre possessions the family had. For example, when relatives came to live with my family in St. Marc, we children shared our food and sleeping space. If we had had toys, those, too, would have been shared among all children in the household. As a student in Port-au-Prince, even though I had very little, what I did have was shared with my good friend, Ulrick, just as Ulrick shared with me. In medical school the same held true; whatever I had, I shared. As a rural physician, I gave most of my earnings to my mother, keeping only what I needed for expenses, and when I reached Canada I sent money home, both to support the family and, in time, to build the house for my mother. As my professional success increased, so did my earnings, so did my giving, and so did unexpected rewards.

Beyond family and friends, however, I unstintingly donate to the Church in proportion to my earnings. I also have supported many programs and initiatives in Haiti, particularly in St. Marc where one of my projects was to pay for the cost of painting the Church of St. Marc. Even when there was no guarantee that the projects to which I donated would come to fruition, I made monetary gifts to endeavors slated to help St. Marc and its people. For example, I was requested to pay for the cost of paving the road in front of my mother's house in St. Marc. I wrote a check, but the work was never started. Another time I was asked to underwrite the cost of building an area in the boulevard for the planting of flowers. That project, too, never got underway and the money was never returned to me. When people ask me if this kind of exploitation does not anger me, I reply that it does not. I don't mind. I tell people, "Now I can be guaranteed that those persons will never again ask me for money." Friends and neighbors in my hometown of St. Marc continue to ask me for loans, which, unfailingly, I give, knowing full well that I am likely to never see the money again.

Cecile's father, George Shahhein, had occasionally traveled to Haiti with Cecile and me and was taken with the dignity, generosity, and kindness of spirit of the people. He was amazed at their positive attitude despite hardship, observing that they help each other even when they have nothing but themselves to share. He said to me, "Their faith is very strong even though their houses of worship are in disrepair. In fact, sometimes I think they are more devout than the people in my own church who enjoy a magnificent sanctuary, a pipe organ, a choir of trained voices, and sumptuous beauty everywhere. In Haiti some of the people worship without a church and seem to be pleased just to be worshipping together." He told me that he would like to donate something tangible and lasting to the Haitian people, something that might enhance their worship service. I discussed with him what might be appropriate, mentioning that I had noticed there was only a very small tabernacle in the church at St. Marc, and that in other churches where we had visited there were no tabernacles at all. "I would like to buy two tabernacles," he announced. "Help me choose which two churches in the Diocese of Gonaïves most need them." This I did, and the following year we hand delivered new tabernacles to the two churches recommended by Bishop Constant.

When then Bishop Keeler became the Archbishop of Baltimore he planned to take his support for Haiti with him to his new Archdiocese. He arranged for Monsignor Galeone, chairman for the Propagation of Faith program, to invite Bishop Emanuel Constant of Haiti to deliver his message to the parishioners of the Archdiocese.

I also introduced to (now) Cardinal Keeler my friend Dr. Laurent Pierre-Phillipe, a benevolent physician known for supporting projects benefiting people in his home region of Haiti and for operating a clinic for the poor in inner-city Baltimore. He was very pleased to have the opportunity to meet the Cardinal. As a result of their meeting, a special celebration of the Haitian community, presided over by the Cardinal, was held in 1998 at the Basilica in Baltimore.

Cardinal Keeler also apportioned some part of the Lenten Appeal of his Archdiocese to be sent to Gonaïves. In addition, arrangements were made with the Speakers' Bureau of Food for the Poor to supply priests to preach in the various churches on behalf of the Diocese of Gonaïves.

National Organization for the Advancement of Haitians

In 1991 a new organization was founded as a non-profit social policy corporation dedicated to the restoration and preservation of democracy in Haiti. Five years after its founding, late in the fall of 1996, I was selected to receive NOAH's Outstanding Achievement Award for Health and Education.

The award ceremony, termed "Rebuilding Haiti for a Brighter Tomorrow," was hosted by the Chairman of NOAH, Joseph Baptiste, D.D.S. His Excellency Jean Casimir, Ambassador to the United States from Haiti, was patron for the event, held in a location very familiar to me. Returning to the Waldorf Astoria Hotel in New York City on a February evening brought back a flood of warm memories of a decade earlier. The reminiscing was bittersweet, however, for while my immediate family was with me, my mother was not.

It was a night for other memories as well, for in attendance was an old friend and comrade from my medical school days. When I saw Charles Benoit, we embraced as only those who have shared and overcome hardship are able. Charles reminded me of the episode the night we had studied together for our final exam for the notorious Dr. D__. Charles asked me, "Do you remember the milkshakes we drank that night? You laughed at me when I became ill, accusing me of malingering. Then, several hours later, you also fell prey." I nodded in agreement, reminding my good friend of the proverb he had prophetically recited, "*Nan lantèman kodenn, poul pa ri.* (At turkeys' funeral chickens don't laugh)." How far we both had come and yet in each other's company we were still the same young men of nearly forty years ago.

As my turn came to make my acceptance speech, I was thinking of Charles Benoit as well as my mother. When I took my place at the microphone, my eyes fell first upon Cecile and our daughters Denise and Renée, then upon Dinah, and finally upon Charles. I paused, looking directly at those gathered to honor me and I began the delivery of remarks I had titled "A Rendezvous with Destiny."

I am profoundly honored, extremely flattered, and deeply touched to be included among those being recognized here this evening. The announcement came to me as a surprise because while I have tried to assist Haiti in its struggles toward reconstruction and revitalization, I did not expect any reward. What I have done and will continue to do is offered simply in gratitude. I am indeed indebted to Haiti for the totally free education that I received;

Only shortly into my speech, the applause began.

. . . grateful to my mother and sister for their sacrifice, love, and devotion;

More applause, which continued as I finished each sentence.

and extremely thankful to my wife and my children for always supporting my professional endeavors and my constant efforts to assist Haiti. I also thank God for His blessings, because, without His guidance, I would not have been able to overcome the many obstacles encountered in my journey from St. Marc to the Waldorf-Astoria tonight.

As I waited before starting the next section, a hush (which nearly always greeted the parts of my speeches when I spoke of very personal experiences) was clearly evident in the room as I continued:

Allow me, if you will, to be personal for a moment. Born of Haitian peasants into abject poverty, hungry and poor, evicted from the meanest of dwellings, I was convinced very early that education was the only way to self-respect; thus, the determination to acquire the best education became permanently etched in my heart.

My gaze met Charles' eyes as we both remembered:

> . . . It is logical that this same road now takes me back to Haiti
> and that the water returns to its source. The circle must be
> closed.

The "Yes" from many in the audience was audible.

> . . . When asked why I continue to devote my resources to Haiti
> when I could continue to climb the ladder in the United States,
> I simply answer that no achiever is successful unless he or she
> takes someone else along. Yes, you heard me right. Regardless
> of the level of your accomplishment, you are not a successful
> individual unless you help others. Therefore, to any idea of mov-
> ing forward personally and leaving Haiti behind, I say, "No."

Applause burst forth.

> . . . To any thought of not visiting Haiti because the country
> lacks the high living standard to which I have become accus-
> tomed, I say "No." To avoiding involvement in the reconstruc-
> tion of Haiti because I did not participate in its destruction, I
> say, "No." To staying away from Haiti on the pretext of inse-
> curity or any other reason, I say, "No!"

With every "No" the applause entered a crescendo.

> . . . Yesterday Haiti planted in me the seeds of education. Today,
> it is fitting that she reaps the benefits of such investment.

Again, silence fell, as I paused in preparation for the conclusion.
The audience anticipated a climactic finish. They were not to be disappointed.

> Ladies and Gentlemen,
> In 1797 Haiti was struggling for her life against the oppression
> of slavery; this movement prepared the country for indepen-
> dence early in the 19th Century.

The applause rose en masse.

> In 1897 Haiti prevented an imperialistic take-over by Germany and the plan of President Hyppolite was to prepare the country for the 20th Century.

And the applause still grew.

> In 1997 amidst strife and turmoil of uprisings and strikes, Haiti continues to fight for the right to control her own destiny. We shall overcome.

Shouts rang out with the applause as the listeners recognized that I was tracing the history of this country that had faced so many travails.

> Now, as we prepare to enter the 21st century, together let us resolve to fight adult illiteracy and invest in the education of our youth. Let us provide for every Haitian access to health care. Together, let us pledge to lift the limits imposed on every Haitian's freedom. And, together, let us pledge to build a new Haiti. We shall succeed!!

The audience rose as one, clapping and shouting, crying and laughing—all, it seemed, in unison.

Notes

1. Ralph Gardner, "The Original Horatio Alger," used annually in the program honoring the Horatio Alger Awardees. Gardner is the author of *Horatio Alger*, or *The American Hero Era*

2. Ibid.

3. *Medical World News*, April 22, 1985.

4. Jerry Kobrin, "Take two aspirin and go hear the doctor speak," *The Orange County Register*, April 10, 1986, p. J2.

5. Kobrin, "Astronaut grounded for exceeding warp speed," *Orange County Register*, April 15, 1986, p. D2

6. "Cal Lutheran lecture on success will feature Dr. I Mortel," newspaper clipping, undated.

7. Rodrigue Mortel, *Commencement Address*, Milton Hershey School, June 12, 1986.

8. "Dr. Mortel receives Penn State Faculty Scholar Medal," *Vital Signs*, June 1986, p. 7.

9. "Haitian Born Doctor Named Fellow by National Academy of Sciences," *Haïti-Observateur*/15–22 avril 1988, p.8.

10. "Career to take Hershey doctor, native of Haiti, to Washington," Jo Griffiths, *The Patriot-News,* 17 April 1988, n. p.

11. "Health Policy Fellows Learn the Ropes in D.C.," *Advances, Newsletter of The Robert Wood Johnson Foundation*, circa 1989, p. 9.

12. Rodrigue Mortel, *Robert Wood Johnson Health Policy Fellowship Evaluation Report*, August 1989, 2.

13. Judith Patton, "Hershey doctor is honored for work in Haiti, Romania," *The Patriot-News*, November 9, 1991, n. p.

14. Steven Trapnell, " 'Churchman of the Year' is doctor whose hands first fold to pray," *New Lancaster Era*, November 11, 1991, A1, 5.

15. Patton, ibid.

16. Ibid.

Chapter 9: Haitian Ties

I have mentioned my family many times throughout this story and while I have paid honor particularly to my mother, my father, Demarant Mortel, also was dear to me. He was a shy man, very quiet, and was not comfortable out of his own environment. He visited America only once, at the age of 77, shortly after Renée was born. The pace of living in this country was overwhelming to him, even though he rarely left my house. He did his best to not be "in the way" and helped by cutting wood. He found the weather in Pennsylvania far too chilly, and asked to go home to Haiti earlier than planned. He was proud of me and the life I had worked for, but said he did not want to return again to America. However, because of my frequent trips to Haiti, I was able to visit with him often. He outlived my mother by several years, remaining in excellent health. He lived with my cousin who was like a sister to me. In 1992, at age 93, my father was struck by a car and suffered a fractured femur. By the time he was transported to Port-au-Prince, he was in shock. Surgery was performed and he was sent home. Subsequently he developed an infection and there were no antibiotics available. Had they been available, he probably would have survived. It was most distressing to me as a physician to know that it was political reasons, specifically the Embargo, that prevented the availability of antibiotics.

217

Embargo—Threat of Doom

My ties to and love for Haiti are permanent. While I have spent two-thirds of my life away from Haiti and long ago became an American citizen, I could never turn my back on the country of my birth. Even though I do not measure love in time or money, I have contributed a significant percentage of each to Haiti. I know what it is like to be poor and hungry. I know what it is like to be lonely. I know what it is like to have little hope. Because of that, I believe my contributions can provide opportunities for others, opportunities they otherwise would not have. Moreover, I believe that by helping others I am honoring and repaying the sacrifices others have made for me.

Haiti is poor and its people oppressed. The political situation has nearly destroyed the country and its people. Yet there is a dignity and perseverance in the people that provides hope that life will improve "as soon as. . . ." In my own small way I am trying to expedite the "as soon as. . . ," helping to make that *sooner* for some of my countrymen.

I found the greatest challenge in assisting my homeland occurred after an embargo against Haiti was declared in early 1992. This embargo followed the coup d'état made against Jean-Bertrand Aristide in September 1991 and Aristide's subsequent rescue by the United States. Because I viewed the resulting embargo as outrageous, I found myself being pulled into the political situation more than I cared to be. But I had to make an effort to help, at least by voicing my extreme indignity over the excessive action against Haiti by the Organization of American States (OAS).

Any embargo instills fear, especially to an island that cannot sustain itself and to a people who cannot survive without assistance from the outside world. This embargo was especially devastating to the poor of Haiti inasmuch as they saw it as their death knell. Unable to bear the cost of transportation for their crops to the cities and ports, gasoline for pumps, or any imported goods, villagers faced certain disaster. Most of them had few or no options. Seeing flight as their only chance for survival, those who could afford it began pooling their scant savings to pay for the building of boats to escape to the United States, Cuba, or any other place that might harbor them.

Many of the boats, overloaded with passengers and their meagre belongings, set out for the United States. The émigrés believed they would be rescued by the American government which had provided a safe haven for their president. To their disheartening disappointment, however, they were turned away from Florida and sent to Cuba, where the United States set up a temporary camp for them at Guantanamo Bay, the site of a U.S. naval station on the southeast coast of that island country. This camp quickly reached its capacity of 12,500 refugees. Once it no longer could accommodate the vast numbers of emigrants fleeing Haiti, the United States government sent all new in-coming "boat people" back to Port-au-Prince, ignoring the frightening probability that the passengers would never survive the voyage.

In early August I was the keynote speaker for the Annual Meeting of the Association of Haitian Physicians Abroad (Association des Médecins Haitiens à L'Étranger [AMHE]). I had looked forward to addressing this organization, for I had been urging the leadership to make a public statement against the embargo. They had refused, wavering because many members were not clear in their own minds if they wanted to take a political stand. Some said they did not want to offend Aristide who had found asylum in the United States.

What most concerned me, however, was that many of the "Haitian Physicians Abroad" had not been back to Haiti since they had left their country following medical school. It irked me that they wore their Haitian nationality like a badge of honor yet really had no idea of what Haiti had become. Some of these physicians had adopted a paternalistic attitude, a posture of "knowing what was best for Haiti" without having made any effort to see for themselves what the embargo had done to the homeland we all shared.

With great disquiet I began my speech that evening to the membership of AMHE but did not address the specific political issue in the way the members had been anticipating. Rather, I began with a tribute to the medical profession in general and the association in particular. I referred to the struggle Haitian physicians always face in achieving status and prestige, and I deliberately complimented the assemblage with these words: "Today I wish to recognize and applaud you for the compassion, the courage, and the tireless effort with which you apply your skill and knowledge for the benefit of every human being." I meant those words most sincerely, for it had been a struggle for each of us to rise to the prominence we now enjoy.

I segued to my next point by reminding them that ". . . we are more than simply physicians. We are *Haitian* physicians, and that adds another dimension to the scope of reward and recognition. We should not be ashamed of our humble origins, but rather be proud of our ascension." Moving toward the thrust of the message, I said, "Haiti is not a country we should abandon, but an alma mater we should cherish, the helping hand we should remember and to whom we should show gratitude. . . . Haiti gave us a free medical education and prepared us to be competitive with the majority of practicing physicians in foreign lands. It is only by looking at the cost of medical education in the United States today that we can realize the extent to which our own education was subsidized by the Haitian government." I suggested that we as Haitian physicians have the responsibility to contribute to the good of Haiti and to the individual dignity of its people:

> As I told this Society six years ago, to whom much is given, much is expected. You and I who were privileged in receiving the most generous gift of a free education also have the responsibility of reaching out to the poor, to the sick, and to the oppressed Haitians at home and abroad. As Pierre Bonnefil said in his article on racism in America, "It is sad, but many of our Haitian professionals forget where they came from and they live a life of isolation and denial of their roots. The Haitian community would benefit greatly if those *more* fortunate would share their time, their talent, their expertise, and their financial support to those *less* fortunate."
>
> Ladies and gentlemen, there is much to do; there are many

needs to be met. This Association should take a leadership role in identifying and addressing these needs. AMHE could and should become the visionary organization, but somehow neutralizing forces have either paralyzed the society or kept it in a holding pattern. Haiti is changing. AMHE cannot persist in doing business as usual. We must change. This Association cannot continue seeing only individual trees; we need to look at the forest. We need to change. The Association needs leaders, not followers; needs to be proactive, not reactive; needs movers, not blockers; and needs doers, not talkers. Let us change. The membership needs to realize that, like Haiti, divided we will fail, but united we will succeed. We must change.

My challenge to the Association was a harsh admonition to "wake up;" to denounce the racism we all have faced; to recruit new and active members and educate the second generation of Haitian physicians; and to become active in the efforts to help our country and her people. I had been annoyed at the presumption of the United States government in imposing on Haiti what the U.S. thought was best. I did not like to see this same kind of arrogance in the AMHE:

Wake up, AMHE. Be proud of your past achievements, but widen your scope of activity if you want to be more than a travel club. Wake up, AMHE, and take a close look at yourself and realize that in 19 years you have not reached the second objective of your mission statement. Wake up, AMHE; we are out of the loop and must immediately take steps to become the leader that U.S. agencies, as well as Haitian governments, call upon when health policy matters involving Haiti are being discussed. You need to understand the political context of health policy and find ways to influence in a positive manner.

Wake up, AMHE, tell Americans about this body of professionals and show them that not all Haitians are objects of charity. Show America that we are strong and intelligent, that we are capable of contributing to the welfare of both our country and of the western hemisphere.

Wake up, AMHE, we are the last of our kind. The United States and Canada no longer admit foreign physicians. The second generation of Haitians do not feel the same responsibility to the homeland. . . . in a matter of two decades, our Association may disappear, the next generation will melt into the American mix, our grandchildren will forget, and our people will be abandoned by those of us who can help them the most.

. . . Let us not do for Haiti what *we* think Haitians need. Rather, let us help Haitians to do what *they* want to do. We must do what needs to be done to alleviate human suffering regardless of the cause, the race or the creed. We must help Haiti regardless of *who* is in the National Palace.

As impatient as I was with the AMHE membership, I was even more intolerant of the seeming disregard by the United States for the basic needs of the common people of Haiti who were suffering the most as a result of the embargo. The United States government's inaction raised the ire of humanitarians all around the world. I keenly felt the effects of this cruelty, both personally and for all the people of my homeland. I wrote to every single minister of the OAS, asking for a lifting of the embargo. A guest editorial I wrote for *The Washington Post* appeared 10 August 1992; it demonstrates my passionate cry for ending the embargo policy:

Haiti is my homeland. It has always been a rather poor country—poor in material things, that is, but not in hope. But today, hope in Haiti is scarce—as rare as sutures, syringes and general anesthetics. People of all ages in need of special antibiotics are dying without getting them. Women with episiotomies, unable to be sutured following childbirth, heal slowly and painfully.

Children who depend on their schools to feed them are starving. The Organization of American States' embargo against Haiti, backed by the United States, is depriving poor people there of food, medicine and surgical materials. The embargo, quite simply, is genocide. I have been returning to Haiti for more than 20 years, and I have never before seen the misery and hopelessness I witnessed during my recent two visits.

At the Hôpital Université D'Etat D'Haiti in Port Au Prince, the country's main hospital, general anesthesia has not been available for more than a month. All procedures requiring general anesthesia cannot be performed. Only those using spinal or epidural anesthesia are done.

I went to Haiti recently, carrying two suitcases of suture material. My meager gift was received with the gratitude and enthusiasm usually reserved for humanitarians bearing food for starving people.

The hospital has no oxygen supplies. No syringes. No antibiotics. No vaccines. Patients must get prescriptions to buy their own syringes. The hospital has no sheets or gowns for patients; they must bring their own if they have them. During my visit to the ob/gyn department there, two women who were admitted for ectopic pregnancies underwent life-saving procedures under local anesthesia. Two others who had generalized peritonitis following self-induced abortions died because they could not be operated upon.

My own father, Demarant Mortel, died in Haiti in April. At age 93, he was recovering nicely from a traffic accident. He subsequently developed an infection and needed an antibiotic. None was found. I know that before the embargo, the antibiotic was available. People who would have survived in Haiti a year ago are dying today. How many others, younger than my father, will need to die because life-saving medical supplies are out of reach? How many will develop diseases that vaccination could have prevented? And how many parents, bereaved and bitter, need to suffer wounds that will never heal?

The United States has also cut back food assistance to Haiti. Students who normally get their only meal in school are not being fed. Many have stopped going to school. During my recent visit, a school employee visited the home of a student who had missed a test, only to discover that he had died of starvation. The university hospital often runs out of food, so patients' relatives bring food from home. That is the work of the embargo.

If the embargo were intended to deter the backers of the September 30, 1991 coup and force them to reinstate the ousted President Jean-Bertrand Aristide, it has failed to do so after nearly nine months. Yet innocent people are suffering and dying. Why continue a policy that has not accomplished its purpose, but instead is killing the people democracy needs to protect? Can a better-targeted policy be found? Can lives of children, pregnant women and innocent people be spared?[1]

This editorial was reprinted in a number of newspapers, including *The Miami Herald*. Yet, despite many voices raised in support of my plea, Amy Wilentz, a very vocal critic of the call to end the embargo and author of *The Rainy Season: Haiti Since Duvalier*, responded negatively and did much harm to a country she professes to care about. Her "Op-Ed" piece in *The New York Times*, 13 August 1992, claims rather callously that "It is true that the people of Haiti are starving. But they were starving long before the embargo began." She continues with the argument that "such necessities as food and medicine have never stopped entering the country." She then states, "I have seen stolen medicine meant for the country's poor traded to Dominican soldiers. . . . The same thing happens with food."[2]

I was quite annoyed at Wilentz's presumptions. She apparently did not know that medicine had been available to the people prior to the embargo but was not available to the general population during the proscription. She did not know the true situation. It had been five years since she last had been in Haiti, while I was visiting the country regularly. I saw firsthand the desperation among my people, and had to watch my own father die for lack of antibiotics, medicine that had been available prior to the embargo.

By September, newspaper columnists were confirming my claims and supporting my plea. Lucinda Fleeson, staff writer for *The Philadelphia Inquirer*, reported directly from Port-au-Prince,

When an international trade embargo was imposed against Haiti last year, medicine and food were supposed to be exempt from the sanctions. But now, a year later, Simphar Bontemps, a surgeon and hospital director, can't get critical medical supplies to keep patients alive. . . . in a country long submerged in poverty, the embargo has helped create new depths of misery. . . . Bontemps . . . said his 100-bed Catholic mission, Hospital St. François de Sales, ran out of anesthesia in July.[3]

In a second article, Fleeson continued her investigative reporting of the embargo-induced conditions in Haiti and told of the travails suffered by Haitians who had tried to escape as boat people from the hardships and had been returned to Haiti. Most returnees tell the same story of executions, tortures, kidnaps, and arrests. "The army just arrests people whenever or wherever they feel like it," said William O'Neill, deputy director of the New York-based Lawyers Committee for Human Rights. His group had made several factfinding missions to Haiti and had documented hundreds of cases of illegal arrests—"and that means in reality there have been thousands," O'Neill stated.[4]

The issue of Haitian refugees being turned away from the United States without even a hearing quickly became a highly debated topic in the news media. On the "Opinion USA" page of *USA Today*, an interview with Randall Robinson reported my charges that the United States displayed a discriminatory policy against Haitian refugees. Robinson made the point that "if a person is facing persecution and can support that claim, then that person has a right to a hearing and if that person can demonstrate persecution is being fled from, then we're obliged to provide safe haven."[5]

On 10 September, *The New York Times* printed my response to the editorial of 13 August by Amy Wilentz,

"Haiti's Lies". . . is dead wrong in its plea to keep the Organization of American States embargo to restore President Jean-Bertrand Aristide to power. The embargo has failed to do so after nearly 10 months, yet innocent people are suffering and dying.

The poor Haitians do not need "spiritual sustenance." Rather, they need food assistance. They do not need "the illusion that the international community supports their quest for democracy." Rather, they need action and aid from the international community in their search for democracy. . . ."6

The same day that my letter appeared in *The Times*, an editorial in *The Philadelphia Inquirer* took up the cry to lift the embargo. The editorial plainly made the point that the embargo was not working. The writer enumerated the reasons, including the fact that the impoverished poor were suffering while the military and wealthy elite were barely affected. The piece concluded with the point that President Bush's policy of ". . . (sending) home fleeing Haitians intercepted at sea without giving them a chance to make a case for political asylum" was both a violation of U.S. laws and "a betrayal of American principles."7 Further, the writer took the OAS to task, repeating that the embargo must be lifted and failure must be admitted.

A year later, in August 1993, the UN Security Council suspended the embargo, but in October re-imposed it, with five U.S. warships arriving in Haitian waters to patrol against boats attempting to break the embargo. Eventually, more than a dozen ships from a number of different countries joined the blockade. On 9 November 1993 *The New York Times* published a front page story, reporting that "an oil embargo and other sanctions designed to help restore democracy to Haiti are killing as many as 1,000 children each month, according to a study by international public health experts at Harvard University. . . . In the small town of Gantier . . . Haiti's suffering is everywhere evident. At the town's small medical clinic, the only health care center within miles, a white ambulance sits idle for lack of gasoline. The clinic's pharmacy is almost bare."8

This *Times* article prompted me to write another letter to the editorial page editor:

The Harvard public health officials who prepared the study . . . are right. Children in Haiti, as well as their elders, are dying needlessly . . . the reality is that the fuel shortage is preventing even necessities from reaching the people. Supplies may reach Port-au-Prince, but there they remain, as people die. . . . the OAS and UN embargoes not only fail to accomplish their intended purposes but instead kill the people they are meant to protect, while a small minority is getting richer just by the very nature of the embargo.

. . . Although assistance from the international community is welcome, the Haitian problem is a complex one that requires a Haitian solution. It is unlikely, however, that such a solution can be found without dialogue, negotiation and compromise. No single party will win or lose, but the biggest winner will be the (now) suffering Haitian people.[9]

By the summer of 1994 the situation between the U.S. and Haiti was very tense. The Clinton administration was considering U.S. military intervention backed by the UN resolution that gave the United States the authority to intervene. The editorial position in *USA Today* (6 July 1994) warned against such military action[10] and by mid-September, military intervention had been averted. In a letter (unpublished) sent 28 September to *The New York Times*, I wrote:

If we as a country have been willing to play a role in Haiti's demise, then we should also vow to help Haiti rise from the ashes. We will gain nothing unless we commit long term to the success of the new administration, the protection of human rights, and the resurrection of the country. Otherwise, in no time at all, Haiti will be weakened and revert to its present crisis situation.

As scheduled, U.S. troops landed at the commercial airport of Port-au-Prince to prepare for the return of President Aristide and the peaceful transition of government. The soldiers were in full battle dress as they exited from the army helicopters, armed and ready for combat. They were very surprised at the welcome they received from thousands of cheering Haitians. Over the next few days, 20,000 American troops had landed. Most of the Haitian army had melded into the general population, so there was no need for the American soldiers to demand a "surrender." As expected, general uneasiness increased as the date for Aristide's return drew near. Finally, on 10 October, in an official ceremony, General Raoul Cédras stepped down. As part of the observance held outside army headquarters, the flag of command was passed from General Cédras to Jean-Claude Duperval as temporary custodian until the arrival of Aristide five days later.

On 15 October 1994 President Jean-Bertrand Aristide returned to Haitian soil.

Embargo Lifted

Despite dire predictions from many quarters that Haiti was collapsing, I visited the country in November of 1994. What I observed was that Haiti had started on the long road to recovery and was showing signs of life again. Upon my return to the United States I told a reporter that "Haiti is starting to get its strength and spirit back. There is a sense of hope there, with the embargo lifted, with Aristide back, and with the American military occupation. Haiti is not yet back to work and there aren't jobs open. But life has come back. People are very upbeat. With the embargo lifted, gasoline prices dropped from a high of $18–$24 a gallon to $4 a gallon. In contrast, however, food, largely imported, remains expensive and hospitals are still short on supplies."[11]

While I was able to broker donations to assist the country's people, the 20,000 U.S. troops on Haitian soil was a different matter. The Haitian people held mixed feelings about the American military. On the one hand, Haitians wanted the American military to provide them safety; on the other hand, they did not want any foreign military to become involved in restructuring their government. Another concern for the citizens was that armed U.S. soldiers were visible everywhere. In addition, tanks with mounted guns were very much in evidence in the streets. I personally was uneasy that the American military was involved at all levels in the Haitian government, yet their purpose did not seem to be clear to either the Haitian people or themselves. Most important, many Haitians felt humiliated by the U.S. military occupation.

I personally believe that the military had overstepped its bounds and I advocated the withdrawal of American troops from Haiti. In late November I submitted the following editorial to *The New York Times*:

> A recent visit to my homeland provided me with a picture totally different from what I had expected. The display of military force in Haiti is nothing short of overwhelming. I could hardly believe my eyes as I watched tanks and large military trucks and equipment swarm up and down the streets of the capital; many of the vehicles were equipped with mounted machine guns that were aimed (although mercifully not fired) at passing civilian pedestrians.
>
> There are also numerous incidents of the U.S. military entering private homes at gun point and searching these homes for firearms without benefit of search warrants. Residents in my hometown of Saint Marc have been arrested without a warrant, have been mistreated, detained in U.S. military controlled detention centers without cause, and kept incarcerated without a court hearing. One of these detainees, a good friend of mine, was arrested at gun point, held without a hearing of any kind, released after four days, and given a card indicating that the U.S. military had arrested him by mistake, that he was not guilty, and that, in fact, he was innocent.[12]
>
> . . . On Thanksgiving Day, U.S. Defense Secretary William Perry told American soldiers at the presidential palace in Port-au-Prince, "You are restoring democracy to this country, and it is moving more quickly and more effectively than anyone imagined."
>
> If the incidents I witnessed and heard about are prevalent,

then restoring democracy looks a lot like military occupation. If such measures can be taken in Haiti, under the guise of restoring democracy, what, in turn, might be the future of U.S. endeavors in other countries?

Aid to Many Hospitals

My philanthropic efforts on Haiti's behalf are far closer to my heart than my political ones, and it is that area to which I devote my resources. My growing interest in Haiti's welfare began on that sunny January day in 1973 when Dr. Vincent Stenger and I met the two nurses from the Hôpital Albert Schweitzer on a Haitian beach while vacationing with our families. That chance encounter gave us the opportunity to tour the facility and it was this visit to Schweitzer that started it all. As mentioned earlier, I was very impressed with the organization of the Albert Schweitzer Hospital program. Even though the hospital is limited to serving the district assigned to it by the government of Haiti, the high quality of the care it provides is second to none. Its charter designates the Schweitzer Hospital to serve the people of the Artibonite Valley, a district of approximately 200,000 people. While it is possible to be referred to Schweitzer from another district, an individual person cannot present himself as a patient.

Once I had seen the Schweitzer Hospital, I knew their organizational and operational system would be the best plan for other districts of Haiti as well. Both because I wanted to learn more about its operations and because of my admiration for the medical practice that was conducted at Schweitzer, Cecile and I volunteered each year for several successive years to spend two weeks working in the hospital. After studying its systems, I then suggested the same system of care delivery be started in the St. Marc district. The hospital in St. Marc, Hôpital St. Nicholas, was, like all of the public hospitals in Haiti, operated by the Haitian government. As a public hospital, St. Nicholas had all of the negative features of a cumbersome bureaucracy and none of the benefits, such as adequate government funding.

While there are private *clinics* in the larger cities, there are few private hospitals in any of the cities except for Port-au-Prince. Therefore, when an individual wishes to be admitted to a private hospital, that person usually goes to Port-au-Prince. This lack of quality medical care (either private or public) throughout the rest of the country is one of the many reasons why the population of Port-au-Prince has exploded; the capital city has the best, and sometimes only, private hospitals and quality medical care.

No hospitals in Haiti are regulated by any standards or controls. While each hospital has an administrator, this position is held by one of the physicians on staff and not by a person especially trained in hospital administration. Most hospital positions are political appointments, unintentionally providing much autonomy to the general employees who do not have to be accountable to the administrator. In such a system with few or no "controls," hospitals are neither efficient nor effective in their daily functions.

Fortunately, a "Concordat" exists between the government and the Catholic Church which, among other things, allows for much of the nursing services in the public hospitals to be provided or supervised by orders of nuns. This arrangement assures more consistency of quality care. On the other hand, even though public hospitals are free to the citizens, the system still allows for unscrupulous physicians to take advantage of patients in that these unprincipled physicians make it very clear that if patients pay them personally, they will receive better care.

Even without a well-regulated government system, I was determined to assist the St. Nicholas Hospital in St. Marc. Beginning in the mid-1970s, I periodically shipped supplies to the hospital and hand-carried additional materials on each visit I made to Haiti. This process continued until the late 1980s at which time I sent twenty-five cartons of supplies, surgical instruments, and pharmaceuticals. Not one of the items reached the patients. All cartons and their contents—everything was stolen. As a result, I had to stop shipping items. I do, however, continue to hand carry items and to send packages directly to the nuns who, in turn, take the supplies and equipment to the hospital.

As mentioned earlier, several years ago when the Milton S. Hershey Medical Center replaced all of its beds with state-of-the-art models, I asked the hospital administration what would be done with the beds being replaced. I was directed to the supplier who told me that I could have the old beds if I could arrange to have them shipped out of the United States. Delighted with this unexpected opportunity, I began in earnest to find a way to transport the beds and to ensure they would arrive at the hospital and not be stolen from the dock warehouse in Port-au-Prince or St. Marc. I eventually was put in touch with a Lancaster, Pennsylvania Mennonite organization, which is part of a larger mission organization, Christian Aid Ministries, based in Berlin, Ohio. Christian Aid Ministries arranged to ship 100 beds to St. Nicholas Hospital. The 100 beds arrived at St. Nicholas as promised—and in good order. In exchange, I offered the remaining several hundred beds to be sent to a hospital in Romania. Further, the Ministries offered to ship any other goods or supplies that I wished to send to Haiti or any other needy country.

In August 1990, following the fall of the Communist dictatorship in Romania, I was invited by Christian Aid Ministries to visit that country to assess the medical needs of the hospitals there. I spent ten days evaluating the need for medical equipment and supplies, a process that had never been done before and an experience new to me.

We first flew to Budapest and were transported by truck across the border of Romania. It was eleven o'clock at night, and at the border was a line of vehicles about two miles long waiting to enter Hungary to purchase food. Each driver had to have papers checked before being allowed to cross the border into Hungary—just to buy food.

When we arrived at the hospital to distribute supplies, what I saw was more terrible than anything I had ever seen in Haiti. I was permitted to see only the first two floors of an orphanage and not the ground level where I had been told the children were kept under filthy conditions. I have no doubt of the authenticity of the photographs journalists smuggled out of the country at that time.

There was one bright spot in this visit, and a reminder of the generosity of one people for another. As I walked through the hospital ward I recognized the beds from the Hershey Medical Center. This was the only thing that brought a sense of satisfaction at all to my visit, seeing the beds from the Medical Center being put to good use.

In contrast to the hospital and orphanage, we also visited the palace in Bucharest. One of the rooms in the interior was pure gold. Everything, everywhere was gold. I couldn't help comparing this ostentatious display of splendor with what I had seen in the city's hospitals and orphanages.

Outside of Bucharest, no buildings in Romania had indoor plumbing and neither the pharmacies nor the grocery stores had anything on their shelves. I ate only tomatoes and potatoes the entire time I was in Romania, except for the one evening when we were invited to dinner at the home of a physician. Here we were served sardines and other vegetables in addition to our usual tomatoes.

I had no idea, of course, that I would have difficulty leaving the country, but when I arrived at the airport to confirm my return flight reservation and to check in, there was no one at the counter. Finally I found an employee who said to me, "That flight was canceled a month ago." I was told that I might be able to get a seat on a flight to Switzerland and that I should return at 3:00 a.m. This I did, and at nine o'clock the following morning a plane arrived bound for Switzerland. At noon I boarded, but there was no seat for me. Sitting on a folded down bench, I finally arrived in Switzerland only to discover that I had missed a connecting flight. I then got on the next flight to Germany, eventually arriving in Chicago, one day late for my meeting there.

I have found the Mennonite organization to be very reliable and we have forged a partnership, one that is universally beneficial for countries in need. I have worked with other organizations as well, most of which are truly altruistic and only a few that are unreliable. For example, when I was contacted by Haitian Physicians Abroad I collected, donated, and sent 30 cartons of supplies to the Hospital of the Haitian Community. None of the cartons ever arrived and no one seems to know what happened to the shipment.

I later found another organization known as Food for the Poor who, like the Mennonite Christian Aid Ministries, is helpful, dependable, and grateful for any donations. When in 1995 the Hershey Medical Center replaced 400 mattresses, I asked if I could have the old ones. "No problem," said the supplier. "Fine," said the officials of the Medical Center. "However, the mattresses must be removed from here within a week." Not to be deterred by the near impossible, I called my friends at Christian Aid Ministries. They were interested, but unfortunately had no place to store 400 mattresses until they could arrange for shipping. I then contacted Food for the Poor in Deerfield, Florida. They were able to help immediately and a large van was sent to collect all of the mattresses, a hundred of which were shipped to Haiti, designated for St. Marc. The other 300 were to be sent to wherever there was the greatest need. I was very gratified to receive confirmation when the shipment arrived in Haiti. Elation, however, turned to dismay when I discovered that the mattresses, while on the manifest at Port-au-Prince, never got to St. Marc.

In 1996 Dr. Simphar Bontemps, Medical Director of Hôpital St. François de Sales, contacted me to ask if I could find a way to obtain a "C-arm," a piece of X-ray equipment that was badly needed in his facility. I went scouting, making telephone calls and personally contacting people who might be able to assist. Eventually a used C-arm was located and donated on the condition that it be delivered safely to the receiving hospital. Again, I contacted Food for the Poor who helped Dr. Bontemps work out a plan to assure safe delivery of this piece of equipment. Their only requirement was that the crating cost of $700 be paid by the person scheduled to receive the shipment. I suggested that the crate be shipped directly to Dr. Bontemps at the hospital. This was accomplished successfully.

In addition to collecting supplies, I have made many attempts to encourage my compatriots to volunteer their time and services to Haiti and particularly to the Albert Schweitzer Hospital. I knew there were enough Haitian-born physicians in the United States to make a contribution if each one would volunteer even a week at a hospital in their homeland. However, despite my efforts, nearly everywhere I tried I was unsuccessful in recruiting the number of volunteers needed.

Never once was I openly rebuffed in my recruiting efforts; rather, my entreaties were met with enthusiasm and promises. Unhappily, in most instances that is as far as the interest went—promises, with no follow-through. For example, I once spoke to an informal gathering of Haitian-born obstetrics/gynecology physicians in New York City, telling them of the urgent need to be of service in Haiti. This group applauded my plea and presented me with a plaque for my efforts on behalf of Haiti. More importantly, twelve of that group agreed to go to Haiti to donate their services. Over a period of time, however, eleven of the twelve called, with a variety of excuses. Of those twelve who originally had volunteered, only one, Dr. Jacques Guillaume, actually went to Haiti and spent time at the Schweitzer Hospital.

Connecting with Albert Schweitzer Hospital

Another group from which I tried to recruit volunteers was the AMHE. I did my best to convince the members of this organization to spend a week or two helping at the Schweitzer Hospital. I even presented a proposal from the Schweitzer Hospital, inviting the AMHE to participate in a partnership. The AMHE members thought the idea was exciting—"fantastic" was their word, as I recall. The AMHE formed a Task Force and the president of AMHE wrote to the Executive Director of the Schweitzer Hospital who, in turn, responded with great enthusiasm. Because one of the missions of Schweitzer is to recruit native Haitians for leadership positions in the hospital organization, the Executive Director saw this potential link with the AMHE as very positive to this long-range plan. Unfortunately, but perhaps not unexpectedly, nothing more came of this coalition, although three physicians—Drs. Andre and Marie-Claude Rigaud; and Dr. Andre St. Louis—made their own arrangements to volunteer at the Schweitzer Hospital. These three volunteers, at my invitation, attended one of the biannual "Schweitzer Alumni Meetings" held in Pittsburgh by the Grant Foundation.

Another opportunity for Haitian-born physicians to become involved in the Albert Schweitzer Hospital in Haiti occurred when the AMHE planned a joint meeting with the Haitian Physicians Association (Association Médicale Haitienne [AMH]) based in Port-au-Prince. The meeting was scheduled at Club Med Haiti in July of 1997. The only drawback was that many members of AMHE were very reluctant to agree to a meeting in a country they believed to be unsafe (even though it was their homeland). Regardless of these fears, however, the conference was scheduled and subsequently held. To everyone's surprise, it turned out to be the best AMHE conference attended to that date.

As soon as the conference dates were set, I offered to plan a side trip to the Albert Schweitzer Hospital for those who were interested in visiting the hospital site. What I had in mind was a satellite symposium held at the hospital, a program I thought would appeal to many of the conference attendees.

By May, plans for the satellite symposium at the Schweitzer Hospital were confirmed. Mrs. Mellon was to welcome the visitors, followed by remarks from the Executive Vice-president of the Grant Foundation. Next on the program were to be three scientific presentations followed by another presentation scheduled only as a "cover" for a very special and secret event. I had decided that this symposium would provide a perfect occasion to honor Mrs. Mellon personally for her support of the Schweitzer Hospital and to make note of her birthday anniversary, the day I had selected for us to visit.

Like almost everyone else who had known Dr. and Mrs. William Larimer Mellon, I held them in the highest regard. Both were very generous and had devoted their lives and fortune to this hospital. They themselves lived quite humbly. For example, Dr. Mellon could have had a burial vault of gold had he wanted it. Instead, before his death, with his own hands he built two wooden boxes. These were to be used as coffins for himself and his wife. Dr. Mellon had chosen the hand-hewn coffins for his interment to show by example that one does not, nor should not, need to spend money on elaborate burial rites and that a simple burial could serve the same purpose as a more ornate one. He wanted to emphasize that it was not prudent to spend lavishly for a funeral—something Haitians generally did, whether or not they could afford it. In 1989 Dr. Mellon, as he had anticipated, died first, leaving his wife a widow. The second coffin remains at the compound where Mrs. Mellon fully expects to be interred beside her husband.

Early in the development of this hospital, the benevolent Mellons had chosen "Reverence for Life" (*Révérence pour la Vie*) as the motto for their mission, although the words were not actually displayed anywhere. Faithful to their lack of ostentation, the Mellons had not spent funds on exhibiting the motto. Other persons, including members of the board, believed that, with the new addition to the hospital, this motto should be displayed. The board decided to offer for sale, at $300 each, eighteen bronze letters, one for each letter of the motto. These letters would be mounted on the exterior of the new addition. Seeing this as an appropriate opportunity to honor the Mellons and their work, I purchased three letters, V I E, with plans to bequeath them during the satellite symposium scheduled to be held at Schweitzer Hospital.

A month prior to the Haitian Medical Convention, I mailed letters with the complete information, outlining the activity calendar for the day at Schweitzer, to the Board of Directors, and all Executive Committee members who had registered for the week-long event. Thirty physicians responded to the invitation to attend the satellite symposium scheduled parallel to the events of the second day of the conference. Gratified at this number, I confirmed plans and made reservations with the Schweitzer Hospital for thirty visitors on 22 July.

Our visit to Albert Schweiter Hospital was a highlight of the convention for those who took the tour. The visiting physicians had the opportunity to see the full range of programs and services of the institution. Few of the members had ever been to the Schweitzer Hospital, so there was great interest in the facility and its mission. Everyone was in good spirits and talking with great excitement over what they had seen. The visitors were expecting only a modest lunch in the hospital and did not know they were in for a rare treat, one that even I had not known about in advance. Mrs. Mellon had arranged for this delegation to be served in her own home, quite an honor because, at her advanced age, Mrs. Mellon did not host many events.

St. Marc Beneficence

In addition to making speeches and writing letters on behalf of Haiti I have supported numerous projects there, many of which I mentioned previously. The major recipient of my efforts, however, has been my home area of St. Marc. For many years I have been sending medical supplies and materials to the hospital; donating money for church funds; contributing to numerous civic projects; giving money to friends; and financially supporting members of my family, both immediate and extended.

My only income is what I earn, but I strongly believe that "the more one gives, the more one receives." My own desires are modest and the thought of living extravagantly has rarely, if ever, crossed my mind. It is hard for me to imagine reaching some degree of success and not helping others.

Because of my religious convictions, I have tried to be especially responsive to the needs of the Catholic Church in Haiti. For example, a few years ago the parishioners of the Church of St. Marc asked me for my advice on raising funds to cover the costs of repainting the church. After meeting with the priest and the building committee, I offered to pay for the entire project in tribute to my mother's membership and my own service there as an altar boy many years ago.

Shortly after the church had been repainted, officials from my home city of St. Marc approached me for a donation to erect a small decorative architectural structure in front of my mother's house. This structure was to serve as a divider in the roadway and as a commemorative to my mother. Again, just as I had done with the church, I agreed to underwrite the cost, and the configuration was built. However, when it was completed and I saw how ugly it was, I asked that it be removed.

Some years earlier, following my mother's death in 1989, I had wanted to create an appropriate and lasting tribute to her memory. Because of her strong religious faith, I thought it would be most fitting to donate something tangible to the parish, a building or program that would continue in perpetuity. I was aware that the population of the parish had tripled and that there was a desperate need for additional churches. Thus, building a church became a major possibility as a memorial. Dinah and I held a number of discussions with the priest at which time I offered assistance with open hands, noting that I would be receptive to paying a significant portion of the cost for the building of a new church for the parish of St. Marc.

Progress on developing a plan was slow and three years passed before preliminary drawings and a rough cost estimate were available from the diocese. In addition, there was interminable discussion as to what the new church would be named and even how the parish of St. Marc would be reorganized. Finally, my own enthusiasm began to waver. In the meantime, during the course of these three years of indecisiveness on the part of the diocese, I had come upon that small group of parishioners who had been meeting to worship every Sunday under a mango tree, and I built a small church for them.

After further family discussion, I began to think that perhaps building a school would be a more appropriate way to honor my mother. I will never forget her stories of yearning for an education and how fervently she had wanted to attend school. In addition, the memories of the eviction fifty years earlier had never left my soul or my consciousness. The anguished words of my mother still haunted me: "If I had had an education, this would not have happened." And, always, I recalled with lasting gratitude the sacrifices she had made to assure me of the best possible education and a better life. As I thought about the many speeches I had made in my lifetime, I realized that in most of those speeches I had emphasized the importance of education. The anecdotes I had told of my own background often centered upon my mother's forfeiture of her own comfort in order for her daughter and then her son to have the education denied her.

After considering all factors, I made yet another trip to speak to the pastor of St. Marc's Church about an alternative plan. I knew that the pastor very much wanted to build a school, and that he likely would be receptive to my suggestion of building a school rather than a church. We talked at length and I then met with Bishop Constant. The Bishop welcomed the meeting and wholeheartedly agreed with the parish priest as to the necessity for a school that would meet the needs of the parish.

Now thinking in terms of a school rather than a church, I held further discussions with advisors and my family before I began a comprehensive assessment of possibilities and options. One of the ideas I had considered previously was to transform my mother's house into a school. That possibility was discussed briefly, then dismissed because the house would not readily lend itself to any increasing needs of the school, either in population or program expansion. Other possibilities were then raised, as I also owned the house next to my mother's home as well as another house in the same block on a half-acre of land. This latter purchase had become possible when I heard that a cousin of mine, living in the United States, was about to sell the house. I contacted this cousin, who was delighted to hear of my interest, as she did not want to risk carrying cash from a sale in St. Marc to the airport of Port-au-Prince. With the acquisition of this land, plans for building a larger school and possibly a residential house would be assured. I believe this to be an act of Providence, as the acquisitions of this land assured the construction of a school in an appropriate location.

Then, like an answer to a prayer, I met Maude Paultre, a former teacher, whose father had been the pastor of the largest Protestant church in St. Marc, a church that also sponsors its own school. Known for her patronage to her fellow Haitians, Mm. Paultre had hoped eventually to leave a legacy to her country. Through a mutual friend, she had learned of my intentions to build a school. We met and discussed our shared desire to improve conditions for those in St. Marc who had the motivation to learn to read and write and to develop job skills or competencies to help them rear healthy families.

Since Maude Paultre could not be in Haiti to oversee any of the plans, she suggested that I purchase the ten acres of land she had in

St. Marc, not more than a ten-minute walk from my mother's home. The land was offered to this purpose for substantially less than market value. I accepted the offer with great joy and gratitude. We could move forward!

We faced three choices: (1) build the school on that land, (2) sell the acreage and use the profit for operating expenses of the school on the property I owned in the city, or (3) develop a model city on the land and use the proceeds to sustain the school. I contacted an architect to look at the ten acres I had purchased from Mm. Paultre and to determine if and how the land might be developed into building lots. In addition, a meeting with an officer of a local bank assured me of financing should I decide to develop the land. I soon realized, however, that I simply could not devote the time needed to be a land developer.

What did come out of this meeting, however, was the formation of the Mortel Family Charitable Foundation. Incorporated in Pennsylvania and administered by a trust company, the officers of the foundation, which include family members, will make all decisions relative to the foundation.

My design was for a multi-purpose school that would make the most effective use of resources, particularly for the poorest three-year-old children who, without proper care and nutrition, have little chance of surviving to the age of five. Classes for the children will be held in the morning, human development programs and trade skills will be taught to adult women in the afternoon, and an adult literacy program will be offered in the evening.

I made some initial contacts to various church officials as to the logistics of finding an appropriate order of nuns to manage the school. Again, God answered our prayers and in July 1998 I received a letter of acceptance from the Congregation des Soeurs de Saint Joseph de Cluny, notifying me that they would provide the services to the school. I was completely filled with happiness at their willingness to be a part of our endeavors. Not only are they a most highly respected teaching order, but also their religious community is located in St. Marc, thereby relieving our concerns for housing.

We are in full agreement that the greatest need in Haiti is education of the population and we have focused our efforts to meet that need. Considering that one of every four children in Haiti dies of infection and malnutrition before reaching the age of five, we had planned for the school to target three-year-olds who have no means of attending any other school. We would provide them with food and clothing as well as a traditional education. Opening the school to three-year-olds should have a greater impact (both on education and survival rates) than opening and restricting enrollment to those of typical school age. Each succeeding year we plan to add a new class of three-year-olds while continuing with the preceding year's group. A child would start at age three and remain in the school until the age of fourteen or until he/she has completed the equivalent of eighth grade and is ready to attend the lycée or to join the work force.

The literacy program will be aimed at illiterate adults of both sexes. This is critical to my own belief that everyone should have an opportunity to learn to read. Perhaps our program can offer a future to those like my mother who left the village of Savary long ago, a child who so desperately wanted to go to school and never could.

The third component of the school will provide programs designed for the development of women, for in the Haitian culture the woman is the main pillar of the family. The man, while viewed as the bread winner, in reality may or may not remain with his family. It is, therefore, critical to help the women learn a trade, build their self-confidence, and provide them with the necessary ingredients to meet their responsibilities to family and society.

This diocesan school will serve the population of peasants and farmers who originally came from the surrounding rural communities because they could no longer farm the land. Their goal was to find work in the city, but with the high (80%) rate of unemployment combined with their own illiteracy, their hope for a new life never materialized. Their children have neither clothes nor shoes and they suffer malnutrition among other ailments. Hence, it is very important to recruit these children and offer them an environment where they can receive not only preschool education but also a nutritious meal along with vitamins and minerals essential to proper growth.

Our plans were to be operational by the end of the 20th Century. We were greatly assisted in our endeavors when the charitable organization Food for the Poor expressed interest in the school. In August 1998 I met with the president of the organization to present a proposal for possible funding for the school and went prepared with detailed plans and blueprints for the school, as well as plans for developing the land for the model city. Once he saw the amount of careful planning that had gone into the proposal and realized that there was the financial backing to support the operation of the school in perpetuity, the president guaranteed that Food for the Poor would totally finance the construction and furnishing of the school, from the mortar to the pencils and tablets. I was first astonished, then elated. I could not believe it. I had gone with the hope of finding some support, but to have my proposal totally accepted and to be told that all I needed to do was to provide a list of what would be needed is incredible. God's hand was evident. The president asked me how soon we could start construction, "Is January 1999 good?" Taken by surprise, I told him that demolition of standing buildings was scheduled for January, a step necessary before construction could begin. "Good," was his reply. "We will break ground in February."

Of course, construction plans rarely proceed at the speed the builder desires. We ran into several obstacles, none of which were insurmountable, but all of which took time. The guest residence was completed in early 2000 and has become the temporary headquarters for the school. The house is a very comfortable, two-story dwelling with four bedrooms, a living room, dining room, kitchen, and two-and-a-half bathrooms.

We have named the school "The Good Samaritans" in gratitude for the many persons who have made this endeavor possible. We are eagerly looking forward to its dedication in the fall of 2001.

Thanks to the support of Food for the Poor which is underwriting nearly the entire cost of construction, the Mortel Family Foundation can concentrate its efforts on raising funds to operate the school. A major campaign is underway to establish a trust whose interest will provide yearly operating expenses. All of us have faith that, as God has led me to fulfilling the dream of providing this opportunity for the children and adults of St. Marc, so, too, will He show the way to conduct a successful fund-raising campaign.

Those of you who read this book are part of that fund-raising, for any profit from the sale of this book goes into the Foundation. In addition, there is a Pledge Card in each book, asking that you consider becoming one of the Good Samaritans by making a donation towards the continuing operation of "The Good Samaritans School," or as the children would say, "Lekòl Nou!"

Notes

1. Rodrigue Mortel, "End the Embargo Against Haiti," *The Washington Post*, Monday, August 10, 1992, section A, p.1.

2. Amy Wilentz, "Haiti's Lies," OP-ED, *The New York Times*, Thursday, August 13, 1992.

3. Lucinda Fleeson, "Embargo on Haiti falls hard on poor," *The Philadelphia Inquirer*, Monday, September 7, 1992, 1+.

4. Fleeson, "A village of would-be refugees cries out in Haiti," *The Philadelphia Inquirer*, Tuesday, September 8, 1992, A1+.

5. "Let Haitian refugees into USA," *USA Today*, Wednesday, September 9, 1992, 15A.

6. Rodrigue Mortel, "Embargoed Haiti's Suffering Increases," EDITORIAL/LETTERS, *The New York Times*, Thursday, September 10, 1992, n.page.

7. "Revisiting Haiti," *The Philadelphia Inquirer,* Thursday, September 10, 1992, A18.

8. Howard W. French, "Study Says Haiti Sanctions Kill Up to 1,000 Children a Month," *The New York Times*, Tuesday, November 9, 1993, A1, A8.

9. Rodrigue Mortel, letter to Philip M. Boffey, Deputy Editorial Page Editor, *The New York Times*, November 12, 1993.

10. "Go slow with any plans for using force in Haiti," *USA Today*, Wednesday, July 6, 1994.

11. Mary Klaus, "Local doctor predicts Haitian cure, *The Patriot-News*, Harrisburg, PA, Monday, November 21, 1994, B7.

12. This arbitrary arresting of citizens without cause was apparently

widespread. A citizen would be stopped, arrested, and held for as many days as the occupying military decided was warranted. There was no attention given to rights, no opportunity for legal council, no regress at all. Following a period of time, ranging from hours to days, the innocent citizen would be released with a small printed card, indicating his name, reason for being detained, and the date. On the reverse side of the card is pre-printed, "Milité Ameriken arete moun sa pa erè/ Li pa koupab. Li inosan," which translated simply says that the bearer had been arrested in error and was not guilty (pa koupab), but rather was innocent.

Epilogue: Closing the Circle

Faith and Family

Cecile has often said to me, "How many lives can you live?" I know she means that in a solicitous way, as she does worry about the schedule and pace I keep. I also know she is concerned, but I try to keep it light by responding with such answers as, "I would like to live as many lives as I can live well within the time allotted to me." I thank God that I have been healthy and that I have had the desire to do as much as I can. I have become who I am today by the grace of God and with the help of my family. I would not want anyone to think that my success is the result only of my own hard work. I would not have been able to achieve what I did without my deep and abiding religious faith and the unconditional love and support of my family.

Faith

. . . the faith and fire within us[1]

The greatest motivation for anyone is religious faith. I was blessed by being born into a family where the Catholic faith was taken very seriously. My mother was a devout Catholic and she instilled in me the belief that a strong religious faith was the most important characteristic a person could have. She lived her faith and she expected nothing less from me. As a youngster I took this for granted, but it provided the foundation for my lifelong faith.

I never struggled with the questions, "Who am I? Why am I here?" My personal questions dealt more with "How am I going to get to where I want to be." I never really had to deal with "Why do I want to accomplish the impossible, risking life and limb." I knew I wanted to accomplish because I believed that was my destiny. I believe that God has endowed everyone with an instinctive drive to succeed, but that achieving success is defined differently for each person. I have heard many statements made that the only reason people strive for success is for financial gain. I personally don't believe that, and it is certainly not my reason for striving. I am of the opinion that most of us are trying to complete something worthwhile with our lives. This is true for artists as well as scientists. A musician wants each composition to be better than the last, a painter cleans off his canvas and begins again until he has painted what he wants to communicate, and a writer edits and rewrites, polishing the text until the words convey the message. A scientist, likewise, strives for the best possible result, continues to research, regardless of his past discoveries, always looking for new truths, new drugs, new ways to improve life. The Apostle Paul, one of the greatest men who ever lived, said this well, "Forgetting what lies behind and looking to the future, I press on towards the mark of the high calling of God in Christ Jesus my Lord." In spite of all St. Paul achieved, he continued to strive.

We all have goals we want to accomplish, be it a burning desire, an obsession, or something only slightly felt. Many times in my life I could have said, as Faust did when he believed he had reached the center of beauty and truth, "Stay, thou art so fair." I could have been content as a village physician in Haiti, as an obstetrician in Montreal, a gynecologist in Philadelphia, a medical department chairman in Hershey. But I could not stop. God had plans for me, leading me always to continue to strive. At every crossroad of my life, I have paused and asked God for His guidance. He has never led me astray.

Each one of us has some idea as to the kind of person we want to be. But the obstacle for most people is that they do not know *how* to be the person they want to be. They have goals, but not clearly defined objectives. What many people forget is that goals alone are not enough. Those who want to achieve their goals must have a plan and must be willing to sacrifice to make sure that plan works. They must be willing to face a challenge and work to overcome it. The way we react to challenges determines the destiny of our lives. With God guiding us, we can face any challenge, but we must work with Him and take the time to know His plan for us.

Whatever God wills[2]

I was blessed, first by having a mother who was both devout in her religion and determined in her actions. She was my first "role model," although like most children I did not realize that. All I knew was that my mother loved her family and was resolved that we would follow her faith. That became the foundry for my life. Our household revolved around faith. We saw my mother pray and we saw her come away from prayer with a sense of being comforted, and always with renewed strength and the germ of a plan to resolve whatever dilemma she faced. To her, the Haitian belief, "Whatever God wills" was the credo by which she lived. She held total trust in God and instilled that trust in us. Religion was my mother's motivating force and that, in turn, became mine.

My serving as an altar boy was but one stage in my devotion to my religion. It pleased my mother that I was chosen to assist the priest, but my own reason for wanting to serve during mass is that I felt a closeness to God. In His house all was well, and even at a young age, I felt a calmness unlike any other feeling I had anywhere else. At that time, I was sure that I wanted to enter the priesthood, but God had other plans for me.

When I was eleven, our family was evicted from our $4 per month home because we could not pay the rent. I watched my mother cry in despair as nine of us, including the cousins who were living with us, were forced into the streets of St. Marc. I will never forget her anguish. I will also never forget her praying. She did not simply wail at her misfortune; rather, she prayed for guidance. From her prayers came a determination to do whatever it would take to save the family. I watched her faith strengthen through this troubled time, as she prayed and planned; prayed and worked; and prayed and saved one small coin at a time. Thus, it was through prayer that my mother was led to a plan of becoming a market woman so that in three years she was able to purchase a small house.

Observing my mother was a very powerful lesson for me in the power of prayer. Without my quite realizing it, watching her overcome her adversity instilled in me both faith and determination. These two motivating factors became the cornerstone for the rest of my life. They governed my every decision and led me to discover that God had given me a great gift of intellectual ability, spirituality, and vision.

Who rises from prayer a better man, his prayer is answered.[3]

As a youth I would occasionally lack determination, but as soon as I started to backslide, I would stop and think about the future, trusting God to show me the right direction. I recall in particular a group of friends whose company I thoroughly enjoyed. We had just entered manhood, the age at which we were permitted to wear long pants. How we strutted and believed we were unique in discovering life. And in discovering girls! Like most young people, we thought there had been no others like us, and that we should have the freedom to do exactly what we pleased. We had fun, cutting classes and having a general good time. Not unexpectedly, my grades plummeted. After I failed a grade, I knew I had to do something or I would never make it to the university. I looked at myself and at my mother and in both faces found disappointment staring back. I gazed at my friends who continued to beckon me to join them in their pleasures. I then turned to God and asked Him to show me the way. Embarrassed by my own failure, I prayed to Him Who had never failed me. I regained my confidence and with it my determination to better myself. It was then I knew for certain that I could not succeed alone.

When I moved to Port-au-Prince at age 17, my charge was

clear. I was there to study. I tried not to let it matter that that I had
no money and often went hungry. I told myself, "You wanted to be
in a good lycée to prepare yourself for entrance into the university,
so here you are. Study and be content. You have a future to prepare
for." I asked myself, "Am I fulfilling the role for which God and life
have prepared me? Am I making the most of my time, my intellect,
and my energy; and am I sustaining the confidence of those who
trusted and believed in me?" I knew the future of my entire family
rested on my getting into the university and preparing for a professional career.

*Faith consists in believing when it is beyond the power of reason
to believe.*[4]

It was also at this time that I began to realize I had an ability to
set a goal and to concentrate on the steps necessary to fulfill that
goal. It was as if I could see the end result and knew what it would
take each step of the way to achieve it. Prayer and faith, I am sure,
were what enabled me to envision my future, for I continued to be
devout in my religion. I don't mean to imply that I did not find time
to enjoy the companionship of friends. Friends have always been an
important part of my life. Rather, what I had learned from my experience with my school chums in St. Marc is that I needed to find
friends with similar values and goals. I was lucky to be able to cultivate friends who also had determination to succeed, friends who
knew they had to study hard and who were very serious in their
work. We had a good time studying together in the park under the
lamplight, but we were deadly serious about our futures.

In medical school there were additional challenges to face. I
was now in classes with the very best students from the entire country of Haiti. The academic competition was intense, especially
among five of us who throughout our time together ranked as the top
five students in our class. All of us were intelligent and ambitious. In
addition, I was known among the group as the one full of enthusiasm. Perhaps I was more enthusiastic than the others, but to me I was
just being myself. I have always enjoyed life and welcomed what it
brought. Later, when I learned that "enthusiasm" means "to be

inspired by God," I saw how well the term does describe me, for everything I do is motivated by prayer and faith.

In this faith I wish to live . . . (François Villon, *Ballade pour prier Notre Dame*)

Graduation from medical school was a high point in my life. It also provided a new dilemma. I very much wanted to do a residency in a specialty, but because of the political situation, no new graduates were permitted to accept a residency. Rather, all medical school graduates were required to provide one or two years of medical service in the villages. In those villages, there were no medical consultants to bring to any of the cases. However, one might say that I had the best consultant possible with God by my side.

I could not have survived in Montreal without my strong faith. The city was cold and I was trying to subsist on as little as possible in order to send money home to my family. As I also was very homesick, prayer helped me feel closer to my mother. When I prayed, I tried to imagine her, a world away, praying for my safety. As bad as conditions seemed to me, I knew they were nothing in comparison to what my family had endured in order to send me to Port-au-Prince years earlier. My endurance may have been tested in Canada, but my determination to find my destiny beyond Montreal led me forward.

Soon my plans to find a residency in the United States fell into place. I could see it all before me, as if I had been handed a map. However, without my faith I never could have survived the tragic week-end duty at Mercy-Douglass Hospital. Reasoning tells me I had been placed in an impossible situation, but that does not change the fact that I lost patients, that persons lost their lives because of an irresponsible decision on the part of the hospital. As a result of that event, I almost lost my confidence as a physician. I know I did my best, but my best was not good enough to overcome the situation. Finding solace in the Church helped me to deal with my own feelings, but I regret to this day the loss of life. Even now that incident haunts me, but I have tried to learn a lesson from that, to never, ever place a new resident in a situation that has the potential to explode.

More things are wrought by prayer than this world dreams of. [5]

In every situation I have ever faced I prayed for guidance in making decisions:

- — Whether or not to accept offers of new positions, many of which promised great financial rewards;
- — Whether or not to take a sabbatical;
- — Whether I should accept a chairmanship;
- — Whether to take on a directorship;
- — Whether I should follow my lifelong passion for research or continue to contribute through my expertise in surgery;
- — Whether I should uproot the family yet another time if it means a better life for us in the long term
- — Whether I can give back to my family, my country, and my profession;
- — Whether the time requirements are worth the end result—to the particular project, to my family, to my personal satisfaction and desire to make a difference, to leave the world a better place.

With prayer, in every instance things fell into place.

I never enter the operating room without praying, "Dear Lord, You have put one of Your creatures into my care. Lead me safely through this surgery, for I am only the hands; You are the head." I always pray for skill in the surgery I am about to perform, as well as for an end to the patient's suffering. My own religious convictions have positively influenced my work with patients diagnosed with cancer. I spend time with these patients, counseling them, listening to them, praying with them, and consoling them. One of the most difficult tasks I face as a physician in a specialty where there is a high mortality rate is helping patients who are facing death from their disease. I try to help them die with dignity, suggesting they make as many personal choices as they wish regarding their final care. It is my own strong faith that helps me to help them. People who believe in something can accept death

much better than those who don't. The belief that life is a contin-
uum from earth to the other side helps me lead patients to a realization that death is just a passing, that life will continue and their
pain will be gone.

Throughout my medical practice and my personal life, my
prayers have been led by the question, "What is His will for me
today?" I place myself into His guidance as to how He can help us
to be good Christians in the modern world. What we should want to
know is not, what would this or that person, or this or that church,
have of us, but what God himself wants of us. By responding to that,
decisions become easier and the pathway becomes clearer.

*Faith is the substance of things hoped for, the evidence of things
not seen.*[6]

Finally, I need to underscore that my personal spirituality has
been very much enriched by my involvement in church activities,
beginning with my training in the Leaders in Ministry Program.
This training led to my first becoming a member and then chairman
of the Liturgical Committee of my parish church. I also developed
many strong personal friendships, particularly with Bishop Constant of Haiti and Cardinal Keeler, Archbishop of Baltimore. These
friendships allowed me to take the initiative in forging partnerships
by which parishes and dioceses of the United States have "adopted"
counterparts in Haiti.

Because of my many commitments, I have little time to travel
for pleasure. I take the most enjoyment from accomplishing something. One exception I make is time for spiritual reflection. I am a
devout Catholic and find renewal of both body and spirit while
engaged in religious endeavors, be they the celebration of a mass or
traveling in the company of the Church leaders. I recall with exu-
berance the joy I experienced on a religious pilgrimage a few years
ago. When now Cardinal William Keeler was serving as Bishop of
the Harrisburg Diocese he organized a pilgrimage for interested persons in the diocese to attend an Eucharistic Congress. Held every
four years, in 1985 the site selected was Nairobi, Kenya. It was

absolutely inspiring. It made me realize all the more the power of faith and the Catholic Church. There was a palpable synergy there, whether we were in discussion or quiet prayer. The twenty of us from the Harrisburg Diocese followed the week of the Eucharistic Congress with a trip to Egypt. That, too, was a pilgrimage, for we were enveloped with the historical and Biblical significance of our Christian and Old Testament heritage. Having Bishop Keeler as our personal guide enhanced the excursion in a way that could never have been matched by a tourist guide, regardless of experience and knowledge.

. . . thou good and faithful servant[7]

In the fall of 1998, following an application and acceptance process, I entered training to become a deacon in the Catholic Church. As there was no deaconate program in Haiti, Bishop Constant petitioned Cardinal Keeler for me to be enrolled in the program in the Baltimore Archdiocese. I will be ordained by Bishop Constant in the spring of 2001 in my home parish of St. Marc.

This path to service to the Church seemed appropriate, as for several years I had been thinking about expanded ways in which I could serve. From the time I first became a physician I had wanted to give back to my people. I found that possible first on an individual level by meeting some of my patients' needs. As I widened my own world beyond Haiti, I found myself in a position to serve in a larger community and to repay some of the many blessings I had received during my lifetime. With each passing year and additional responsibility, my sphere of influence widened and I was able to touch the lives of even more persons.

The circle grew with each transition in my professional career: from country doctor in Haiti to leading a medical department, from a researcher to director of a cancer center, and from presenting papers to organizing international scientific programs to aid developing countries. What better way to transition yet once again, from physician in service to mankind to deacon in service to the Church? My ordination will bring me full circle to the birthplace of my faith.

Family

At the end, only two things really matter to a man, regardless of who he is; and they are the affection and understanding of his family. Anything and everything else he creates are insubstantial; they are ships given over to the mercy of the winds and tides of prejudice. But the family is an everlasting anchorage, a quiet harbor, where a man's ships can be left to swing to the moorings of pride and loyalty.[8]

The greatest support anyone can have is a loving family, a family in which each member is willing to make individual sacrifices for the overall good of the family unit. At each stage of my life and career my amazement is continually renewed as Cecile never ceases to offer her unconditional support in whatever decision I ultimately make. It is our custom for the two of us, and then the four of us, to discuss all conditions of a choice or decision, all implications for my career and for our family, and any adjustments necessary to our life. Based on everyone's input, the final choice is mine and what will be best for my professional life. If Cecile were Haitian-born, I could better understand her deference to my career, but she is not. Rather, she is purely and unquestionably unselfish. A professional in her own right, she was a registered nurse who had her own full-time career until our first child, Denise, was born. We decided that Cecile would take a hiatus from working outside the home and become a full-time mother. Three years after the birth of Denise, we were blessed with a second daughter, Renée. What resulted was that Cecile assumed total responsibility for our home and children and dedicated herself to all that implies. Without Cecile's complete devotion to the family, I would not have been able to achieve professionally to the extent that I have.

Everything has its price

While I am eternally grateful for Cecile's dedicating her life to our family so that I could accept professional opportunities as they were offered, I regret that I had precious little time with the girls, particularly in their early years. I was fortunate in that the entire family could accompany me on many of my travels, but I very much missed out on the day-to-day tending to the children, reading them bedtime stories, pushing them on the swing set, taking walks in the neighborhood, playing games in the evening, and going to the town park or the pool in the summertime. I have many photos of Denise and Renée in childhood, but not nearly the memories that their mother holds in her heart. That is the price I have paid for my professional success.

During the early years at the Medical Center (summers, 1973–1978) I was able to take only one week's vacation each year. I tried to make that week special for the family. We always went camping, either in the mountains or at the shore, and the entire week was totally devoted to doing things together as a family. The children loved having Cecile and me completely to themselves as we devised activities that could include all of us. Like most children, the girls particularly loved playing in the sand at the beach and I found myself building forts or allowing myself to be buried in the sand.

By 1975 I was working day and night to bring to fruition the initiatives I had taken in building the Division of Gynecologic Oncology. The number of patients had increased dramatically. In addition to seeing patients, I was teaching in the College of Medicine and trying to continue my research, as well as traveling throughout the world, both performing surgery and teaching surgical procedures I had found effective. In fact, the Division and my own work were so successful that I ultimately found myself in a prison of my own making, working fourteen-hour days.

Finally, I was able to hire Dr. William Nahhas and Dr. Stephen Curry. Both men were outstanding, and with their arrival I was then able to spend a bit more time with the family. With Cecile making all the arrangements, each year the family soon spent two weeks doing things together. As we had found camping a good way to enjoy simple pleasures, we continued that routine, varying only the vacation site from year to year.

That's where Daddy lives!

With the arrival of Drs. Nahhas and Curry, I was able to schedule one day a week in a research laboratory, rotating among the various special research areas. Because my long-term goal was to develop an academic division in which well-balanced research would be the foundation for medical education and patient care, I wanted to be well-grounded in current laboratory techniques and protocols. This was very important to me as I had not had any kind of laboratory work in my medical school training in Haiti. I knew I had to make up for lost time, especially if I were to spearhead the plan for a comprehensive approach to cancer care at Hershey Medical Center.

However, the realization that I would have to redouble my efforts to spend more time with my family hit me square in the eye one Sunday following church services when Cecile and I, with the girls in the back seat, drove past the Medical Center. Unexpectedly, yet with great assurance in her voice, Denise pointed to the Medical Center and announced, "That's where Daddy lives."

We should go and live in Paris[9]

In 1978 my intense desire to conduct basic research, as well as seeking an opportunity by which to spend time with the family, led me to apply for and receive a research appointment in Paris. I was granted a year's sabbatical and we all sailed for France. We loved that year. The work was not as demanding as I was accustomed to, and we found ourselves with time for many wonderful excursions. We traveled every week-end to parks, chateaux, Parisian landmarks, and historical sites. We particularly enjoyed junkets to the Méditerranée and the Côte d'Azur, clipping along the AutoRoute Sud to the sea. We sometimes headed across the English Channel to England and occasionally traveled to the province of Brittany, on the west coast of France, where the Haitian consul was a longtime friend of mine.

In addition to the travel, we entertained friends we had made in Paris and friends and family from the States. My cousin Roger lived in Paris at this time so it wasn't long before we were a part of several social circles. There was always something we could do as a family and for that reason I remember this year with particular fondness.

Denise developed a fluency in French enough so as to have the lead role in the school play. She particularly remembers Paris, though, for a more unpleasant experience when she was hospitalized for a week. The nurses had a difficult time finding a vein for the IV that was ordered and Denise, to our surprise and great embarrassment, cursed them in French!

We so loved Europe that we seriously considered remaining there, especially after hearing of the nuclear power plant "incident" only a few miles from Hershey at Three Mile Island. However, duty returned us to Hershey.

Listen, my children and you shall hear[10]

Beginning in 1981, following the death of Duvalier, we began traveling regularly to Haiti, usually spending a week or two at a time. This gave us an opportunity to visit with my family and for the girls to become familiar with their paternal heritage. My parents and my daughters could not converse through a common language, but they most certainly communicated. We built a beach house along the coast not far from St. Marc so that we would have a place of our own in Haiti. At the time "Villa Cecilia" was intended to become our second home and we built it with the idea of perhaps retiring there. There was no electricity, just battery-operated lights that the girls found a novelty. Our evening meal was our own "fresh catch of the day"—lobster, conch, or crab. We cooked on a charcoal stove and played Monopoly in the evenings. During the day, in addition to swimming and playing on the beach, the girls rode donkeys and horses; that and playing with the house-man's dog was great fun, particularly for Denise, who became very attached to that little dog.

During our stays in Haiti we made numerous side trips, most notably to the Citadel, built nearly two centuries ago by Henri Christophe to defend the island against an anticipated attack by the French. The siege never materialized, but the fortress remains in all its imposing splendor. The fortification is situated on a rock foundation at the very top of the bluff and can be reached only by donkey or walking. Because of its elevation, the buildings are often enshrouded in clouds. The girls thought of the Citadel and its environs as a fairy tale castle, and I said nothing about its real history to spoil their enjoyment. There would be time for that later.

Back in Hershey I made opportunities to become involved in the girls' school activities. I formed a Parent-Teachers Organization at the school and arranged for speakers, special events, and field trips. One of the most enjoyable times for me—and for Denise and Renée—was Halloween. Unknown to them, I would dress in a costume, completely concealed, and visit their school during the afternoon of their Halloween festivities. This brought delight to all the children and gave me a chance to attend an informal event without wearing the label of "doctor." I was simply Denise and Renée's daddy. The evening the children went for "trick or treat," I wore a different costume. Invariably I would take the children by surprise when I came upon them as they approached a friend's house. We had a great time!

When I became Chairman of the Obstetrics and Gynecology Department I found myself yet again with very little time to spend with the family. The children were still small and while it bothered me a great deal not to have the time to spend with them daily, Cecile's being there is what has kept us a strong family unit. I promised all of them that we would continue our extended vacations together.

I looked forward to a second sabbatical as much to be with the family as to participate in the Robert Wood Johnson Fellowship. Because of the fellowship, we spent a year together in Washington, DC beginning in September 1988. Just as in Paris, we spent every possible free moment together as a family exploring the nation's capital and its surroundings. The girls were twelve and fifteen, old enough for them to absorb American history, both in the monuments and its living chronicle. I found myself wondering what connections their own minds were making among the sophistication that is Paris, the primitiveness that is Haiti, and the dichotomy that is Washington, DC. I thought about asking them, but knew what their responses would be. What mattered is that we were a family doing things together.

Let us remain together still[11]

To recoup some of the time I had lost with the girls when they were children, we have traveled to many places the past dozen years, both for vacations and for my medical meetings. Of course, we have more time to "play" when we are on holiday, because when I am traveling on business I don't have time to sightsee with the three of them. What matters, though, is that we enjoy one another's company, however limited.

We were in Taipei, Taiwan the year Denise turned thirteen. I was visiting the hospital on business, and happened to mention to my host, the chairman of the ob/gyn department, that my daughter was disappointed not to be home for the event of officially becoming a teen-ager. I was only making conversation as one father to another, sharing stories of our children. However, on the day of her birthday he held a party for Denise, and what an elaborate event that was. Its surprise was outshone only by its extravaganza. Not many thirteen-year-olds have such a birthday party to remember!

We also have been to Montreal, as I wanted the girls to see where their father first set foot in America, and have traveled to numerous other cities around the world. Even now in her mid-twenties, Denise arranges her work schedule to accompany Renée, Cecile, and me.

In 1991 we were scheduled to go to our beach house in Haiti when the coup against Aristide occurred. We knew the country would be in turmoil and I did not want to endanger the lives of my family, so we canceled the trip. I feared that things would never quite be the same for the girls; that foreboding was borne out when Villa Cecilia fell victim to the aftershocks of the coup; the generator for the house was stolen, along with other items. We have since leased this house and when we visit my family we stay in St. Marc.

The price I have paid for my professional life has come at great cost to me personally. While I am close to my daughters, I do regret the many times I was not there for them. I suppose there are many fathers who have not spent time with their children, but I don't know how many regret it to the extent I do. All I could offer was my best effort to make the time we did share one of quality and great love. However, had it not been for Cecile, I don't know what the result might have been. She has been the family's strength, its anchor, its center, and its solace.

The Circle Closes

As a circle closes and water returns to its source, so I have returned to my beginnings.

Even though I left Haiti many years ago to continue my education, to realize a career in academic medicine, and to provide a better future for my family, my heart has held an abiding love and depth of caring for the country of my birth. From the time I was a village physician able only to help support my immediate and extended family, I have always contributed what I could. My sphere of helping Haiti soon grew wider to include friends, the city of St. Marc, and the Albert Schweitzer Hospital, as well as other hospitals and churches. Over time, as my resources increased, so my giving grew. Money, time, supplies, and materials—with each passing year I provided even more assistance as I saw the needs of Haiti increase. Before long I realized, that, like the parable of the loaves and the fishes, as I expend additional personal resources, new opportunities arise which allow me to replenish those resources.

The best is yet to be . . .

At this stage of my life and career, I more fully understand what Robert Browning, the British poet, meant as he reflected upon his life. Browning's lines, "Grow old along with me, the best is yet to be, The last of life for which the first was made,"[12] are viewed by many as a call to "rest and enjoy" their later years. Browning would probably be dismayed at this misinterpretation, as his message was meant to be much more encompassing of our lives. I see this "last of life for which the first was made" as meaning that our first and early struggles, work, friends, experiences, and education all prepare us for the crowning efforts of our life's work. Positions of responsibility, challenges, honors—everything we have faced, overcome, or achieved throughout our lives and everything that helped to shape us—all of this is but preparation for the ultimate contributions we make. These arcs in our circle of life ready us for the culminating legacies we leave.

While our names are written in water, our deeds live on.
Another closing of the circle has been the assistance I have been able to give to the churches of the Diocese of Gonaives through monetary gifts, building a small church for a group of devout parishioners, and facilitating the adoption of parishes in the Diocese of Gonaives by United States parishes located in the Diocese of Harrisburg and the Archdiocese of Baltimore.

And, finally, with the Mortel Family Charitable Foundation I will be able to fulfill my dream of honoring the memory of my mother through building a special school in St. Marc and financing its operation in perpetuity.

In addition to the endowment we are making through operating the school in St. Marc, the Mortel Family Charitable Foundation has also made a five-year commitment to the College of Medicine to endow a Visiting Lectureship both in oncology and in obstetrics and gynecology. This pledge is made as an appropriate way to acknowledge my years as Chairman of the Department of Obstetrics and Gynecology and as Director of the Cancer Center in support of the educational programs I first introduced. This gift allows for the Department Chairman and the Director to bring a nationally or internationally recognized leader in the field to teach students and residents and to deliver a public lecture.

Some work may yet be done
Like Ulysses, I am ready to move forward again to where "some work of noble note may yet be done. . . . I cannot rest from travel, to rust unburnished, not to shine in use. . . For my purpose holds to sail beyond the sunset and to touch the Happy Isles."[13] After more than twenty-five years of helping the Republic of Haiti from afar (including countless trips to provide direct assistance), I now have the means, the time, and the contacts to bring influential people together to assist my homeland in a broader and more last-

ing way. Through this effort I can reach beyond the churches and schools to touch the larger community.

What I had not expected, but which greatly furthered my work, was the offer made by "Food for the Poor" to finance the construction, equipment, and supplies. We are guaranteed to be ready to open our doors in the fall of 2001.

The web of our life is the link from which we have gone back to our center.

The final link in the web which intertwines my life with Haiti and the final closure of the circle which binds me to the source of my life is the hope that I can devise a strategy to assist in the improvement of the medical school education in Haiti. I have traveled worldwide, presenting and teaching. I have taught new surgical techniques and reported on protocols for cancer treatment. I have performed unusual and often daring operations and I have been an outspoken promoter for basic research. I have donated time, provided supplies and equipment, sought funding, and arranged for Haitian and other third-world physicians to receive training in host institutions. But what I have yet to do for Haiti is to find the means by which to assist the medical schools so that physicians from Haiti will have the training and advantages so long missing from their education. I am particularly advocating the institution of appropriate methods to teach basic sciences using well-equipped laboratories. If I am able to reach this goal, I truly will have come home. Like water I will have returned to my source, and the circle will be closed.

Prospice

As to what challenges yet lie ahead, I welcome them. I view life as a fulfillment of duty and an unreserved acceptance of whatever life brings of toil, suffering, happiness, or service. As long as I have the strength, energy, and enthusiasm to achieve God's plan for me, I embrace every opportunity to continue to serve Him through serving humankind. I praise God that He has given me the gift of life and the skills by which to work through problems and discern a clear vision of the solution. If the measure of a man is what he has done for his family, colleagues, countrymen, and fellow sojourners in this life, I have been blessed indeed, for real success is marked by what we give in return for what we have been given.

Notes

1. Thomas Hardy, *Men Who March Away*.

2. Common aphorism in Haiti.

3. George Meredith, *The Ordeal of Richard Feverel*, ch. 12.

4 Voltaire, *Questions sur l'Encyclopédia*.

5. Alfred, Lord Tennyson, *The Passing of Arthur*, l. 409–410.

6. Hebrews, 11:1.

7. St. Matthew, 25:21.

8. Admiral Richard Byrd.

9. Anonymous. Reported in S. Butler. *Notebooks*, ed. G. Keynes and B. Hill, 1951, p. 193.

10. Henry Wadsworth Longfellow, "Paul Revere's Ride, 1861.

11. Percy Bysshe Shelly, "Good Night."

12. Robert Browning, "Rabbi Ben Ezra," 1854.

13. Alfred, Lord Tennyson, "Ulysses," 1842.

References

"1.7 % Increase Proposed for Basic Research Next Year." *The Chronicle of Higher Education*, 14 April 1993, A1.

1996–1997 Bulletin, V. xxvi, no. 1. Hershey, PA: College of Medicine, 1996.

Abbot, Elizabeth. *Haiti: The Duvaliers and Their Legacy*. NY: McGraw Hill, 1988.

Abrams, Maxine. "The Best Cancer Specialists in the U.S." *Good Housekeeping,* October 1992, 53–72.

Abrams, Maxine. "The Best Doctors for Women." *Good Housekeeping,* August 1997, 53–72.

Antoine, Guy S. (*gstenio@juno.com*) "A personal reflexion (sic) on Kreyol." Posted on ListServe, *bcorbett@netcom.com*, 12 January 1997.

Aristide, Jean-Bertrand. "Real Democracies, Not Formal Ones." *Novib Network* 2, no. 5 (October 1996): unpaginated.

Aristide, Jean-Bertrand, with Christophe Wargny. *Jean-Bertrand Aristide: An Autobiography*. Maryknoll, NY: Orbis, 1993.

Aurand, Ellie. "Pennsylvania's New University Hospital Opens." *Penn State Journal* 3, no. 7. (October 1970): 1.

Averette, Hervey E. "Society of Gynecologic Oncologists: Reflections on the Beginnings." *Gynecologic Oncology* 55 (1994): 6.

Bentivegna, Joseph F. *The Neglected and Abused: A Physician's Year in Haiti*. Rocky Hill, CT: Michelle Publishing Co, 1991.

Bezilla, Michael. *Penn State: An Illustrated History*. University Park: The Pennsylvania State University Press, 1985.

Blanchet, Max. (*Tiben1940@aol.com*) as reported in the "Human Development Report, 1996" of the United Nations Development Program. (on ListServe, bcorbett@netcom.com) 1997.

"Board of Visitors," *Penn State University Cancer Center*. 26 October 1995.

Brown, Karen McCartney. *Mama Lola: A Vodou Priestess in Brooklyn*. Berkeley, CA: University of California Press, 1991.

———. ListServe. *bcorbett@netcom.com*. 19 October 1996.

265

Byrd, Admiral Richard C., no source.

"Cal Lutheran Lecture on Success Will Feature Dr. Rodrigue Mortel." Newspaper clipping, n.d., n.p., unpaginated.

Curry, Stephen L. "For Whom We Care." Presidential Address, Society of Gynecologic Oncologists, February 1996.

Davis, Wade. *The Serpent and the Rainbow.* NY: Simon and Schuster, 1985.

"Department of Ob-Gyn Achieves *U.S. News & World Report* Ranking." *Vital Signs,* The Milton S. Hershey Medical Center, circa August 1994, 2.

De Regt, Jacomina P. "Basic Education in Haiti." In *Haiti—Today and Tomorrow: An Interdisciplinary Study,* eds. Charles R. Foster and Albert Valdman. Lanham, MD: University Press of America, 1984.

"Dr. Mortel Receives Penn State Faculty Scholar Medal." *Vital Signs,* The Milton S. Hershey Medical Center, June 1986, 7.

Evarts, C. McCollister, MD, Dean, College of Medicine, The Milton S. Hershey Medical Center, quoted in "Director's Message," *Annual Report 1995/96.* Penn State University Cancer Center. September 1996, 1.

"Executive Message," *Penn State Geisinger Cancer Center.* (newsletter) Fall 1997, 1.

Fleeson, Lucinda. "Embargo on Haiti Falls Hard on Poor." *The Philadelphia Inquirer,* 7 September 1992, A1.

———. "Official Haiti Spokesman Blames Terrorists, Opponents." *The Philadelphia Inquirer,* 8 September 1992, A1.

———. "A Village of Would-be Refugees Cries Out in Haiti." *The Philadelphia Inquirer,* 8 September 1992, A1.

Fonda, Dave. Listserve: *bcorbett@netcom.com.* 17 September 97.

ForHaiti@aol.com, 14 February 1997, posted on *bcorbett@netcom.com.*

"Foundation Feasibility Study Moves into Phase II." *SGO Issues* 10, no. 2 (Fall 1991), 1.

Fowler, Wesley. Presidential Address, SGO Annual Meeting, San Antonio, TX, February 1992.

French, Howard W. "Study Says Haiti Sanctions Kill Up to 1,000 Children a Month." *The New York Times,* 9 November 1993, A1, A8.

GCF Bulletin, Winter/Spring 1999. Gynecologic Cancer Foundation.

Gardner, Ralph. "The Original Horatio Alger." Information printed in every annual program honoring the Horatio Alger Awardees.

"Go Slow With Any Plans for Using Force in Haiti." *USA Today*, 6 July 1994, unpaginated.

Greene, Anne. *The Catholic Church in Haiti: Political and Social Change*. MI: Michigan State University Press, 1993.

Greene, Graham. *The Comedians*. NY: Viking Press, 1966.

Griffiths, Jo. "Career to Take Hershey Doctor, Native of Haiti, to Washington." *The Patriot News* (Harrisburg, PA), 17 April 1988, unpaginated.

The Grolier Multimedia Encyclopedia. Online, figures for 1993.

"Haitian Born Doctor Named Fellow by National Academy of Sciences." *Haïti-Observateur*, 15–22 Avril 1988, unpaginated.

Hamburg, Jill. Listserve: *bcorbett@netcom.com*. 20 November 1996 (Bloomberg Financial Services).

Hardy, Thomas. "Men Who March Away."

"Health Policy Fellows Learn the Ropes in DC." *Advances*, newsletter of the Robert Wood Johnson Foundation, circa 1989, 9.

Hebrews, The Book of

Heinl, Robert D. and Nancy G., with revisions and expansion by Michael Heinl. *Written in Blood (The Story of the Haitian People)*. Lanham, MD: University Press of America, 1996.

"Hershey and Geisinger Ranked by *U.S. News & World Report*," *Vital Signs*, Penn State Geisinger Health System, August 1997, 1.

Herskovits, Melville J. *Life in a Haitian Village*. Garden City, NJ: Anchor, 1971.

Inghram, Glenn. Listserve: *bcorbett@netcom.com*. 19 October 1996.

Ives, Kim. "The Coup and U.S. Foreign Policy: The Unmaking of a President." In *The Haiti Files. Decoding the Crisis*, ed. James Ridgway. Washington, DC: Essential Books/Azul Editions, 1994.

Jean-Pierre, Jean. "The Diaspora: The Tenth Department." In *The Haiti Files. Decoding the Crisis*, ed. James Ridgway. Washington, DC: Essential Books/Azul Editions, 1994.

Keever, Wythe. "Goal of School Program is to Inspire Students." *The Patriot-News* (Harrisburg, PA), 17 November 1987, Metro East 25.

Keynes, G. and B. Hill, eds. *Samuel Butler's Notebooks,* 1951.

Klaus, Mary. "Local Doctor Predicts Haitian Cure." *The Patriot-News* (Harrisburg, PA), 21 November 1994, B7.

Klotz, Richard Russell. *The Rise and Demise of the Hershey Junior College*. Hershey, PA: Educational and Cultural Center, 1973.

Kobrin, Jerry. "Astronaut Grounded for Exceeding Warp Speed." *The Orange County Register* (California). 15 April 1986, D2.

Kobrin, Jerry. "Take Two Aspirin and Go Hear the Doctor Speak." *The Orange County Register* (California). 10 April 1986, J2.

Laguerre, Michael. "Haitian Americans." In *Ethnicity and Medical Care,* ed. Alan Harwood. MA: Harvard University Press, 1981.

Lawless, Robert. *Haiti's Bad Press*. n.p.: Schenkman Press, 1992.

"Let Haitian Refugees into USA." *USA Today*, 9 September 1992, 15A.

Leyburn, James G. *The Haitian People*. New Haven: Yale University Press, 1966.

Longfellow, Henry Wadsworth, "Paul Revere's Ride," 1861.

Lord Tennyson, Alfred. "The Passing of Arthur."

Lord Tennyson, Alfred. "Ulysses," 1842.

Lowenthal, Ira P. "Labor, Sexuality and the Conjugal Contract in Rural Haiti." In *Haiti—Today and Tomorrow: An Interdisciplinary Study,* eds. Charles R. Foster and Albert Valdman. Lanham, MD: University Press of America, 1984.

Lundahl, Matt. "Peasant Strategies for Dealing with Increasing Population Pressure; the Case of Haiti." Cited in "Developmental Strategies and Basic Needs in Latin America: Challenges for the 1980s," eds. C. Brundenius and M. Kundahl. In *Haiti - Today and Tomorrow: An Interdisciplinary Study*, eds. Charles R. Foster and Albert Valdman. Lanham, MD: University Press of America, 1984.

Manigat, Leslie F. *Haiti of the Sixties: Object of International Concern*. Washington, DC: Washington Center of Policy Research, 1964.

"Many Crises, Little Time: Aristide Still Needs Help." *USA Today*, 17 October 1994, 10A.

Marquette, Rob. "Hershey Medical Center Dedicates New Cancer Center." *The Sun* (Hummelstown, PA), 15 November 1995, 9.

Marrone, Sandy. "From Poverty to PSU's Chief Cancer Fighter." *The Patriot-News* (Harrisburg, PA), 13 March 1995, B1–5.

Medical World News, April 22, 1985.

Meredith, George. *The Ordeal of Richard Feveral*, Chapter 12.

Metraux, Alfred. *Voodoo in Haiti*. n.p.: Schocken Books, 1959.

Moffatt, Denise. "My Story." Speech delivered at the Cancer Survivor Rally. Middletown, PA, 1996.

Morison, Samuel Eliot. *The Oxford History of the American People*. NY: Oxford University Press, 1965.

Morrow, C. Paul. "'Who Are We?' A Paean to Gynecologic Oncology." Presidential Address, Society of Gynecologic Oncologists, Orlando, FL, 19 February 1991.

Mortel, Rodrigue. "Commencement Address." Milton Hershey School, 12 June 1986.

———. "Embargoed Haiti's Suffering Increases." Editorial. *The New York Times*, 10 September 1992, n.page.

———. "End the Embargo Against Haiti." Editorial. *The Washington Post*, 10 August 1992, A1.

———. "The Impact of Sabbatical Leave on a Clinical Discipline." The Dean's Lecture Series, Fall 1994, The Milton S. Hershey Medical School.

———. Letter to Philip M. Boffey, Deputy Editorial Page Editor, *The New York Times*. 12 November 1993.

———. *Prospectus: The Gynecologic Cancer Foundation*, 1990.

———. "Quo Vadis: The Vision Triumvirate (The Next Twenty-Five Years)." Presidential Address, Society of Gynecologic Oncologists, February 1995.

———. Report to the Membership: Gynecologic Cancer Foundation. SGO Annual Meeting, San Antonio, TX, February 1992.

———. Report to the Membership: Gynecologic Cancer Foundation. SGO Annual Meeting, Palm Desert, CA, February 1993.

———. Robert Wood Johnson Health Policy Fellowship Evaluation Report. August 1989.

———. "SGO Research and Education Foundation Report to SGO Membership." February 1991.

"Mortel Named Associate Dean and Cancer Center Director." *Penn State Medicine* (March 1995): 9.

"Mortel Speaks to AAUW." *The Sun* (Hummelstown, PA), 4 September 1985, n.page.

"Mortel Success in Establishing New NCI Section." *Vital Signs,* The Milton S. Hershey Medical Center, February 1993, 5.

Nicholls, David. Past and Present in Haitian Politics." In *Haiti—Today and Tomorrow: An Interdisciplinary Study,* eds. Charles R. Foster and Albert Valdman. Lanham, MD: University Press of America, 1984.

Norton, Michael. "Haiti Faces Education Crisis." Associated Press. ListServe, *bcorbett@netcom.com,* n.d.

Patton, Judith. "Hershey Doctor is Honored for Work in Haiti, Romania." *The Patriot-News* (Harrisburg, PA), 9 November 1991, n.page.

Penn State University Cancer Center: Benchmark Report. September 1995. unpaginated.

"Penn State University Cancer Center Established." *Vital Signs,* The Milton S. Hershey Medical Center, 18 September, 1995, 1–2.

"Permanent Charities Provides Grant." *GCF Bulletin* 1, no. 2 (Spring 1997), 2.

"Report from the Education Committee," International Gynecologic Cancer Society, n.d.

"Revisiting Haiti." *The Philadelphia Inquirer,* 10 September 1992, A18.

Riegel, Robert E. and David F. Long. *The American Story, Volume Two" Maturity.* NY: McGraw-Hill, 1955.

Rodman, Selden. *Haiti: The Black Republic.* NY: Devin-Adair, 1954.

Rotberg, Robert I. *Haiti: The Politics of Squalor.* Boston: Houghton Mifflin, 1971.

Ruckdeschel, John, Michale Gallo, and Paul Carbone. "Report of the Cancer Center Advisory Committee, Penn State University Cancer Center," July 2000.

"Seventeen Medical Center Doctors Name 'Best in America'." *Vital Signs,* The Milton S. Hershey Medical Center, circa August 1994, 2.

SGO Issues 10, n. 4 (Fall 1991), 6.

SGO Issues 11, n. 3 (Summer 1992), 6.

SGO Issues 11, n. 4 (Fall 1992), 2.

Shelly, Percy Bysshe, "Good Night."

"SGO Profile," *(SGO) Newsletter.* April 1991, 3.

St. Matthew, The Book of

Thompson, Ian. *Bonjour Blanc: A Journey Through Haiti.* London: Hutchinson, 1992.